**Geoffrey Elliott** was born and brought up in London, ........... ed for many years as a merchant banker with the enigmatic Siegmund Warburg, before moving to New York as a Managing Director of Morgan Stanley & Co.

He learned Russian at Cambridge University while serving in the Intelligence Corps, qualified as an interpreter and makes a hobby of learning foreign languages. While criss-crossing the globe on behalf of his investment interests he pursued every clue to his father's clandestine career, and wrote *I Spy* after his retirement to Bermuda. An Honorary Fellow of St Antony's College, Oxford, he is a director of several major companies, and is married with two children.

# I SPY

## The Secret Life of a British Agent

## Geoffrey Elliott

ST ERMIN'S
PRESS

A *St Ermin's Press* Book

First published in Great Britain in 1998
by St Ermin's Press
This edition published in 1999 by St Ermin's Press
in association with Little, Brown and Company

A CIP catalogue record for this book
is available from the British Library.

ISBN: 0 9536151 0 3

Typeset by M Rules
Printed and bound in Great Britain
by Clays Ltd, St Ives plc

St Ermin's Press
in association with
Little, Brown and Company (UK)
Brettenham House
Lancaster Place
London WC2E 7EN

For Thomas and James

# Contents

# Illustrations

Glamorous grandmother: Walburga Rice in about 1900

Ethel and Kavan Elliott

Kavan, Ethel and Leo Elliott, 1916

Elliott and his mother, Walburga, in about 1936

My mother, Sonia, 1940

Kavan and Sonia Elliott

Elliott and an uncomfortable author, 1940

Colonel Hudson, a Montenegrin veteran and General Mihailovic, 1942 (courtesy of Times Newspapers)

Elliott under Croat interrogation, February 1942

Spangenberg Castle: Oflag IX A/H – Elliott's 'home away from home', 1942–5

David and Maria Redstone: from Siberia . . .

. . . to the Savoy

The Romanovka House, Yakutsk, after the siege

The Romanovka Group and their lawyers, Irkutsk, 1904

Sir Dick White, Director of MI5, later Chief of SIS

Antony Terry

Elliott at rest . . .

. . . and at play, 1952

Away to the races: Elliott with Jamaican Premier Bustamente and
    friends, in about 1953
The last lap, Berkshire, 1970s

# Author's Note

It is easier to say what this book is not, rather than what it is. It is neither hatchet-job, nor hero-worship. Nor a work of history, though I have tried to provide a minimal historical context for some of what went on. Nor, at least in the conventional sense, is it a spy story; it is, though, the story of a spear-carrier in that down-at-heel theatre of the absurd and the cruel, that blend of The Crazy Gang and Grand Guignol, which is the essence of the espionage world. My father had two wives and several mistresses, but, although they are a key part of the tale, it is not really a love story either, partly because though they all loved him, I'm still not sure he loved them back, at least for very long.

I have taken two conscious liberties in the telling; any other errors or unkindnesses are unintended and entirely my responsibility. In the first place, I have not used the real names of Kati and Margit. I had mixed feelings about telling their stories in any case, but could not tell Elliott's without them. For this reason they are not thanked below by name, but I am deeply grateful to them for talking to me and for keeping my father somewhere in their hearts, after everything that happened. One of the oddest conclusions from this whole exercise is my conviction that, had they, my mother and Pamela, his second wife, actually met, they would all have got on rather well.

Second, while not altering the sense, I have used filial licence to put the staccato dictated notes which tell Elliott's side of the story into more readable narrative form.

It is invidious to single out a special category among all the many kind and patient people who helped provide bits of this story, who troubled to reply to my often misguided enquiries, and who allowed me to intrude into lives and memories. I am especially indebted to Sir William Deakin DSO, whose professional and personal generosity were the key to getting started. The postgraduate students who have helped with the archival research, notably Peter Palmer, as well as Neville Wylie, Kyril Haramiyev and Tina Podplatnik, deserve a special vote of thanks, as does the SOE Adviser's Office.

Others to whom much is owed include: Rachel Ames, John Austin, Professor Phyllis Auty, Lord Amery of Lustleigh, Richard Aldrich, Monika Bachmann, David Brighty, CMG CVO, Anthony M. Brooks DSO, the late John Bruce Lockhart CMG, Anthony Cavendish, Jonathan Chadwick, Jean and Robert Chapman, Sir Humphrey Cheam, Jean Clissold, Aidan Crawley, George Cushing, Basil Davidson, Sir Douglas Dodds-Parker, Stephen Dorril, Steven Earl, Susan Edwardes, James and Stephen Elliott, Vladimir Farkas, Dominic Flessati, Antonia Gerard, Sir Alexander Glen, Lord Greenhill of Harrow GCMG, Jean Hannant, John Harrison, Don and Nancy Holmes, Peter Lunn, Malcolm Mackintosh, Peter and Helen Makower, Eric van Maurik, Charles Moser, Jim McCargar, Linda Osband, David Price, Renata Propper, Robin Ramsey, Sir Steven Runciman, John Saumarez Smith, George Schoepflin, Stephen Schofield, Lalita Sreenivasan, Maureen Staniforth, Bela Szasz, Antony Terry, Thames Investigation Services, Al Ulmer, Istvan Vida, Laszlo Vargas, Dr G.P.M. Walker, Auberon Waugh, Phyllis Wender, Mark Wheeler, and Tibor and Judit Zinner.

Practical and moral support has come from all my friends at St Antony's College, Oxford, as well as the Bodleian Library, the Imperial War Museum, the Public Record Office, the National Westminster Bank, the British Council, the Bermuda Public Library, the Marx Memorial Library, the staff of Privatair, in whose high-altitude care much of this has been written, the Concierge Desk of the Ramada, Vauxhall, and almost last but very much not least – since they provided one key clue – the Barrow-in-Furness branch of the Royal British Legion.

And, towards the end of it all, in a Hertfordshire garden, bordered by birches which could have been transplanted from Russia, I met Vera Broido-Cohn, memorable daughter of a memorable revolutionary couple who were among the leaders of the Yakutsk Uprising. She told me the stories and sang me the songs, making me wish I could open this book up again and focus it far more on the Redstones and their struggle.

That most authors thank their wives for their support I used to regard as little more than a standard courtesy. I know now that without that support, nothing is possible, and I am deeply grateful for it.

*Emsig wallet der Pilger! Und wird er den Heiligen finden?*
*Hören und sehen den Mann, welcher die Wunder getan?*
*Nein, es führte die Zeit ihn hinweg, du findest nur Reste,*
*Seinen Schädel, ein Paar seiner Gebeine verwahrt.*

[The pilgrim strides out eagerly. And will he find the saint?
Hear and see the man who performed the miracles?
No. Time has borne him away; you will find only remains,
His skull, a few of his bones preserved.]

J.W. Goethe

# 1

# A Game of Circles:
# Hungary 1946

This is how it was, as best I can tell.

Kavan, sometimes known as Joe, drove across the Austrian border into Hungary on 8 December 1946 – his thirty-eighth birthday, though that was happenstance. *'Jo napot kivanok. Az utlevelt, legyen szives.'* Asking an important-looking foreigner for his passport, the scruffy border guard was warily polite. *'Tessek,'* the driver replied neutrally, handing over his British passport, its dark blue cover and gilded coat of arms as worn as the injunction from the Foreign Secretary inside the front cover requesting and requiring in haughty italics that, as one of the King's subjects, the bearer should be allowed to pass, 'without let or hindrance'. As the guard could not read English, or indeed much of anything else, the impotent echo of Empire rather went over his head.

Except when it meant going back into England, crossing any frontier was a birthday present in itself. The rites of passage across the fifty yards of damp tarmac, the thud of stamp on passport, the frowning, suspicious looks of the officials in the limbo between this world and the next, had become an invigorating act of absolution and self-renewal. Love gone rancid, shabby deceits, scrapes over money which, untended, festered like sores into lasting embarrassments, all the crap could be left behind, unwanted small change on the powder-flecked glass top of the dressing-table after another night of sweaty, yeasty promises.

When the red-and-white pole swung back down into its iron cradle, it sterilised memory. He was once again the actor striding nonchalantly on to a new stage, another opening of another show, his personality shaped by the script, fact and fiction tweaked into new alignments. There had been so many first nights: London, to less than rave reviews, then the Ambleresque amble through Zagreb, Sofia, Cairo, Malta, Sarajevo, Spangenberg Castle, Hamburg . . . and now Budapest.

London never worked for long, however sincerely he promised himself that he would try harder. Sonia putting what her twittering bloody girl-friends called 'a brave face on things', twisting her handkerchief and sobbing that he could have all the freedom he wanted, all the women in the world, if only he would promise that at the end of it all he would come back to her and the three children. Promises were easy enough. He had made many. Remembering what you had promised, and to whom, was not so easy. But the poor cow just didn't see it. Nor did her parents, lobbing their moralising mortar shells at him from behind their cigarette smokescreen, all Russian doom and gloom. For Christ's sake, who did they think they were, presuming to know or, even worse, to lay down the law to him on how family life should be lived? 'Vee sink Sonia vud be khappier if you vud be more time at home,' they eyed him reproachfully, coughing up the guttural Slav Hs like a droshky driver getting ready to spit.

Climbing the three cold flights of stairs to see his own mother in her two rooms of awkward memories, the traffic rumbling its way towards Highgate, the kettle forever whistling gently on the Belling stove out on the landing kitchen. When he last took her out for her ritual whisky and orange at The Greyhound, that ratty little man had pushed a County Court debt summons at him along the beer-slicked bar. He had looked up at him almost apologetically when, in a flash of rage and shame, Kavan had shoved him roughly away and he had stumbled to the floor. 'Only doing my job, old son,' he cringed. The next day his mother and sister had scraped together £7 13s to keep the bailiffs off his back for a few days.

Sure, the furtive involvement with 'the Firm', as Antony Terry and the others liked to call it, exchanging arch looks, brought a touch of flesh and blood to his flaccid London life. But when you were just one of their Joes, an 'Honourable Correspondent' rather than an insider, and once you had got over being impressed by their flattery and flummeries, the chummy dinners, all silver, mahogany port and war stories in the discreet Artillery Mansions flat, an Alex Korda vision of a British gentleman's pied-à-terre, even that side of things was better abroad. London was myth; abroad, where the action was, lay reality. Far better too than the weekend courses being preached at about the Communist menace and communications in those stuffy secret classrooms in the King's Road, still shored up after a wartime bomb blast and occupied, according to a small black-and-white plaque on the wall, by the Central Asian Research Bureau, whose blue-jacketed janitors deterred casual callers with the tough politeness of retired policemen.

By contrast, the firm with a small 'f' whose slowly rising junior sales manager he ostensibly had been since 1936, and on whose behalf he was now just as ostensibly entering Hungary, was mind-numbingly boring, unless, like the career-minded Johnnies, you could simulate a grand passion for soaps, detergents, edible oils, sausages and ice-cream. Though the firm was a sprawling and highly profitable multi-national enterprise, working for them in London meant little more than a metronomic commute in and out of Blackfriars Station, marooned among mackintoshed managers and accountants hiding their lives from each other behind the *Daily Telegraph*, their briefcases more likely to hide pallid pornography that they dared not leave at home, Shippam's fishpaste sandwiches and a spare collar, than grand plans for rebuilding the world's washing powder industry.

Inside the granite monument to margarine, the meaning of life boiled down to shuffling papers and playing committee games with a platoon of snooty sober-suited old-young men, the vividness of their old school ties in inverse proportion to the schools' reputation, and humourless Dutchmen, rimless glasses and a whiff of herring, seconded by the bargeload from The Hague, where the real power centre of the firm lay, to keep an eye on the British. 'In matters of commerce,' an office wag had once recited to him at a sales lunch, 'the fault of the Dutch is giving too little and asking too much.'

When he recycled the quip to Terry and an owl-eyed *bon viveur* from the Firm, with a knowing chuckle over a tabletop of pink gins at the Travellers', the owl-eyed one had trumped him, remarking with carefully cultivated mock diffidence that the nineteenth-century quip was nothing to do with trade, but a fine example of *l'esprit de l'escalier* by

Lord Canning, after some very hard bargaining with a fabled Dutch courtesan, whose obdurate refusal to reduce the price of the ultimate favours at her disposal had forced an indigent and by now desperate Foreign Secretary to settle for a still costly bird in the hand rather than something more deeply satisfying in the bush. Sessions like this were fun, though gin with a dose of Angostura bitters took a lot of getting used to, and if you could keep your end up and conceal with a quizzical eyebrow the fact that you hadn't got a bloody clue who Lord Canning was.

Drinking the evenings away with his brothers Leo and Basil in The Coal Hole on the Strand was a more deliberate, far less lighthearted defence mechanism, putting off until the last train of the day another round of razor-backed recrimination, shouting, screaming and the inevitable tears, followed by the stiffness and silence of the bedroom, the children lying awake next door, all ears and ignorance. God rot them, each and every one. At least marriage was one prison sentence from which, with luck, you could get time off for bad behaviour.

With the blessing of its London Chairman, a close friend of the shifty-eyed military man who ran the Firm itself, rejoicing in his title of 'Chief', the firm with a small 'f' cheerfully paid his salary, let him make what he could of a job in export sales and, sometimes because he deserved it and sometimes to reinforce his cover, even threw him the occasional promotional bone. From his earliest days well before the war, its Personnel Department had grown used to professing polite confusion about his precise whereabouts to Sonia, or indeed any of the duns or other women's husbands who came looking for him.

The dour gang in the executive suite at Blackfriars had even professed to be enthusiastic about the Firm's idea, discreetly floated from Broadway Buildings via the bar at White's, that he should be posted to Budapest, convincing themselves that whatever else he might get up to, they could get some real value if he applied even a part of his energy and his language skills to revitalise their war-smashed business.

It being a commercial world, their motives were not entirely altruistic. One well-manicured hand washed another. Helping the Firm with cover and logistical support, including the transmission, cloaked in the humdrum traffic of business, of anything from men to money, put the firm with a small 'f' in a strong position to ask for and expect to get quiet government help in other areas. No small thing at a time of shortages, restrictions, licences and pervasive bureaucracy. The Chairman, not a stupid man, was given to boasting in complete confidence to his wife, who told only her closest bridge friends, that overall his shareholders came out ahead from the series of Faustian compacts at which he had connived over the years.

Though the Hamilton clock on the Studebaker's battered walnut dashboard showed it was almost midday, the freezing fog still ran its thick fingers through the pine trees and around the brooding watchtowers of the Hegyshalom checkpoint. The fur hats of the border guards were backlit by a sallow halo from the sodium lamps. In the exit lane on the other side of the divider strip a truck driver, head down, hands pressed flat against his sides in a stance that could have been drummed into him only in the army or jail, breathed clouds of condensed fear into the chill air while three soldiers, supervised by a blank-faced man in a leather coat, unloaded his cargo of wet potato sacks with methodical menace. The 1937 V8 saloon had seen uneventful service as a staff car for the commander of the US 14th Infantry Group in the advance across northern France. Reported stolen to a disbelieving but unconcerned quartermaster with his own rackets to worry about, it had been hidden by its enterprising driver in a dusty Paris lock-up, and safely traded behind a nearby bar in 1946 for six cartons of penicillin. The driver had returned home as an all-American hero with a chestful of campaign ribbons and a kit bag stuffed with cash to carve out a career of unblemished corruption in the Illinois State Legislature.

Resprayed Mafia black somewhere along the way, the Studebaker, like a stray cat, had found itself a marginally more respectable owner when Kavan, for a brief moment giddy with cash and courage from his wartime backpay, won it with an Ace-high bluff in a smoky and very drunken poker game in the rather elegant mock-baroque villa commandeered as a mess by the Office of Strategic Services in Kassel. A rare smile from Dame Fortune since, in the cool eyes of his steadier friends and the careful men of the Firm who watched him closely, though he had the gambler's deep streak of recklessness, he was neither a good nor a lucky player, and a truculent loser.

The Roy Lichtenstein chic of its bulging trunk and the sweeping spare-wheel nacelles on either side of the hood drew the awed attention of the Hegyshalom guards. So did its driver when he swung out to deal with the paperwork. Partly it was the sheer glamour of association with this purring capitalist Juggernaut and partly his own erect swagger, a definitely military air tipped a touch off key by a double-breasted camel-hair coat, which, carelessly belted, collar rakishly uptilted, probably struck the guards as a hallmark of the fabled English Milord, though a more snobbish eye might have associated it more closely with a Warren Street second-hand car showroom.

If Kavan had been briefed about their photograph routine, he gave no sign, though the bright spotlights framing the green-curtained passport guichet were something of a giveaway. Retrieving his passport from the guard's blank scrutiny, he bent forwards to slide it into the disembodied hands of the clerk inside the booth. The latter, by now adept at catching the precise moment when a traveller's face was squarely framed in the window, and lit clearly by the lamps around the booth, pressed a floor button with his foot as he took the papers. The camera clicked discreetly. A long-snouted Leica originally designed for the Gestapo, it was a small part of the sad and vicious tools of the trade looted by the Russians after the war from the blood-spattered headquarters of the German security services in the Golf Hotel in the hills above Budapest.

Inside the booth the weedy Hungarian clerk passed the papers without a word to the duty officer of the Soviet MVD, or Internal Affairs Ministry, a fat slug who the Hungarian, an avid movie-goer, sometimes thought wryly was like Oliver Hardy to his Stan Laurel. Six days out of seven they shared the tobacco fug of the security post for eight hours of mutual distaste and incomprehension, and but for the slight administrative inconvenience which would have followed, each would have cheerfully killed the other long ago. The Russian flicked slowly through a circular file of dog-eared cards, paused, ran his finger suspiciously over every word of the entry on the card, glanced again at the passport and reached for the telephone, an upright brass and bakelite affair which would not have been out of place on the set of *The White Horse Inn*.

'*Govorit* Lebedyev,' he grunted. Whoever sat at the Budapest end of the line was evidently his superior, since he gave the Hungarian clerk the impression of sitting to attention and, had his hands been free and the booth big enough to permit the gesture, he might even have saluted into the electronic void. '*Vot u nas poyavilsya anglichanin, zaregistrirovannyi na krasnom spiske,*' he reported, taking some pride in having spotted an Englishman on the MVD's 'red watch' list. Lebedyev listened respectfully for a few moments, nodded with sycophantic enthusiasm and pulled the passport towards him. After a few more monosyllabic exchanges, he cradled the phone, spat viscously on a worn rubber stamp and banged it on to a fresh page.

Tongue protruding with the effort of writing in Hungarian rather than Russian, he printed carefully under the stamp '*ERVENYES* 1947 12–08', allowing the driver to enter the grey fastness of Hungary and remain for the next twelve months. In their wordless Laurel and Hardy routine, Lebedyev solemnly handed the passport to the Hungarian, who passed it silently back through the guichet, taking no notice of the driver's polite and unaccented '*Köszonom szepen. Viszontlatasra*', though very few of the foreigners who passed through had either the knowledge or the manners to say thanks and goodbye in Hungarian. They usually showed more gratitude, not to say relief, when they left. More out of curiosity and greed than suspicion, the guard took a cursory look inside the Studebaker's leather-plumped interior, took without a word the round yellow-labelled tin of fifty State Express cigarettes Kavan had left on the driver's seat as a votive offering, and waved him on his way.

Back in the booth, Lebedyev farted with double-barrelled satisfaction. By reporting Elliott's arrival he had surely earned a good mark or two with Head Office. And his noisy anti-social act drove his Hungarian colleague to transports of speechless fury.

# 2

# Remains

It took fifteen years, almost to the day, for news of my father's death to reach me. So much for the information superhighway.

A few years earlier, the daily round and common task having furnished all I needed to ask, I had scraped the chewing gum of Wall Street from my shoes and slid away to the warmth and fiscal neutrality of Bermuda, a caring, conservative village-nation marooned in mid-Atlantic, combining piracy and piety on fifty square miles of crowded, gossip-fissured coral rock. Between the ecstasy and the agony of retirement, watching the white longtails skim out over the cobalt waves from their cliffside nests below the house, there was plenty of time to spare.

There was no excuse to put off the project which had hung for years like a hibernating bat in the rafters of my mind, of finding out who Kavan Elliott was and what he was all about. And to put a scaffolding of reality into the loosely billowing tent of fantasy that his name conjured up.

In 1940, when Elliott went off to his various public and personal wars, I was a mewling, nappied lump. His determination not to return to humdrum domestic life despite several grim, growling attempts to make fresh starts, and the inevitable furtive divorce (hushed up because back then it was something vaguely shameful, a social scrofula, to be kept from the children at all costs), meant that I had barely known him, remembering from childhood not a walking, talking, living person but little more than a jumble of impressions and objects. The clipped military-styled rather than strictly military voice, a ramrod shadow on the bedroom wall. The evocative contents of a Swaine Adeney & Brigg's pigskin suitcase, which lay for years in our attic, next to the wickerwork picnic hamper, its unused knives, forks and Thermos bottles still wrapped in tissue, which some wealthy friend had given my parents as a wedding present.

The suitcase, sporting with nostalgic pride the multi-coloured Art Deco labels of grand hotels of the kind which died out with Vicki Baum, held the raw material for a world of fantasies; aromatic leather and cloth artefacts, smelling of mothballs rather than incense, totems of my very personal Cargo Cult, whose central mythic being would one day reappear from his exile, tanned, rich and famous, to take warm-hearted charge of our lives. How often I slid my hands through its neatly packed contents, a cadet Customs Officer. At first with sly circumspection, leaving everything meticulously as I had found it in case he might one day detect the signs of childish rummaging; later with increasing boldness, when it slowly dawned on me (without anything actually being said; very little was ever said on the subject) that he wouldn't be returning.

A khaki barathea uniform, with a major's metal crown on the epaulettes, medal ribbons on one of the breast pockets, a parachute insignia on the sleeve. Inside, the discreet label of Gieves, 'Sporting, Military and Civil Tailor', in Savile Row. A Sam Browne leather harness of belt and cross-strap, its deep patina still unsullied, brass fittings not yet dull; who, I asked myself years later, had the eponymous Browne been, and how did he come to have a belt, of all things, named after him? Khaki silk shirts with detached collars, and a box of brass studs, gold cufflinks and whalebone stiffeners, the mysterious accoutrements of middle-class malehood.

Photographs of military parades, soldiers in oddly shaped caps in far-away places with strange sounding names scribbled on the back. Buildings that did not look like London. Ruined factories and smashed railways in crisp close-up. Rubber-banded rolls of greasy banknotes with un-English colours and an excess of zeros. These forints, levas, Reichsmarks and dinars I discreetly filched in due course to swap at school for American comics. A boozer's silver hip flask, its leather cover well-worn, a thin glass slit down one side to reassure or depress its owner about just how much high-octane happiness was left. A Leica camera, a pair of binoculars. Tins of pomade, a violet-scented hairdressing from Trumper of Curzon Street, their oval lids stamped with nostalgic *Mittel Europäisch* royal warrants.

Lurking like a metal alligator at the bottom lay a long-barrelled Mauser 7.63 mm pistol, with a nine-inch blued steel barrel, its wooden handle grooved to take an extension butt for long-range shooting, nestled snug in a stiff leather holster big enough for Goering's thigh. Slotted inside a pocket of the holster were several clips of ammunition. Fortunately for the neighbourhood, the firing pin and spring had been removed from the gun's heavy bolt mechanism, and despite years of desultory fiddling I never did succeed in reassembling them, an early indication that matters mechanical and military were not my forte.

Tucked away rather forlornly behind the suitcase and the basket were two or three heavy wooden hat-making blocks, their Kojak crowns as polished as the skull of an alopecia victim. Together with a heavy smoothing iron and a set of rather alarming broad-bladed metal tongs, which would not be out of place in an interrogator's armoury, they had been part of the tools of my mother's trade during a brief spell as 'Mademoiselle Sonia – Milliner of Paris and London'. At least that's what her business card said in bold blue italics, though I suspect the 'Paris' part was a romantic promotional fable.

All this sad flotsam, the remains of my mother's attempt to establish her own life, my father's wolf's clothing, I had forgotten until I saw the photograph. Elliott was little more than a ghost. I knew so little about him (by the time I set out on his trail, there were no family papers to be found). My mother, herself long ago dead, had seldom spoken of him. When she did, it was with a mixture of grudging acknowledgment that there had been a secret side to his life, about which she knew nothing, and a bitter-sweet nostalgia for what might have been – a mixture shared to the chilling echo, as I later found, by other women he also loved and left.

My mother's father, David Redstone, detested Elliott, though as we shall see, for two men of such different personalities, unknown to each other they had some curious similarities. Underneath the carefully buffed patina and tweed waistcoat of a respectable, though unabashedly immigrant, businessman, there lurked in David Redstone the basic instincts of his Menshevik revolutionary youth in Tsarist Russia, convinced that he had never lost his nose for spotting a wrong 'un, especially one as wrong as the seductive, enigmatic Elliott. My grandparents' inability to derail his relationship with my mother at the outset reinforced the subsequent 'I told you so' inquests when my father decamped to the Continent and then to the Caribbean, safely out of range of a volley of alimony writs.

# 3

# Memories Are Made of This

When I had begun to think how to go about the finding out, it jolted me to realise that I actually had no idea whether my father was alive or dead, so far had we drifted away from each other. I asked my quizzical friend, the Lawyer, to see what he could discover. All I could give him was an address in Berkshire, scene of a bizarre encounter with Elliott twenty years or so previously.

I was being driven back towards London in a dark blue Volvo sedan, rather more prosaic than Elliott's Studebaker, from an Oxford where, on a grey apology for a summer's day, the rainwashed spires and brain-washed academics had proved singularly uninspiring.

Like my father, I have lived long abroad. And my visits back to England are nowadays soured by a feeling of being a dyspeptic stranger in the country in which I grew up. Out of tune with its 'luvvy' politicians, its mean-spirited harmonies and its high-camp, hand-clapping, unisex Church. Pinfold-deaf to a language reduced to its lowest common denominator of swallowed syllables and pseudo-Americanisms. Even the landscape has become unfamiliar, a haphazard patchwork of chrome-yellow fields of Euro-rapeseed flanked by new buildings thrown up in minor variations of the same whimsical LegoPark style.

With nothing much to look at except the bristly nape of the driver's neck as we trundled towards London through the peristaltic contractions of a series of roadworks, I decided to telephone the Lawyer – actually a solicitor, who manages to handle minor royalty and major conmen with equally discreet aplomb. Part of his discreet charm for the bourgeoisie is that he, like his father before him, has managed to maintain his firm's profitable presence in a set of panelled rooms in one of the Dickensian rabbit-warrens, the Inns of Court, where the barristers have their chambers. It lies east of the Savoy Hotel, sheltered from the Thames Embankment traffic behind a manicured lawn crying out to be used as the set for a Peter Greenaway movie.

'Ah, yes,' the Lawyer told me rather flatly. 'Our chap checked out the address you gave me. No one remembers an Elliott there. So we sent a clerk to search the Register of Deaths. It took a while, but I'm sorry to say we found out your father died in July 1977. Pneumonia and cancer of the bladder,' he added with the dispassionate precision of the professional. I quickly calculated that Elliott would have been sixty-nine.

A hypochondriac searching for symptoms, I checked my reactions to the Lawyer's news. Grief? Not at all. Elliott could barely qualify as a passing acquaintance, and certainly not as a parent in anything other than biological terms. Irritation? Why hadn't someone on Elliott's side of the family bothered to pass on the news of his death? Guilt? In a very small measure; perhaps I should have started the search earlier and had the chance at least of getting to know him, catching him and his memories alive, forging some happy reconciliation. Surprise? Only in the sense that, given what little I knew about him, had I had to guess the cause of death, I would have said either a firing squad or a frying pan, wielded by a dark-rooted Bulgarian blonde of a certain age at the end of her tether and a bottle of Gordon's gin. In the end, though, the dominant emotion was curiosity. What had this strange man, The Imperfect Spy, The Man Who Hardly Was, really been about? Now that he was beyond the reach of even the most assiduous Yale researcher, I was even more challenged to see what I could find out.

I re-holstered the carphone and worried about the traffic. I had no idea that after so many years of unknowing, I was about thirty minutes away from the first of the many bizarre concatenations of circumstances that made the quest for Kavan so much more of a pleasure than a sadness.

Scribbled weekly calculations in the margin of the *Financial Times* reassure me that I am able to indulge without too much guilt a streak of extravagance whose origins I now don't have to look very hard to find. So when I have to travel, I usually charter a private plane; like yachts in the Mediterranean, villas in the Caribbean and pretty women anywhere, planes are far more economical to rent than to own. One advantage of what is euphemistically called the 'executive jet' (to make it sound like a tool of efficiency rather than the self-indulgent wallow it really is) is being able to come and go when you please, unfettered by timetables or the need to check in half a day before the flight so that the British Airports Authority can cajole you to overspend in their grotesquely mis-named 'Duty Free' shops. But the principal advantage is that by slipping under deferential escort through the unmarked rear entrances of the world's airports, bags loaded directly on to the plane, you are cocooned from the Bedlam of the public areas – where the destination boards click like worry beads, and squinting, androgynous security guards with halitosis and intrusive hands make the worst of a bad job – and shielded from the sheer High Anxiety of it all.

On that trip, Paris was my next stop and as an experiment I had arranged for the plane to meet me at Northolt, the small Royal Air Force field just to the west of London. Smack on the Oxford road it was more convenient than Luton, my normal departure point. Northolt is used mainly by fliers for whom the taxpayer is footing the bill – government ministers, senior military men and the less controversial members of the royal family – but it also provides, rather grudgingly, a limited number of slots for private jets.

The main road ran past wire fencing, low buildings, distant hangars and a pair of ornate wrought-iron gates, once obviously the main entrance but now locked and barricaded. Access, the Volvo's driver told me, was nowadays through a side entrance. The setting tugged at my memory. We drove down a narrow sliproad, which discreetly bisects a row of red-brick semi-detached villas. Across it, framed by high-intensity lights and concertina wire, is a metal barrier, where cars and passengers are given a brisk rubdown by pretty but serious girls from the RAF Regiment, dwarfed but not daunted by their jumbo-sized semi-automatic rifles.

We drove circumspectly along the perimeter track, looping back towards the cluster of buildings alongside the Oxford road. Beside the single-storey white reception building, the sharp-nosed Lear 55, with its go-faster tilted-tip wings, glinted erotically on the tarmac. Memory crowded in. Had Elliott not been at the front of my mind, I wouldn't have made the connection until later; even so it was a few minutes before the pieces coalesced, and I realised I had been here before.

As I did the mental arithmetic, about forty-four years before. If I had been past the airport since, I had certainly never been inside, nor indeed given it a second thought. Now I could replay the mental videotape; it was rather grainy, with jumpcuts here and there, but the episode as a whole came back quite clearly.

October, 1948, I had been a nervous, still secretly thumb-sucking, nine year old. As Elliott had never really been around in any continuous, significant way, there had seemed nothing special about his latest absence. Knowing what I do now, I can see my mother had made a good job of concealing her worries from me and from my two sisters, over what must have been a stressful two weeks.

I had become conscious only of a mounting bustle, the telephone ringing, a car, highly unusually, in the driveway, people coming to talk to my mother, away in the back of the house. 'It's just some people from Daddy's office.' Then, more perceptible fluttering from my mother. 'We're going to meet him this evening. He's coming back from Hungary. The girls can stay here. It'll be too late for them.' We had no car. In those pre-pubescent, public transport days, going anywhere was not so much difficult as disjointed. Going from south London into the centre, and then westwards, was a daisychain punctuated by wet waits, staring at the walls of bus shelters or at holiday posters peeling off the sooty walls of a cavernous station, of bus, train, underground, and still more underground, clattering through tunnels, erupting suddenly into the open between market gardens and the secret, untidy rear views of rows of 1930s' ribbon housing.

Back in 1948, I had no idea where we were going until we had ended up at Northolt, my hand wrapped in my mother's grip. It was the very same single-storey stucco building, then serving as London's pre-Heathrow Airport, into which I strode with a touch more self-assurance forty-four years later. Apart from the paraphernalia of modern travel – a baggage X-ray machine and a couple of computer terminals – it had hardly changed. The swing doors to the rear which lead on to the apron were just where I remembered them. And the neat waiting-room, with its G-Plan furniture, saucers of government-issue digestive biscuits on the varnished table and rows of RAF squadron plaques lining the walls.

Elliott had emerged through the swing doors. Pale was my abiding impression. Since in those days England's prevailing complexion, immigrants and suntanned scrap-metal merchants apart, was fishbelly white, his pallor must have been exceptional. He didn't say much, if anything. My mother said, 'Hello,' and touched his hand. People fussed about. Men in brown hats moved us briskly out of the building. We splashed a few steps in the rain and crammed together in the back of a long black car. Car rides were a rarity. Big cars like this, deftly driven by a man in a peaked cap who was deferential to my mother, and even to me, were a new experience altogether. The car purred out of the gates on to the highway. One of the men in brown hats sat next to the driver. Still, no one spoke. Yellow street lights, traffic signals, shiny wet streets.

I went to bed and woke in the dark. It could have been five minutes or five hours later. Sweating. Head splitting. I had left the gas fire burning. Nudged on, perhaps by some deep-hidden Freudian imp, I went to my mother's room. Actually, suddenly and rather strangely, my parents' room. I slid in, about to ask my mother plaintively for a glass of water when a hand grabbed my wrist . . . 'What the hell do you want, chum?' he asked. The tone was very awake, very level. Not soothing or paternal, not that I had any frame of reference for that anyway. All in all – remembered now – the swoop, the note of menacing inquiry of a store detective catching a shoplifter about to snatch a carelessly displayed scarf from a countertop. I stammered that I had a headache. My mother woke up, put on the light, gave me an aspirin with some water from the glass by her bed. Elliott sat up, silently watching. He had rather smart navy-blue pyjamas with white piping, the sort of thing advertised by Gamage's in the *Illustrated London News* with a line drawing of a bank managerish cove slipping between the sheets with a glossy balance sheet, so much more elegant than my striped Daniel Neal winceyette. He said nothing more. After turning off the fire and opening the window, I went back to bed. It was still raining.

Home had become a stranger place. How very much stranger it must have been for my parents, lying stiffly side by side, he a spare-time spy who had just scrambled out of trouble and was back with his family reluctantly, under the direction of the counter-intelligence specialists of MI5, she a riven wife hoping against hope that he was back to stay but knowing in her heart that he wasn't.

# 4

# A Few of His Bones

At least I had recognised Elliott at Northolt. On the previous occasion I can recall spending any time with him, in 1946, if the headmaster of my pre-preparatory school, an unctuous Welshman of religion, hadn't told me that my father was coming to see me, I would have had no idea who the visitor was, pacing impatiently across the bubbling linoleum in the long, dark hallway. Quite why it had been decided to ship me off at the rather early age of seven to Dr Morgan's flint-fronted academy with its pervasive odour of damp boys and badly boiled beef on the chill and pebbly south coast of England I have no idea.

We were, as you will see, not a conventional English family given to such ritual barbarities. Nor, but you must take my word for it, was I a difficult child best dealt with at a distance. My mother had no money, and Elliott's lifestyle always absorbed for his own urgent needs all his available resources and more besides, so, I wonder now, who was paying the fees? But in any event come to Worthing he did, a tall stranger in a long navy-blue overcoat. We went for a walk one wet Sunday afternoon.

We traipsed along the promenade, trapped in an amber silence of mutual incomprehension, punctuated by his racking cough and my monosyllabic responses to questions about school, one of his loping strides to every two of mine. The school days were of wool-grey monotony and there would not have been much to say even if I hadn't been

tongue-tied by shyness at meeting this strange non-stranger. We walked
past the pier, two rusty, gull-splashed platforms in the slatey, bladder-
wracked foam, whose mid-section had been demolished by Dad's Army
in the war in the forlorn hope that this might deter a German seaborne
landing, and circled slowly back towards the school, shaking hands in
awkward farewell on the steps while Dr Morgan smarmed. One of my
more worldly and better connected contemporaries had assured me that
any visiting relative was good for at least half-a-crown in pocket money
and a father, probably ten shillings. Not so. Being now a little more familiar with Elliott's behaviour, I am only thankful he did not actually tap me
for money.

The visit did not stay long in my mind. It was overtaken in twenty-four
hours by an attack of ringworm, brought on not by the blast from the
past his visit had represented but by the bacterial miasma given off by a
band of small, dirty boys in a small, dirty building eating small portions
of dirty food from which every scrap of vitamin had been diligently
steamed by a pair of shifty, effeminate Poles in the basement. These
claimed lugubriously to be Displaced Persons, but their occasional
flashes of terrible anger suggested to the more imaginative that they
may well have been concentration camp trusties on the run from the War
Crimes Tribunal.

Matron's kindly, if shocked, diagnosis meant the special pleasure of a
bus and train ride, she riding plump and genteel shotgun, to consult a
specialist along the coast in Brighton. Parting my hair under an eerie
ultraviolet light, he murmured sadly as he took his fees about the
school's standards of hygiene, and smeared yellow sulphur paste on to
the angry red circles. On the return journey I covered my shame with
my schoolcap, and for my stoicism earned a private mug of cocoa in the
school's kitchen, more Hogarth than Siematic, while the Poles lurked,
the younger pouting as he cleaned his nails with a breakfast fork.

There was another odd episode in 1947, odd not in itself but because
I can recall so little of it, whereas each moment should have stuck as
firmly in a child's mind as a harpoon. After all, in those days of austerity,
with the tectonic plates of Europe still quivering from the aftershocks of
war, with British travellers rationed to an allowance of a few pounds per
day, and my mother's habitual penury, to go off to Switzerland had more
than a touch of the exotic, if not the bizarre. But off I went with her, and
I can still remember sooty British trains, a cross-Channel ferry moving

in a cloud of seagull droppings, saltspray and beery vomit, French porters in blue smocks and, in Switzerland, a toytown railway running on cogs between snowy mountain bowls. Quite possibly my mother took me – the curly-headed embodiment of their life together – to thrust in the face of a wavering Elliott in an attempt to appeal to his loyalty or his better nature. Yet again, she had the man wrong; there was little room for guilt on the gingerbread of his life. It must have been a disaster, since I cannot actually recall seeing Elliott, my abiding memories being watching from our window the distant skiers crisscrossing the slopes with their vapour trails of snow, a snow that I think once I went down into the street to run through my hands. We ate in my mother's room, the waiters giving off waves of scorn as strong as body odour when they were not lavishly tipped, with intermittent appearances by Elliott, the curt and distant *deus ex machina* of the Palace Hotel.

Apart from a box of disgusting liquorice candies I was allowed to extract from a slot machine on Arosa Station, as a consolation prize, that was about it for infant memories. I needed facts.

The real starting-point for Elliott's exhumation was a one-line reference in *The Embattled Mountain*, Sir William Deakin's fascinating account of his time with Tito's Communist Partisans in 1943, to 'Major Cavan Elliott's DISCLAIM mission', whose aim had been to reach Tito's rival General Draža Mihailovic, leader of the royalist Chetnik guerrillas.

That Elliott had been dropped into what, for the sake of convenience and sad memory, we may as well go on calling Yugoslavia, I knew from my mother; Deakin's reference prompted me to search more widely. I prowled libraries and bookstores, and subscribed to arcane catalogues from wild-eyed mail-order booksellers in the American militia heartland. Among much else, I found *Britain and European Resistance*, a collection of papers delivered at a 1980s' London seminar. One of its editors was Professor Phyllis Auty, said on the cover to be at the University of Vancouver. The book had been published long before I got my hands on it and a telephone call to the rain-drenched shoreline of British Columbia produced the answer that Professor Auty had now retired. I found her address back in the UK and she responded to my neophyte questions with patience and energy. Among many other leads, she introduced me to Bill Deakin.

Taking a book-buying break from his retirement home in a walled hilltop village in Provence to sip champagne in White's, he gave me a tutorial on wartime Yugoslavia, and then, like a diminutive, silver-haired conjurer, produced from beneath his leather armchair a file of papers which advanced my search by several light years. Deakin had been planning a book on four unsuccessful British missions to Yugoslavia, one of them Elliott's. He had abandoned the project, but in preparing for it he had gathered a treasure trove of archive material about Elliott in Britain and Yugoslavia. And, by another chain of coincidence, he had also come to hold a few of Elliott's personal papers and letters, including a sheaf of unedited reminiscences dictated in the early 1960s, apparently for a Berkshire newspaper.

What strange vibrations and confused excitements emanated from those disjointed and, at that stage, little-understood musty memories of someone of whom, at least on paper, I was part, but who always far away was now irretrievably so.

There was one more surprise in Bill Deakin's bundle, as much of an adrenaline rush of *déjà vu* as the step backwards in time at Northolt. Tucked among the notes was a photograph of Elliott, wearing the uniform I remembered so clearly from my attic ferreting. There were the shiny Sam Browne, the campaign ribbons, the buttons and badges. A half-smile told the photographer nothing. His hair glistened, no doubt from the Trumpers pomade unsuccessfully rubbed in to tame his springy waves into the flat curves more appropriate for an officer.

The photograph, signed in his tiny, tidy script 'With all love Kavan, Xmas 1945', is a puzzle in itself. Why was it taken? To whom did he give it? Presumably not my mother, otherwise why was it in his papers? On whose bedside table had it sat for all those years? The photographer's studio was just a grenade's throw away from the headquarters in London's Baker Street of the Special Operations Executive (SOE) for which Elliott had worked during the war, and which, in 1945, its job done, was allegedly winding itself out of existence at the urging of a Labour Government jittery about running in peacetime what their Hampstead supporters would surely frown on as a subversive organisation, whose only targets could be the fraternal countries of the socialist bloc. Was the studio session some end-of-term gesture, the secret world's equivalent of a gold watch? Had Elliott given it as a memento to some SOE girlfriend, apple-cheeked, khaki-knickered daughter of a good Home Counties family with a Baccarat crystal accent and the sexual appetite of a stoat on heat? The answer came very late in the day, at a point when I had in fact almost lost sight of the question. Like so much else, it came almost by accident. And like so many other landmarks in Elliott's life, it involved a woman.

Encouraged by the glasnost of the SOE Adviser, who watches over what remains of the SOE archives from his friendly Whitehall eyrie, I set out eagerly on the Yugoslav trail. I peered myopically at microfilm of faded Gestapo records, yellowing pages of reports by the Ustashe forces of the wartime Fascist Government of Croatia, and old Belgrade newspapers. I met, fifty years on, not only the SOE officer in charge of putting my father on to the plane to make his drop into Yugoslavia, but also the plane's pilot. Branching out, hungry for more, I feasted on clumsily typed annual reviews by the pre-war Bulgarian secret police, the Public Prosecutor's files of the Hungarian Communist regime, the records of the Allied Control Commission in Germany, archives in Jamaica, police court reports rather closer to home and the comprehensive bookstacks of the Marx Memorial Library, a dowdy temple where the altar light still flickers bravely for the god that failed. I badgered ageing academics and retired spies of several persuasions, some furtive, some petulant, some helpful: people who might have known some of the story.

Elliott had relatives, for sure. But who? Where? Uncles and aunts swam in the cotton-wool memories of childhood, but had not been seen or heard of since. I remembered Elliott had two brothers, Basil and Leo. One had been a policeman in London. Which, I had no idea. They were most probably dead anyway, but nothing ventured, nothing gained. I wrote to London's Metropolitan Police. The diligent Steven Earl of their Pensions Department, improbably but successfully an author in his spare time of books on piracy, found an Elliott widow on his computer and kindly agreed to forward a letter, without divulging her address. Back, bread on the waters of the Indian Ocean, came a letter from Elliott's sister-in-law, Basil's widow, in South Africa. Through her I met Elliott's sister Ethel, and a plethora of hitherto unknown and unseen cousins, friendly but perplexed at this odd irruption of a ghost train from a long-forgotten branchline. They provided kindness, photographs and random memories. Their last sight of Elliott had been after a family party, a drunk, prematurely old man, insisting aggressively and, as it turned out, correctly that he was quite capable of taking the endless ride from Cockfosters at one extremity of the Underground to the mainline station of Paddington, and thence, God knows how, to rural Berkshire on a pre-dawn milktrain. He probably didn't buy a ticket.

The late Aidan Crawley, journalist, politician and businessman, shared with me his memories of Elliott in pre-war Bulgaria. And from the enigmatic Antony Terry MC, far from the madding crowd in New Zealand, came memories, clues and papers, some of these personal and important, at least to me. Terry had been close to Elliott at critical periods in the latter's life, and was himself just as puzzling a cocktail of duplicitous charm and amorality. He had been a long-term stalwart at least of the SIS supporters' club, if not actually a playing member of the team itself. Partly through and partly despite Terry, I tracked down two of the women who had, like my mother, reluctantly and warily loved Elliott, fluttering in his candle-flame until reality or calamity dawned.

My biggest benefactor of all, though, was luck, the consistent good fortune with which either evidence has popped up, connections have been made, or random names have turned into people – almost as if there was someone turning the pages for me. I accumulated material; and material about the material.

The world's finest jigsaws are hand-fretworked by the gentle craftsmen of Stave Puzzles in Vermont. Not for them the right-angled, straight-edged outline or the chocolate-box image of an overfed, overwhiskered cat. Their puzzles, custom-cut to order to one of three ascending degrees of difficulty to suit the puzzler's threshold of pain, are arbitrary in shape, sometimes even three-dimensional, tormenting and obscure in subject, and often, to confuse the puzzler even more, incorporate the rebus, a sequence of mini-shapes scattered through the body of the puzzle, which, when slotted home and identified in their correct sequence, spell out some proverb or old-wives' saying. Tipping the 1,000 tissue-wrapped pieces out of their chic blue-and-green box, one's initial reaction is dismay. Poking with a disconsolate forefinger at the cluster of meaningless, often monochrome shapes, the puzzler hopes that somehow, something will gel. So it was with Elliott. So too with the brief history we will come to later of Siberia, revolution and my grandfather.

I risked becoming like Trollope's Sir Thomas Underwood, who spent so much time gathering information on the life of Lord Verulam 'that the labour which he had so longed to commence became so frightful to him that he did not dare touch it'. In the end, though, the sheer menacing weight of all those piles of files mating on my floor and oozing out of cupboards pushed me into action.

# 5

# South from Kentish Town

It's a long, long way from Kentish Town to Budapest, and not that easy to reconstruct. 'Much obscurity attends the passage of his early life', to apply to Elliott a tag from a Victorian obituary. The death certificate gave me his date of birth as 8 December 1908 and led me to the record of his birth as the son of Ethelbert Burnley, a grocer's assistant, and Walburga Rice, spinster. Named after a saint whose remains defied chemistry by continuing to give off a sweet and fragrant odour for 1,200 years, Walburga's photographs show her to have been a strikingly handsome woman, obviously the source of Elliott's own good looks. Though born Burnley, this did not last, and we may as well refer to him as 'Elliott' from this point on. Ethelbert Burnley quickly vanished into the gaslit nether-world of Edwardian London, and Elliott and his mother moved just before the First World War to Glasgow, where his sister Ethel was born. Then, back to London. Ethel recalled the first appearance there of a tall man whom she was told to call 'Father' and whose name they were told they would now adopt. This is the Herbert Elliott named in Elliott's mar-riage certificate as his father, and described as a 'professional accountant' (experience suggests that it is often the unprofessional ones who give you better value). The family moved often, a penny-pinching, 'my old man said follow the van', ramble through working-class North London.

At one point Elliott and his sister were parked for several confused and lonely months in a Catholic orphanage on the northern fringe of London, remembered by Ethel as a period of Dettol, unfamiliar ritual, black wimples and cold, constipating lavatories, while Walburga roiled through some mysterious crisis of men and money. Walburga and Herbert, eventually more settled, produced two sons of their own, Elliott's half-brothers Leo and Basil. Ethel told me that, apart from the small, lost period inside the whitewashed walls of the convent, there had been no trace of Catholicism and nothing remotely Irish in her childhood, which makes all the odder Elliott's later espousal of Irish roots and his claims of a 'traditional Irish family upbringing' (whatever that may mean).

One or two official forms now mouldering in the archives, including the personal details in his wartime intelligence file, give the spelling of his first name as 'Clian' and his religion as Catholic, though most show the name as Kavan and his religion as Church of England. To confuse matters even more, he became known to many of his military and spy-world colleagues as 'Joe', or 'Balkan Joe', evocative of some mustachioed Ruritanian balladeer.

So many seemingly solid families have a structure built on skeletons, secrets and shame. Many have an outer circle, often of elderly ladies, who by comfortable custom and kindness are regarded as cousins and aunts even though the blood lines may not be that clear. In Elliott's case, there was a birdlike lady, sharp as a tack, with wispy hair like fine-spun icing sugar, known by all of them as Aunty Heidi, who had always, or at least as long as they could remember, shared their various homes, as a prop, confidante and foil for Walburga.

Ethel told me that, as a child, Heidi had half-whispered to her, outside Walburga's hearing, with a touch of drama and a hint of gloating, heightened by a couple of bottles of Mackeson's Stout, about 'your Mum's little secret'. She said she was sworn to secrecy and would be free to speak only after Walburga's death. Inevitably, Aunty Heidi died first, the story untold.

Was it to do with Elliott's own illegitimate birth? Walburga and a dashing Irish horse coper on his way to seek fame and fortune in the New World, snatching a quickfire knee-trembler in the wet back alley behind a Kilburn pub? A wild Irish branch to the family, distilling poteen from potatoes in the cellars of a tumble-down Gothic castle in the middle of a desolate Kerry bog, while the wolfhounds bayed and the priests prayed?

As we shall see, Elliott embroidered many of the episodes in his life, but even though his declared parents, Ethelbert and Walburga, bore names redolent of eleventh-century Saxon royalty rather than Ireland, it is hard to think that the Irish link would have been entirely fictional. Perhaps Heidi did get around to telling him, after all, but not Ethel? It remains a missing piece of the puzzle. As does the fate of Herbert Elliott.

Ethel, whom I met late in her life, was very fond of her brother, but three-quarters of a century later remembered Elliott the child as 'a real little con-man', fantasising, wheedling, always coming out on the right side. With this went a crass recklessness even with the halfpennies and intermittent threepenny bits of his pocket money, a weakness noted ruefully over the years by friends, family, shopkeepers, school bursars and off-licence proprietors, which caused a bad problem towards the end of his life. Ethel recalled, 'I always tried never to have any money on me at home, because Kavan would always be after me for it.' When she was twenty-one, he told her grandly, 'Buy yourself whatever you want as a present, I'll pay you next month.'

'Don't do it, girl,' was her mother's canny advice, 'you'll never see a penny.' She was right.

Elliott, Ethel told me, left school at fifteen. He was bright, but with no special aptitude, except perhaps a touch of the devious. In his last term, he won a certificate for diligence in music studies; when his dumbfounded mother and sister pressed him to explain, since he could barely master the scales, he confessed that he had for weeks been forging his mother's signature on certificates fraudulently attesting to hours of assiduous practice on the battered, credit-financed living-room piano.

Ethel found him a clerk's job at Stubbs, a City of London credit investigation and debt collection agency, where she worked as a telephonist. She then moved on to another firm. Elliott continued to leave home like clockwork in the early morning, returning for supper full of office gossip with a predictability admirable in a young man. One evening, some six months later, Ethel ran into a former Stubbs' colleague. What a pity, he said casually, that her brother had lost his job so soon. She learned that Elliott had actually been fired from the agency after only a couple of weeks, following some unpleasantness over discrepancies in the office petty cash. But for months he had kept up the steady, totally false façade of a hard-working clerk. Where he had spent the long, boring days of pretence, what he had used for money, no one knew.

What fed him? I don't mean eggs, beans, bleeding stewed tomatoes and chips in a steamy ABC café on Holborn Viaduct, or a pint of tepid Burton Ale and a pork pie in a noisy saloon bar, its ceiling yellow with nicotine . . . but what perked his interest, shaped his mind? I don't see him poring over Italian Renaissance miniatures at the British Museum. Nor on excited tiptoe, flushed with false optimism, as the greyhounds scrambled around the White City oval in their eternally futile chase after the bobbing mechanical hare. Nor can I picture him crammed in the hoarse camaraderie of flat caps and cheap gaberdine raincoats on the terrace of Highbury Stadium watching the stars of the Arsenal team, Brylcreemed hair parted in the centre, baggy knee-length shorts flapping, kick a sodden football through the mud.

Nor am I convinced about books, though *Stamboul Train*, that primer for the searcher after Continental adventure, did appear in 1932 and might have made some mark on Elliott. I suspect for Elliott, as for millions of others, the formative influence was the cinema, just then beginning its transition from the small-scale to the architectural and cultural overkill of Gaumont British Pictures and Hollywood. It was a cheap way to pass the day transported into a world of black-and-white glamour, suave leading men and pouting blonde starlets making up in mammary development what they lacked in brainpower (Elliott's ideal recipe for a woman), the quays and stations, seagulls and steam framing the adventure ahead, plots which always ended with the hero safe and sound basking in the approbation of his brother officers, and the adulation of the ladies.

These were evenings and afternoons of escape, doubling up as celluloid lessons in elocution, deportment, the right degree of nonchalance with which to flick open a cigarette case or the cylinder of a revolver, the tone to take with foreigners, the caste marks and accents, Hollywood version, of the officer and gentleman, the suave secrets of seduction. In the interval, when the hydraulic pump thrust the pink spotlit Hammond organ rearing priapically over the lip of the pit, the elderly musician flashed his false teeth at the audience and the white ball began to bounce hypnotically from word to word of the popular song sheet projected on to the screen, there was time to stretch the legs, cast an eye over the giggling shop girls on their afternoon off, and try your luck with them or a Walls ice-cream. The cinema and its stars showed just how easy it was, at least in a one-dimensional world, to create a whole new personality, a new image. All it took was a clever scriptwriter, a voice borrowed from the commentators on British Movietone News, and a Burnley from the cobbled streets became Clian the Irish Rover, or a gallant subaltern from *The Four Feathers*.

Back on the streets, blinking like a coalminer at the end of his shift, Elliott found himself one afternoon confronted by his mother with the truth about his non-existent job.

He reacted with an alacrity his family found alarming and suspicious – was someone after him? – arriving home the next night to announce baldly that he was off to Zagreb in Yugoslavia in the morning. He had answered, so he said, an anonymous advertisement in the *Star* newspaper for men with language skills; the box number had turned out to be an agency in the West End, which after a brief interview had offered him a job teaching English and French to the aspiring children of Croat business and professional men. They had given him a one-way train ticket and expenses of thirty shillings to be deducted from his wages when he got there.

The basic implausibility of the story, for he knew nothing of teaching or, as far as she knew, French, sent Walburga into a nightmare of worry about male white-slave traffic, made all the worse when she looked in the atlas in Pears Cyclopedia and found how close Zagreb was to Turkey and similar vice-sodden foreign parts. However, Elliott was determined to go, and go he did. But not before she opened his battered cardboard suitcase and found half-a-dozen dictionaries, one clean collar and a frayed tie. She and Ethel set about laundering and ironing to supply Elliott with shirts, underwear and socks. The next morning he stepped out briskly down the hill in his Gamage's raincoat, brown trilby hat cocked. The boat train from Victoria Station took him to the Channel and to the unknown. In a very real sense, I don't think he ever came back.

In an expatriate community, voracious for new faces as new objects of sexual and professional speculation, Elliott's novelty value and undoubted charm made for a good catch, and he was swiftly absorbed into a pleasant whirl of parties, drink and indiscretion.

When the Learjet whistles you from London to Zagreb in little over three hours, when news is beamed worldwide in an instant from the remotest Montenegrin mountainside or African alleyway, it is hard to visualise the comfortable isolation of the few hundred foreigners in pre-war Zagreb, cocooned by language, snobbery and hard currency from the travails and concerns of the city's 150,000 people, winding the gramophone, swinging the tennis racquet and rattling the cocktail shaker; the political ozone crackling in the European air, the blood, guts and rhetoric of local politics, were something for the diplomats to fuss about.

That the only acceptable form of news – English newspapers dumped, fraying and grimy at Zagreb Station four or five days after publication – was out of date made it somehow more palatable and easier to absorb. That the principal lifeline to London meant spending almost three sooty days and jolting nights on the train, climaxed by the salty nausea of the cross-Channel ferry, made the green and pleasant lands of home something which worked better as an image than a reality. It also meant that visits from head office, relatives and creditors, and other vexatious disturbances of the tranquil daily round, were relatively rare and rarely an embarrassing surprise. And for drifters like Elliott, it was far easier to recreate a past without too much risk of exposure.

Elliott swiftly shed the chrysalis of Kentish Town and moved easily between the languid civility of the embassy round and the fluttering gentility of the English wives and their dinner-parties. He was eyed by the wives often with frank appraisal, sometimes with annoyance if he was suspected of having kept a husband out half the night in one of Zagreb's sweaty *maisons de rendezvous*, chatting mindlessly to the often pretty, always tired girls with hairy armpits who dreamed secretly that one day some rich prince would appear among the froglike clientele to whisk them away to a comfortable life in Stuttgart, Sorrento or Streatham.

Elliott's 'language school' was a couple of dusty rooms with creaking tables. Their windows opened only on to the smelly central airshaft that in most Zagreb buildings served as a rubbish tip, a space to string out the perennially grey laundry and as a loudspeaker, magnifying every yell, shriek, grunt and babble of the tenants. His pupils were mainly the idle and uninterested children of the rich, whose giggling apologies for English diverted the efforts of one or two serious-minded ladies with an interest in literature. Sporadic letters to his mother brought exotic stamps and anodyne news. After a few months, Elliott said that he had been taken on as a soap salesman by Lever Brothers, now Unilever, in their office in the Croat capital – a step upwards that evoked sighs of satisfaction back home: 'Always knew he would come right in the end.'

He lived not in the splendours of the Esplanade Hotel, seven vaguely classical storeys erected proudly in 1926, but in Grisogono's Pension, where a few pennies a day brought him a plain room, an iron bedstead, and a handpump for spraying insecticide into the menacing cracks in the ceiling when the bugs became too much to bear. Down the hallway the communal toilet was best visited with alacrity, averted eye and stout shoes. Round the corner, in the wide market square, reared the statue of the Croat leader Yollatchik, brandishing his sword in the direction of Budapest. Whether Elliott ever saw that as a portent for his own movements in later years, I rather doubt. Not a portent man, by and large.

A rainy evening. Ethel came home, tight-pressed in a tram up the bustling, Cockney gulch of the Archway Road. 'I'd bought some black cloth to make a skirt for the office. Mother was terribly superstitious, and something made me throw the package in the hall cupboard as I came in, so she didn't see me carrying black.

'When I went into the kitchen, she was sitting fretting by the fire, a telegram crumpled in her hand. It said Kavan was very ill with pneumonia. We didn't recognise the name of the person who had cabled. My mother said she was going to go out to Zagreb the next morning. But I persuaded her to let me call Lever Brothers from the box across the road to see what they knew.'

'Never heard of him,' said their personnel people. When Ethel, noisily, suggested they were wrong, an aggrieved voice assured her that all the files had been checked. As the day ended and the street lights flickered back into sulphur yellow half-life, Ethel recrossed the road with a handful of pennies and called Lever again, on the offchance. This time, without a hint of apology, a clerk said that they had found out about Elliott, that he was being well looked after and would come home when he was fit to travel. A couple of weeks later, a gaunt Elliott returned, a ten shilling leg of lamb doing duty for the fatted calf. But only briefly. He said that he had people to see and then had to go back to Zagreb again.

That Lever Brothers in London had no record of Elliott is perhaps not surprising. But the confusion may herald the first faint shadow of the ambivalence in Elliott's flickering relationship over the years with the giant Anglo-Dutch concern.

When he married, for the first time, in September 1935, Elliott gave his occupation as 'Sales Manager, Milk Products'; in today-speak, which transmogrifies technical colleges into universities, I suppose that might be no more than just a milkman, but back then it probably did have some significance. An ever so slightly embarrassed and mildly uncommunicative

Unilever say today that they have no record of how and where he came
to join them, and almost no information on his time with them. British
wartime files record that Elliott was Unilever's representative in Zagreb
from 1934 to 1939, and Elliott's own notes say that he spent 'many years'
in Croatia; a biographical sketch he provided in the 1950s for the
Maugham-evoking *Who's Who in Jamaica* said that he had joined
Unilever in Vienna in 1929.

Bill Deakin told me that he had seen a reference, in a now mislaid
British War Office file, to Elliott also having served for a time before the
war as Unilever's representative in Budapest, which if true (although
there is no evidence) might explain his fluency in Hungarian and his
later return. He is remembered today by someone with forty years of
Central European experience as one of only two non-Hungarians – the
other an Austrian – she has ever met who spoke the almost impossible
language fluently and without an accent.

His language skills were formidable; together with the extravagance,
a profound aversion to the great outdoors and to dancing, and an all-
consuming restlessness, they are my only legacy. Perhaps in those
shabby months when he was pretending to keep up a job, he had actually
holed up in some North London library, discovering in himself the ability to absorb languages. In addition to the Hungarian he concealed from
the border guards and those around him in the Hutter es Lever office, he
spoke German, French and Serbo-Croat fluently, and passable Russian.

Where the Russian came from is another small puzzle. My mother
Sonia was circumspect enough about her assimilation in a new country to
think of Russian very much as a secret language, to be used only with her
parents and sister. Sparingly at that. And never with her children, in case
we became tainted by that awful English stigma of being a foreigner.
Perhaps, nevertheless, Elliott's ready ear made him a quick learner.

A Yugoslav journalist writing in the 1970s claimed, totally without
substantiation, that Elliott had spent time before the war in the Baku oil-
fields in southern Russia, but I very much doubt it; if he had any Baku
connection, it was more likely as a small part of the motley regiment of
British clandestine planners who spent inordinate amounts of time over
the pre-war years working on increasingly fanciful and always futile pro-
jects to sabotage the wells.

How the language teaching, the first links with Lever, and then the initial contact with the fine-meshed nets which SIS strings out in the

shallows to pick up resourceful people with a bent for the bent, all came together, we can only speculate. We do know that at some point in the late 1930s Elliott became General Manager of a Lever offshoot, Astra, in Zagreb.

Certainly, in the 1930s the British Consulate in Zagreb, the British Council's earnest reading-rooms, newspaper correspondents' offices and shabby upstairs bureaux occupied by obscure trading concerns, housed a disproportionate number of clandestine operators. The British business community in Zagreb was small, only fifty-two strong by 1939, according to a military intelligence estimate prepared in London. A tight-knit world in which a muttered request one evening over billiards, or in a nightclub boozily watching a fat lady do physiologically improbable tricks with doves, to run a little errand for Old Fruity at the Consulate would have been readily accepted by Elliott as good fun, a good cause. What was the risk in handing over an envelope at the railroad buffet to a man in a black Homburg hat, or taking a few photos of the Yugoslav air-force base outside the city on the next trip south? All we know reliably is that somewhere in this period, Elliott, to use the SIS vernacular, 'came to notice', and, after clearance by London with a rapidity that suggested some earlier familiarity, was taken on as an occasional undercover go-between and message handler.

That this grew into a far more intense involvement in clandestine activity is suggested by an unsigned, unheaded and undated note attached to a file on Elliott's wartime service. If, as the context strongly suggests, the agent described is indeed Elliott, he was a busy young man, combining – as he did later in life – a superficially conventional business career with a heavy cloak-and-dagger schedule. On the intelligence side, he was successful in 'penetrating the German financial set-up and . . . certain German smuggling organisations in Zagreb', 'arranging for reporting stocks and movements of petroleum products in the Balkans', and 'using his company cover to assist communications and liaison with other Balkan countries'.

On the subversion and sabotage side, so the anonymous memorandum tells us, he again – anticipating what he would get up to after the war in Hungary – used his office and private residence for the storage of 'materials' and for agent debriefings, allowed the company laboratory 'to be used for experimental purposes', arranged for distribution of Allied subversive propaganda and, as a crowning blow, 'organised the adulteration of all stocks of superheated steam oils in Yugoslavia', a manoeuvre whose boldness seems remarkable, even if its real economic impact is not easy to assess.

Although unsigned, another file entry indicates that the memorandum was written as some sort of reference or testimonial for Elliott by T. J. Glanville, perhaps as part of the vetting for his post-war recruitment as an SIS 'asset'. Glanville was another figure in the grey hinterland between British business and the secret world. Officially listed in the 1930s as a humdrum accountant in the Zagreb office of Price Waterhouse, he emerged as British Vice-Consul in 1939. He flitted again across the clandestine stage in the exotic world of Lisbon in 1941, allegedly attached to the British Embassy's Commercial Section.

Using major commercial enterprises to provide cover for British intelligence agents is hardly unknown. Unilever was as likely, or unlikely, a home as any one of half-a-dozen others. In those pre-war years, Rex Pearson, Unilever's senior director in Switzerland, was close to SIS, whose dapper and devious Deputy Chief, (Sir) Claude Dansey, involved him in the formation of the Z Organisation, a deep-cover reinforcement, heavily reliant on international businessmen, for the understaffed, underfunded and under-achieving Passport Control system. Elliott's lack of formal education brings to mind Dansey's claim that he 'would never knowingly employ a university man' for secret work. Z was not Dansey's only claim to fame; he had the distinction, perhaps not so rare, of having been seduced as a schoolboy by Robert Ross, then twenty-four, the Canadian homosexual who later claimed to have been Oscar Wilde's first lover, and to whom *The Importance of Being Earnest* is dedicated.

My own Christian name is another little part of the Unilever enigma. One of the few things positive or negative I can remember my mother telling me about my father was that he had been a good friend of Geoffrey Heyworth, who as Sir Geoffrey, and later Lord, Heyworth was a main Board director of Unilever from 1931 and its dynamic Chairman from 1942 to 1960.

She said that I had been named Geoffrey because of their friendship. She if anyone should have known, but I wonder how within the Unilever/Lever organisation, a stratified, quintessentially English structure in the UK, hidebound and humourlessly Dutch in Europe, a salesman, however bright and upwardly mobile, could have built that kind of relationship with a distant senior director? Elliott was not the toadying type, so I assume there was in fact some unknown link between them. A clue to it may lie in Heyworth's own background. Twelve years older than Elliott, he had joined Lever as a seventeen-year-old school-leaver on one of its lowest rungs, as an accounts clerk. Ambition, and a yearning for abroad and adventure similar to Elliott's, had transplanted him within a year to Canada, where he spent much of his Lever service, aside from a spell in the Canadian army in the First World War.

Had Heyworth been asked to take an interest in Elliott? If so, by whom? If he acted as Elliott's protector in a business that might not take kindly to tough guys whose minds seemed less than 100 per cent set on their careers, it might explain why many years later Elliott's employment with Unilever came to an abrupt and premature end within weeks of Heyworth's own retirement.

A clue that the Gestapo suspected even before the war that Elliott was not quite the straight businessman he claimed to be is to be found in the rather chilling pages of the *Sonderfandungsliste GB*, or 'Wanted List, Great Britain', compiled in May 1940 under the supervision of the German counter-espionage chief, Walter Schellenberg. It identified the men and women to be arrested, and the organisations to be raided, after a German invasion of the UK. The list can be scoffed at for its haphazard, sometimes downright bizarre targeting of politicians, émigrés, labour leaders, businessmen, artists, writers and people with alleged espionage connections. Obvious names were omitted. And some of those included could hardly have been judged dangerous even by the Gestapo at its most paranoid. What did they fear from the toupéed *tapette* Gerald Hamilton, model for Christopher Isherwood's Mr Norris, all the more since they listed his last known address as Shanghai? As Noël Coward ('suspected to be living in London') fluted later to the novelist Rebecca West, who was also listed, 'My dear, the people we should have been seen dead with.'

The list is sloppily edited. For instance, that the controversial Robert (later Lord) Boothby should merit inclusion is not surprising. He was Churchill's Parliamentary Private Secretary after all, but given his proclivity for the company of teenage youths, it was a piquant slip which led to his address in London's then elegant Pall Mall being printed as '17 Tall Male'.

However, for something pulled together in a hurry, Schellenberg's pasty-faced filing clerks did not do a bad job, steel-rimmed glasses glinting as they ploughed through card indexes, newspaper cuttings and informants' reports. One example of their thoroughness, and possibly an indication of a mole in the Motor Vehicle Licence Department, is a careful listing of the registration numbers and owners' home addresses of British cars and even motorcycles seen in suspicious circumstances in Germany. If the sinister Professor Dr Franz-Alfred Six, who would have headed the round-up, had seized even half those listed, and closed only a handful of the newspapers, publishing houses, trades unions and businesses they had targeted, England's intellectual and commercial leadership would have been crippled. As head of the Gestapo's Ideological Enemy Section, Six, a former university professor, had the dubious distinction of having indoctrinated Adolf Eichmann, among others, in the finer points of Nazi morality.

An 'Elliott' is identified in the list as an 'intelligence agent' based in Yugoslavia, of interest to Department IVE4, a counter-espionage section of Heydrich's Reich Security Agency. In later encounters, the Gestapo boasted to Elliott that they had a comprehensive file on him from before the war, and showed him some of their photographs taken secretly in Yugoslavia in the 1930s. So whatever Elliott was doing in Zagreb at that time, it was clearly of professional interest to the efficient German intelligence machine.

Also on the list were Geoffrey Heyworth and the dusty commercial backwater of Stubbs Agency, where we once saw Elliott briefly employed. Had this in fact been some SIS front and had Elliott been persuaded, in some bizarre pre-echo of the plot of *The Spy Who Came in from the Cold*, to feign financial hot water so as to present a tempting recruitment target to some hostile service? Stranger things have happened. And were about to happen.

# 6

# Marriage à la Mode

Where did Elliott meet my mother? When I was growing up, she spoke of him only with sad and terse reluctance; now, when there is so much I would like to ask her, she is not there to tell me.

One of my sisters remembers my mother saying that she had met Elliott in 1933 at the Russian ballet, when Maynard Keynes's ballerina wife, Lydia Lopokova, brought a show to London from the newly established Cambridge Arts Theatre. The ballet was the sort of place I might have expected my mother to be. But why Elliott? None of his friends recalls him as in any way intellectual or musical. What spin of the wheel brought him to such an effete venue? The sheer chance of a spare ticket? An instinctive reaction to the distinctively foreign-looking posters outside? Trawling on someone's behalf for émigré contacts?

But meet they did. After the event, parents and parents-in-law are omniscient. 'Never trusted him,' 'They'll bury her in a Y-shaped coffin,' they mutter. My mother's parents were no exception, but, like all parents in this situation, there was little or nothing they could do, except put a brave face on things, stick up a wedding marquee in the tiny back garden, and grit their teeth through the Registry Office formalities. Given the conflicting stew of religions involved – Catholic, Russian Orthodox and Jewish – a civil ceremony was a sensible compromise.

Though the photograph is in black and white, my mother radiates happiness and colour, holding a small bouquet, her arm laced through Elliott's. His suit is stiff, newly bought off the peg from the Fifty Shilling Tailor and a touch too short in the sleeve, and he has the slightly distracted air of a guest suddenly dragged in to stand in for a couple of sighting shots while the real groom spews up the shrimp cocktail and Votrix British Vermouth over the cat. Whether he had told my mother what I discovered only years later, that a few weeks before the wedding he had changed his name by deed poll from Burnley to Elliott, I have no idea. I doubt it. A honeymoon photograph on the terrace of Fouquet's on the Champs Elysées shows the adoring, adorable bride, while the groom, cool and restrained, is looking quizzically at something or someone in the middle distance.

Elliott always looked good. As a schoolboy, 'a nice-looking lad, and so smartly dressed too', you can hear people cooing as they look at his photograph. The eager-beaver twenty-two year old, in a photograph rather enigmatically inscribed by his mother as 'what the ideal Sunday School Teacher ought to look like'. As a military man, or at his peak as the trim colonial businessman at the races in Jamaica, he always looked the part. He was a touch over six feet tall, thin, always well-dressed, holding himself stiffly in a consciously military chest-out, shoulders-back posture; later in life, whatever North London accent he may have had growing up was smoothed into a clipped close approximation of officer English tones, with a slight resonance suggesting an Australian who had passed out of Sandhurst without quite eliminating the lipstick traces of his mother country. Almost always that sense of holding back. The only two photographs of many I have seen in which he seems to be genuinely happy are one taken very late in his life with his two half-brothers, in which he is slumped in an armchair holding a glass of dark-brown liquid which would surely have blown the fuses on a breathalyser, and another in which he is fondling two Alsatian puppies with more affection than, judging from other photographs, he usually showed with people.

The Japanese characters for the business term 'joint venture' are said to translate literally as 'same bed, different dreams'. So, I suspect, it must have been for the joint venture of my parents' marriage. Looking back, I can see that my mother was only the first, almost certainly only one of the first, in a line of women who fell for Elliott and with whom he fell permanently and irrevocably in love, until the next time. Like my mother, the women who loved him were petite, pretty, cheerful, long-suffering, naïve and foreign; the ones who saw through him tended to be of tougher, shrewder stuff. As the barely English daughter of very Russian parents, who had scrambled halfway round the world before grounding in their tiny home in Golders Green, my mother dreamed of roots – English roots – a semi-detached suburban nest, a husband swinging athletically up the ladder of middle management in some securely English company, and the statistical norm of children to be privately cosseted *à la Russe* but publicly educated in conventional English ways. Instead, what she got, despite or because of the warnings of her parents, was a husband who was himself semi-detached, a restless and unhappy searcher for adventure for whom, in an almost adolescent way, something, someone or somewhere new was always more alluring than the here and now, especially when the here and now had chafing responsibilities attached. In Stalin's era, one of the thinly veiled euphemisms used in vilifying Jews dismissed them as 'rootless cosmopolitans', a description which fitted Elliott well, though ironically for a man who spent most of his life outside England, he was, like most of his generation, viscerally xenophobic. That cannot have helped. My mother's parents could have won a prize for quintessential, unmitigated foreignness; to the end of her days my grandmother could barely cope with English, and their life was firmly governed by her exotic metronome of peasant superstitions, Russian Orthodox beliefs and holidays. Moreover, he must have been painfully aware of what they thought of him.

# 7

# Special Operations

The years between their marriage in 1935 and my own uneventful arrival in April 1939 are not just a closed book but a book that is lost without trace, though memory and anecdote suggest that Elliott soon made his escape back to Yugoslavia, in a welter of those half-promises and convincing compromises characteristic of the confidence man with a subconsciously complaisant victim. In fact, no confidence man can succeed unless somewhere in his target's heart there lurks larceny or love. 'I'll be back in a couple of months. Maybe in six months or so we'll move to Berlin.' A holiday in Switzerland, another walking in the Alps. 'I'd really love to have you move to Zagreb, but it's just too uncomfortable. And risky too.' My mother once confided in a friend, who in turn, forty years later, shared the rare insight with me, that right from the start, 'I knew I couldn't keep Kavan at home. I didn't really mind where he went, or who he was with, as long as I felt one day he'd come back. Until the war, he always did.'

In May 1940, some now unknown circuit of clandestine connections brought Elliott to the vast asphalt steppe that was the parade-ground of the Officer Cadet Training School at Mons Barracks, Aldershot. It was there he first met Antony Terry, who told me that both he and Elliott had entered 'by the intelligence back door' to get themselves commissioned as officers in case spying work called for the extra security blanket of a military uniform. Most of those in Elliott's unit, No. 168, were youthful, upwardly mobile sergeants ('yums', they might be called today) selected from the Regular Army as potential officer material. Terry and Elliott, neither of them with the basic skills that a rigorous British public school might have implanted, had a hard time keeping up with the crisply pressed regular zealots, with heads shaved, bedclothes, uniform and kit compressed for each dawn inspection into improbably neat cubes, and circles of bicycle chain slipped down their trousers to hold a neat, permanent one-inch fold over the tops of their blancoed gaiters.

'Unlike Kavan, I had no previous Intelligence background,' Terry recalled. 'We were pitchforked into the unknown world of Bren machine-guns, pull-throughs, organisation and administration, how to run a court-martial and, above all, DRILL. Neither of us knew anything whatever about that sort of thing . . . and we discovered that superhuman effort was needed with all the smart sergeants who had learned all the tricks, in order to avoid being Returned To Unit shamefaced as "non-officer material". Life in those hot summer days on the parade-ground and rifle ranges and classrooms was pretty harassing. However, we managed somehow to beat the system . . . . Hitler's Blitzkrieg in France . . . led to our training being drastically curtailed, and for better or worse we were confirmed in our commissions so that we could go off and fight the war, each in our own way.'

Elliott's sister Ethel gave me a photograph of him in uniform holding me, aged six months, as though I was an unexploded bomb he had forced himself to volunteer to defuse. The plain British royal coat of arms used on his General List cap badge led to its wearers being derided as the 'Post Office Rifles'. Two months later, Elliott was transferred to the Intelligence Corps, exchanging the postman's prosaic badge for an emblem of a flower surmounting a wreath of leaves, claimed by men in smarter regiments to depict 'a pansy resting on its laurels'. In the 1950s, I myself stood, an apprehensive new Field Security trainee, on an unkempt parade-ground in the Intelligence Corps Depot in the wet Sussex countryside, that same much-mocked badge in my stiff new blue beret. Anyone watching the untidy ranks of pimply youths from the Corps' Linguist section swish from behind the wooden barrack huts to assemble in fluting gawkiness on the asphalt square, as if in some provincial try-out for *Soldiers in Skirts*, would have felt the taunt quite apt.

In May 1940, Elliott reported to the London Area Reception Depot in Duke of York's Barracks in Chelsea. This was another coincidence, for I noted with pleasure when I saw this on his file that I had, all unknowing, been to the same echoing halls in 1957 to be interviewed by two men in tweeds, one of whom, following some subliminal John Buchan script, spent the interview shrouded in invisible silence behind an opened, unturned copy of *The Sporting Life*, emerging only as I prepared to leave to grunt, 'Came across your father once. Good man', with gruff solicitude from beneath a bristly ginger moustache.

From Chelsea Elliott took the District Line tube to Whitehall, where MI(R) – Military Intelligence (Research) – became his first documented wartime employer. A shadowy group established towards the end of 1938 under the cover of the War Office General Staff, 'R' distinguished it from the various other MI designations, of which 5 and 6 are perhaps the best known; at one point there were at least nineteen, as well as an alphabetti-spaghetti of sub-sections. (Ironically, MIR happens to be the English transliteration of a quintessentially Russian word, which can be translated as 'village community', 'world' or 'peace', the three concepts being almost indistinguishable in the minds of centuries of narrow-horizoned Russian serfs.) Certainly 'peace' would fit oddly with the group's operational aims, which a Most Secret memorandum of the era listed as 'Demolition work . . . the preparation of guerrilla warfare . . . the establishment of a system of contacts in occupied territory to collect information and for fomenting insurrections . . .', as well as developing 'destructive devices' for guerrilla war.

In its response to the German seizure first of Poland and then of Norway, the still indifferently organised British intelligence machinery was usually reactive, with little interest in MI(R) schemes for placing British shadow missions in Yugoslavia and Romania, which would inevitably be the next to fall. These missions, the planners enthused, would immediately launch into intelligence-gathering liaison with the local armed forces and the fomenting of all forms of resistance mayhem. They could be composed not only of British officers 'infiltrated into the country in the guise of vice-consuls and clerks', an idea that must have had the Foreign Office reaching for the smelling salts, but also of 'British subjects, such as commercial representatives' resident in the target countries.

MI(R) also had its lines out to the exiles and refugees in London, milking them for information on conditions at home, talent-spotting for embryo resistance leaders who might be sent back to Europe when the right time came. In July 1940, MI(R), the 'D' or Destruction section of SIS, set up with similar aims after the German annexation of Austria, and the propaganda-oriented Political Warfare Executive were merged into the new but already controversial Special Operations Executive. Much, by now too much, has been written, invented or embroidered about SOE; another floodtide of revisionist history will engulf us as its files are released into the public domain, though researchers will find themselves faced with papers that have had to be definitively 'Sanitised For Your Protection' like the toilets in American motels, or, more precisely, the protection of whatever secrets of SIS may still have lurked among the frayed pages, even after several earlier bouts of official 'weeding' by reliable, retired diplomats.

The place SOE has come to occupy in the history of the Second World War, and of British Intelligence, is one of the myriad examples of myth over reality. In the first place, though claimed as a bold and adventurous new initiative, it was not in fact a new concept, merely the reincarnation of old traditions. In Elizabethan times, Walsingham had used 'projectors' and 'explorators' to subvert the Catholic exiles plotting in France and Belgium, and Pitt the Younger's shadowy Alien Office spent large amounts of money fomenting resistance to Napoleon in France, working through intermediaries such as The Swiss Agency and The Swabian Agency, whose rather neutral titles themselves are evocative of the blandly nondescript names used by British secret intelligence fronts through the ages. The hand of the Alien Office was even detected in the assassination of Tsar Paul of Russia in 1790, an accusation given some credence by a vehement refutation from the Foreign Office of any British involvement in an act 'so unworthy of a civilised country'.

SOE's supposedly unique blend of military and intelligence objectives and methods had its forerunner in the British 'interventions' in northern Persia, and Vladivostok and Archangel in the later stages of the Russian Revolution.

SOE's task was the destabilisation of Nazi-occupied territory, waging war by all means except the conventional, a vital diversionary element that would help to keep the Germans off balance in the early years of the war when Britain's conventional military resources were still weak. To support and arm resistance fighters, to explode, sabotage, kill, disrupt and deceive – an imaginative notion, but seen from the Foreign Office, and from the frowsty Broadway Buildings headquarters of SIS, SOE's creation brought daily aggravations and often serious headaches, all the more since neither of them, nor the War Office, had succeeded in having SOE placed directly under their control. 'SOE aroused the suspicions of an upstart felt by older organisations, embittered by political animosities,' one official historian noted. There were many reasons: competition with SIS and the conventional armed forces for scarce resources, SOE's penchant for backing the wrong horses, or worse still the right horses at the wrong time, its endemic disorganisation and insecurity, and, at least as argued by SIS, the real difficulties SOE's trouble-making in enemy country might create for secret destabilisation and intelligence operations which needed permanent invisibility, all the more if, as has been alleged, some of these operations may have involved cohabitation with the Abwehr, the German intelligence service, of a closeness likely to be misunderstood by the uninitiated.

Another problem was SOE's people: men and women who by background and experience were inherently unlikely to get along well with urbane diplomats, bluff military men and the deft intriguers of SIS. As one commentator put it, SOE was an organisation 'among whose high executives many displayed an enthusiasm unrestrained by experience; some had political backgrounds which deserved a rather closer scrutiny than they ever got, and a few could charitably only be described as nutcases . . . .' Elliott was a long way from a high executive, just one of the expendable 'hundreds of mugs who've been trained as thugs', as an SOE wag called them.

Elliott was a natural choice for SOE's Balkan effort. But like all good military journeys his began with a diversion in the opposite direction, to SOE's training area on the Arisaig peninsula in Inverness-shire, through which the narrow road to Skye runs from Fort William. Whoever chose the area, with Arisaig House as its central school, had an astute eye for defensive geography and privacy; local lore has it that it was first identified by a group of Scots military men as the last redoubt, the *Wolfschanze* from which a German invasion of the British Isles might be resisted to the last drop of Glenmorangie. Short of that Armageddon role, it was an ideal university for the forces of the night. Access could be tightly controlled through the single road and the winding railway track. Agents could be trained amid a crazy fretwork of coves and beaches, islands, big and small, or trackless, scrub-covered hills, which in high summer could simulate down to the last Stuka-like mosquito the burning heat of Greece, but which as the weather closed in could equally serve as a good proxy for the Balkan winter. Deep lochs, whose freezing black water clotted the blood even when the sun shone, emulated distant fjords. Its remote railway viaducts and bridges were ideal for demonstrating the finer points of sabotage, and security was preserved by a dourly incurious crofter population, doing beastly things to their sheep in the cold winter nights.

Arisaig was commanded by James Young, who required only two basic qualities in his training staff. First, that they should be able to down at least a half pint of whisky after dinner and still be up, bright-eyed and bushy-tailed, for reveille at 6 a.m. Second, and to some no doubt all the more tiresome when loaded to the gills with alcohol, they were obliged to master the heathen intricacies of the eightsome reel. The spectacle of drunken explosives experts and masters of hand-to-hand combat flailing around the officers' mess must have made their pupils, most of them earnest-minded foreigners, wonder just what British lunacy they were getting into.

Today Arisaig House is an award-winning hotel, its billowing rhododendron bushes, neat flower-beds and gloomy granite walls sheltering a rather different set of guests from the enthusiastic Spanish, Yugoslav, French, Greek and British resistance fighters who passed anonymously through all those years ago, but who are at least commemorated with a discreet plaque in the hallway. The notion that they would today have to pay the thick end of £3,000 to pass a well-fed week there would have amused Elliott and his colleagues no end, as they trained in handling explosives, the numbing routines of wireless communication and the abattoir skills of hand-to-hand combat, trying to stay alive in the freezing, wet underbrush on a Scottish hillside with dogs and a manic training staff baying at their heels.

# 8

# Balkan Realities

In 1942, a dispirited German officer said of Yugoslavia, 'Life counts for nothing. One's own life for very little.' I have on the wall as I write two watercolours, and from a dismissive comment my grandfather once made, I believe that Elliott may have painted them himself before the war. Whatever their authorship, they serve well to highlight the myth and reality of those troubled lands and troublesome people. One is of a Serbian peasant in a woollen cap, heavy moustache, long clay pipe clenched in carious teeth, face tanned and seamed, eyes hooded and watchful: the mythical mountain fighter; a doughty warrior and a stead-fast ally of the West in two world wars. The reality is that for a dinar he would cut your throat. If you were a Croat or a Muslim, or for that matter a Macedonian or a Jew or a Slovene, he would cut it for free. The second picture is of a dusty village street: red-tiled roofs, with two packhorses held by placid men in felt boots; vegetables in yellow, red and green profusion for sale on a long verandah. Scratch that thin, tranquil veneer and underneath is the reality of excrement, rats and blood in the alley.

Our own mythical images of pre-war Yugoslavia and, for that matter, the Balkans generally are a composite of film scripts and a host of charming travel books penned by presentable Englishmen in their lit-erary twenties with money and time on their hands. The Orient Express rocking through the mountain passes, its plush sleeping-cars cradling pinstriped pedlars of Maxim guns, a fat man thought by the conductor to be a Romanian secret agent but in reality the wealthy West Hartlepools manufacturer of 'Snugfit' enema nozzles, glamorous women of a certain age and uncertain origin, a distinguished French diplomat travelling in cosy intimacy with an androgynous adolescent claimed on the passenger list to be his niece, and a pair of whispering, bead-rattling Archimandrites representing a recondite church rooted in some obscure eleventh-century schism; in the 'hard compartments' commercial travellers and tired anonymous men with tired eyes twisted in clammy discomfort in the eerie blue glow of the ceiling lights, sunken cheek by bristly jowl with peasants whose sacks rustled and clucked disconcertingly in the overhead racks. Along the corridor, momentarily silhouetted against the yellow lights of Ljubljana Central Station, shuffled the swarthy sleeping-car attendant, simultaneously in the pay of every serious secret service – as well as the Italians – about to collect with understandable distaste a heavy linen-wrapped package from the unappetising void behind the toilet cistern. Arriving in Belgrade, or for that matter Bucharest, Sofia or Budapest, the traveller would find everything aimed at emulating Paris – the wide central boulevards, the ornate architecture, the purring limousines carrying plump Jewish industrialists and their sleek midinettes to the elegant shops and cafés, the chic strollers on the broad, tree-lined pavements. If they happened to find their way out to the country, they would thrill to see bearded, warm-hearted peasants toiling bent-backed, stopping only to offer a wooden bowl of fresh mare's milk to the weary passing travel writer. Oxcarts creaked along dusty roads, ungainly storks nestled in their twig-cradles on the cottage chimneys. Rolling fields of maize and tobacco shimmered in the sun, stretching for endless *versts* and *desyatiny* towards the jagged horizon of distant mountains.

The myth was sadly just that. The reality always was, and is so obviously today, one of stupidity, poverty and cruelty. Endemic political violence, hard-edged rivalries and territorial ambitions, with a political leadership that has always made up in inflamed self-interest and demagoguery what it lacked in statesmanship. The centuries' old traditions of vendetta, knife and bullet handed on from one generation to the next, a legacy whose wine can be made to fume instantly in the veins of apparently civilised people in response to some perceived tribal or racial threat. The Croat Archbishop Stepinac, a pre-war prelate by comparison with whom the Spanish Inquisition would seem as liberal as an outed English bishop with a moiré mitre and a social conscience, observed in despair that the components of the artefact called Yugoslavia 'cannot be joined except by miracle of God. Here there is no morality, no truth, no justice and no honesty.'

The reality can be traced in part to the drawing and re-drawing of the boundaries of Eastern Europe, first in the sweeping settlements of the Congress of Vienna following the crushing of Napoleon, and then in the radical cartographic surgery that followed the First World War. The new nation states – some, like Yugoslavia, a combination of older, smaller countries, others castrated versions of once larger empires – emerged from earnest deliberations and furtive compromises. Then as today, at conferences in pleasant lakeside locations which offered their portly participants the fringe benefits of eating and drinking well, shopping and fornicating with their pert stenographers between spells of state-craft, the politicians set about their God-given task of settling Europe's problems once and for all. Much lip service was paid to the principle of ethnic justice, the need to create new states based on religiously and lin-guistically homogeneous groups, but the need to achieve a permanent diminution of Prussian power, and the gut politics of revenge, got badly in the way of the high ideals. In the end, the amateur cartographers pro-duced a complex mess that left no one satisfied and is today still being paid for in blood and bullets.

The strains were soon aggravated by economic realities. Central Europe's unproductive agricultural sector was still mired in the Middle Ages. Industrial investment was sluggish and over-dependent on for-eign capital, and this fragile edifice was constantly destabilised by the rabble-rousing of political groups, from the extreme anarchist left to the hard, violent, anti-Semitic right. The growing economic and military strength of Germany was a force that the unstable fledgling democracies and fragile monarchies of the region were unable to resist. Neither Britain nor France – far away and with much else on which to focus – seemed to be able to manœuvre in the complex Balkan environment with the same energy and dexterity as the Nazis, who succeeded in bul-lying the countries of the region one after another into a tempting, ultimately fatal, web of trade and political relationships. As war approached, the British intelligence services, playing second fiddle to the French in the region, did what they could from their main Balkan stations in Istanbul, Bucharest, Belgrade and Zagreb to track what the Germans were up to, to orchestrate counter-propaganda and, very late in the day, to identify reliable local nationals who might form the nucleus of stay-behind intelligence and subversion networks. In Yugoslavia, their attempts to get their point across through timid 'subsidies' to the press – at one stage the *Belgrade Pravda* seems to have been simultaneously on the British and German Embassy bribe lists, to the enduring benefit of the Zurich bank account of its nimble owner – and the activities of the Britanova news agency, counted for little in the face of the serious money the Germans were paying to anyone of influence, and the hard fact that heard from the Balkans, the German voice was loudest. Britanova was subsidised by the Foreign Office, part of a long-standing tradition of covert financial support for the propagation of the official British point of view from which even Reuters, in all respects a bastion of editorial integrity, benefited nicely over the years until the payments, mostly laundered as oversized subscriptions by government departments to Reuters' services, were finally phased out in the 1980s.

As it became clear that the war of words was soon to become a war of bullets and blood, the intelligence and military planners in London turned their sights, belatedly, to resistance and sabotage. Churchill told SOE that the Balkans would be its 'acid test'. Charles Clarke, British Military Attaché in Belgrade, was asked to take Elliott on his staff with the official title of Assistant Attaché, but with the real job of furthering the undercover objectives of MI(R). However, he declined, telling Whitehall that the already delicate position of the Embassy might be further jeopardised if yet another bomb-happy parvenu were added to a team in which genuine diplomats were already few and far between. Elliott had to hang around the crowded hotels and sweaty intelligence offices of Cairo for some weeks, swatting flies, eating ice-cream at Groppi's, dabbing iodine on the red whorls of the dhobi rash which afflicted one military groin in three, doing his best to stay out of the bitchy intrigues of spydom and not to drink too much. 'Did well on the first, not so well on the second,' he noted.

In the summer of 1940, MI(R) found him an alternative home, again camouflaged as Assistant Military Attaché, in sleepy, dangerous Sofia. Bulgaria was a nasty place. Riots, coups and counter-coups, assassination by bomb, pistol, or, rather medieval, dismemberment, were commonplace features of the political scene. King Boris was very much in charge of this basically Slav, predominantly agricultural and irrepressibly bloodthirsty country. He presented himself as a bluff, unassuming monarch, who dealt with affairs of state only out of a reluctant sense of duty and whose real kicks came from togging up as an engine-driver to ferry the royal train in and out of Sofia Station. Myth and reality again. In the real world, Boris was a calculating political operator, who spent the late 1930s happily vacillating, a Balkan Vicar of Bray, courted by all sides, forming alliances according to his changing view of where Bulgaria could gain maximum advantage. As Boris succinctly put it, 'My army is pro-German, my wife is Italian, my people are pro-Russian. I am the only one in this country who is pro-Bulgarian.' But with the tumescence of Nazi power, his highly politicised compass began to twitch more strongly in the direction of the new Magnetic North in Berlin. German know-how was tapped to develop Bulgaria's agricultural base and to expand light industries around it. Inevitably the political and military ties began to deepen, bolstered by seductive German murmuring about territory that Bulgaria could snatch back from Greece if it hitched its oxcart to the German cause.

When Elliott arrived in Sofia, Bulgaria was still technically neutral, an eerie non-combatant oasis, although Boris's pro-German leanings were now beyond doubt. German officers, squeezed uncomfortably into ill-fitting and scratchy Bulgarian uniforms, were already driving themselves demented trying to teach Prussian military skills to Bulgarians, whose techniques of warfare remained mired in the chop, slice and burn simplicity of the Middle Ages. Having finally convinced a nervous and dilatory Whitehall that the diplomatic struggle was over, though George Rendel, the Ambassador, was convinced almost up to the end that Boris could be kept out of the German orbit, the British clandestine services in Bulgaria were given their head. Piecing together the little that remains on British files with the intelligence order-of-battle as documented by the Bulgarian secret police, it would seem that real diplomats were few and far between. Almost everyone on the British Legation staff (with the exception of a Bulgarian police 'mole', probably a secretary but known only as 'R–10') seems to have had links to one or other tentacle of Whitehall's secret octopus, or to have been suspected of having them. The three 'barons' in the Legation were Edward Smith-Ross, the Passport Control Officer and SIS Head of Station; Brigadier Alexander

Ross, the Military Attaché, to whom Elliott reported; and Norman Davis, who seems to have moved between SIS Section D, the Political Warfare Executive and SOE with a seamless smoothness and tough efficiency befitting a man who later became a distinguished Master of Merton College, Oxford. Smith-Ross's front man was one Vadim Grinovich, Russian born but a British subject, who had served in the Legation since 1923. Alexander Ross himself was half Russian and married to a Russian girl. Sir Steven Runciman, then the Press Attaché, remembers him as 'a disaster. He prided himself on his knowledge of Bulgaria. He was fond of the bottle and at Bulgarian parties, as the evening wore on, he became more and more indiscreet.' But this may well just have been part of a well-crafted cover since the secret police noted with grudging respect that Ross's work was 'characterised by extreme caution' and much of what he did was not fully unravelled until after he had left the country. Flitting in and out of the background was an almost unseen American figure, logged by the police as 'Mister Brown' or 'Colonel Tegel', who in all likelihood was 'Wild Bill' Donovan, later head of the US Office of Strategic Services.

But what were they all up to? In the best traditions of the underground services, they were snooping, bribing, suborning journalists, tracking movements on the Danube, photographing airfields, bullying and wheedling information out of the daily less friendly Bulgarian War and Foreign Ministries, and recruiting and training potential stay-behind agents. They questioned and recruited to the British team, or thought they had, many of the White Russians who had fled to Bulgaria after the Soviet revolution. The SIS cover of the Passport Control Office was of special value in talking to frantic Jewish refugees from elsewhere in Europe, or from Bulgaria's own Jewish population. The chance of a visa to Palestine or even the UK was a powerful inducement to co-operation. In the process, the British teams did their best to keep out of sight of the Bulgarian secret police and the increasingly more brazen presence of a German Abwehr contingent led by Major Otto Wagner, masquerading, with or without any intended musical irony, we do not know, as 'Dr Delius'.

Aidan Crawley, Elliott's counterpart as Assistant Air Attaché, told me of some of their own more bizarre adventures: a trip with Elliott to Istanbul, to frighten a Bulgarian arms merchant thought to be overzealous in his efforts to sell his hardware to the Germans; and the attempted sting, when a Bulgarian turned up at the Legation claiming to be the brother-in-law of Hitler's pilot, Hans Bauer. Questioned by Crawley and Elliott with profound scepticism, the stranger, who offered a clutch of authentic-seeming but unverifiable identity papers and birth certificates linking him to Bauer, offered the bargain of the year. Bauer would be prepared to kidnap Hitler and suggested that when next over the northern part of the continent he would divert the Führer's plane to some prearranged point in England. He wanted a fee, modest in the circumstances, of £10,000 in gold, half in advance, the rest when a no doubt rather vexed Hitler stepped off the plane to find himself in Birmingham rather than Bavaria. 'I told him we'd think over what he had said,' Crawley recalled. 'In case it was real, we didn't want the Legation involved, so we said we'd meet again in three days at the Grand Hotel, in the lobby, around 5 p.m. I cabled a full report to the Air Ministry. They got quite excited and told me to see the fellow again, and that meanwhile they had earmarked an aerodrome somewhere near Nottingham and sent quite a contingent of RAF Regiment troops up there to guard it. We had about £1,000 in sovereigns in the slush fund at the time, which I put aside for a downpayment. Went down to meet him at the hotel as agreed, but no sign of him. Kavan and I took turns to go back there for several days, but we never saw him again. I told London it was almost certainly a hoax, but I believe they kept the guard at the aerodrome for months and months!'

According to Elliott's recollection, it was Norman Davis rather than Alexander Ross who assigned Elliott to develop a relationship with Georgi M. Dimitrov, the forty-year-old leader of the Bulgarian Agrarian Party's left wing. A leonine, charismatic doctor from a peasant family, who had worked as a schoolteacher to pay his way through medical school, Dimitrov was known to his friends by his initials 'Gemeto', or 'the GM one' to distinguish him from the eponymous Georgi, the veteran Communist and hero of the Reichstag fire trial. A political leader of singularly un-Balkan courage and vision, Gemeto had remained vocally anti-German despite constant police pressure and the real risk of imprisonment and death (there being in Bulgaria little difference between the two) for political targets of the regime. Never a man generous with praise, Elliott later described Dimitrov as 'an extraordinary man. A real hero truly dedicated to his country.' Dimitrov was working with several other politicians opposed to Boris's policies, collectively known as the

Anglophiles. Although Dimitrov was committed to saving Bulgaria from what he saw as a path of folly, it took Davis and Elliott many voluble meetings in smoky rooms, a junior SOE officer on guard in the hallway, to persuade him to take SOE's gold sovereigns to finance the building of a resistance network. It took them even longer to persuade him to accept weapons and explosives, but finally, in November 1940, Dimitrov agreed to organise six five-man sabotage teams and Elliott became their Mr Chips, teaching them how to handle what SOE jargon called 'chocolate', a buttery plastic explosive made of cyclonite and a plasticising compound smelling slightly of almonds. He used as his training school the sunlit Sofia apartment of Alan Metheun, nominally a First Secretary at the British Legation, who had attracted police surveillance because of his role as Ross's assistant. The prospective saboteurs, among them journalists, clerks and railway officials, would stroll up to the apartment dressed in greasy overalls, carrying toolboxes, pretending to be plumbers and electricians engaged in routine maintenance work. The British believed that these house calls raised no suspicions, the Bulgarian secret police being notoriously inept and the capital having a well-earned reputation for shoddy buildings. We shall see.

As concerns grew about the growing German presence, especially the Luftwaffe, Elliott and Crawley were detailed to make a reconnaissance of northern Bulgaria and, according to their police file, they tried to leave Sofia by a back road on 23 January 1941. Intercepted at a roadblock, they lamely told the police that they were planning a short weekend together in the mountains, a story that had it been believed might have served to confirm the local police's suspicions about British public-school proclivities. Perhaps because of the failure of this initiative the Air Attaché, Group Captain Donald Macdonald, also acting as SIS's representative in Belgrade, made a hurried flight to Sofia a few days later to be briefed by the chief of the Bulgarian air force, General Boydev, on German deployment and the air force's readiness. Details of Macdonald's top-secret mission and a record of his talks with Boydev are noted in the Bulgarian police files.

Section B of the Bulgarian secret police watched in the doorways and the alleys as SIS rapidly built up four separate networks 'dispersed throughout Bulgaria', which were intended as active collectors of intelligence after the German occupation. It tapped the phones, noting with meticulous care the letter code used by the British when they wanted to talk in confidence, though there is no evidence that they actually cracked it. The Bulgarians concluded at one point from their tapping of cable traffic that SIS in Yugoslavia reported directly to Sofia, since 'all the cables from Belgrade are sent to Sofia first'. But they also seem to have built up quite a good picture of the order-of-battle of the British intelligence centre in Istanbul, which in fact supervised all intelligence and counter-intelligence operations throughout the Balkans. The files also show that the Bulgarian Military Attaché in London was alert and rather well-informed, able to give quick career and personality sketches of any British officers requesting Bulgarian entry visas or otherwise coming to notice.

Early in February, SOE and Dimitrov had agreed on the 25th as the date for the handover of the arms and explosives, in their neat oilskin packages, but events moved too fast. Like an over-the-hill striptease dancer, Boris had discarded the last figleaf of neutrality on 21 February and allowed Field Marshal List to establish his German headquarters in Sofia. Two days later, Dimitrov sent word to Norman Davis that he had gone into hiding, having escaped arrest by the skin of his teeth, scurrying out of the back door of his apartment building as the secret police stormed in the front. They had been sent to round him up along with some thirty other opposition leaders – and the Sofia correspondent of *The Times* – for putting their names to a letter to Boris protesting against the pro-Axis policy. Dimitrov had more value to SOE as a rallying-point in exile than as a martyred body in a Sofia police cellar, and, according to Elliott's account, he was instructed by Davis to bring him to safety. Dodging the Bulgarian police watchers, 'sweaty little dwarfs', he later recalled, reflecting the British secret world's conventional view of Bulgarian counter-intelligence, by jumping on and off a series of trams and slipping through crowded streets and busy markets in a lengthy zig-zag across the city, Elliott reached Dimitrov's hideout to brief him on SOE's plan to smuggle him out of Bulgaria. Two days later, Davis and Elliott persuaded a reluctant Rendel to send the Legation archivist on a hastily improvised errand to Belgrade. While he was away Elliott had the use of his car, which had regular diplomatic plates and, unlike Elliott's own battered Buick (perhaps the first in a succession of large, fast cars in which, if someone else paid the bills, Elliott loved to run around), was not on the watch list of every police agent and Axis mission in the city. That evening Elliott gave a small dinner for the Bulgarian Director of Military Intelligence in one of Sofia's grander restaurants, candles flickering in the wall mirrors, plangent gypsy fiddlers, platoons of wine bottles, outrageous bills, fawning waiters, altogether an elegant last-minute leave-taking.

This stroke of tactful duplicity was intended to disarm his watchers and it was successful, for when the dinner ended in a haze of hypocritical plum-brandy toasts, Elliott was able to drive off towards Dimitrov's hideout through the quiet, rain-sodden streets without a trailing posse. As he turned the last corner, he checked his watch: a half hour to midnight, as agreed. A sweeping glance down the pavement and in his rear mirror; the street gleamed empty. Halfway along he slowed to a crawl and swung open the nearside rear door. From a dark doorway Dimitrov splashed across the pavement, scrambled in and flattened himself on the floor. Elliott drove circumspectly away. 'We're okay, Doctor,' he reassured his unseen and breathless passenger, 'I'm clean.' Then, realising that not being a field man Dimitrov might translate the jargon as meaning no more than that Elliott had just showered, some arcane English greeting ritual, he added in Bulgarian, 'No one followed me.'

Elliott had hired a Bulgarian lorry, telling the authorities that it would be used to ship the Legation records down to Istanbul after the imminent rupture of relations; they agreed with alacrity that diplomatic immunity would apply to its cargo. As Elliott drove his borrowed car, Dimitrov now huddled under a blanket, up to the large Legation garage in which the lorry had been parked, one of the Bulgarian guards who prowled the Legation pavements stepped forward to check his papers. Not turning a hair, Elliott wound down the window and growled at the guard to open the door, and to be quick about it! In the darkened interior Dimitrov scrambled out of the car.

In the lorry were four wooden crates about five feet square, three of them actually filled with British files, the fourth hastily lined with strips of a British government-issue pink eiderdown snatched from the bedroom of the Chargé d'Affaires' secretary, to cushion the long and bumpy journey ahead. The heavyweight contingent of SOE officers gathered in the garage gave Dimitrov a pack of sandwiches, a Luger automatic, a Thermos of water, an empty bottle and, in an unconscious echo of Prokofiev, three oranges, nailed the crate shut and attached the diplomatic seals. As Elliott remembered it, the lorry bumped and lurched for a nasty twenty-four hours on primitive roads clogged with military traffic and the terrified detritus of war, through police checks at Plovdiv and Haskovo, and a nerve-jangling delay at the border, where the Bulgarians claimed that the lorry didn't have diplomatic clearance. The smooth intervention of Norman Davis, following the lorry in his car, settled the problem in the time-honoured Balkan tradition with a spray of sovereigns. At Edirne the lorry rumbled into the neutral safety of Turkey. The crate escape had worked. Clambering from his diplomatic coffin in the British Embassy courtyard, reeking of sweat and the petrol that had leaked constantly from the lorry's reserve tank just below the crate, Dimitrov set about writing 'a manifesto to the Bulgarian people' urging resistance. It had painful consequences. SOE gave Dimitrov false Yugoslav papers identifying him as a Dr Grigoriev and escorted him to Belgrade, but the tides of war continued to lap around his wandering feet. Three weeks later, the Germans invaded and Dimitrov was on the run again.

We will never know for sure just who did what in Dimitrov's escape. Elliott's account is factual, circumstantial and, unlike later reminiscences, not obviously self-serving. And yet neither Julian Amery, then a leading light in British intelligence and later a distinguished politician, in his memoirs, nor Dimitrov, in his own story re-told from his own diaries by his son-in-law, but relying for the story of the escape on an interview with Davis himself, makes any mention of Elliott. The diaries identify Davis himself, 'the English Professor', as the driver of the pick-up car and as having actually travelled in the front seat of the truck alongside the driver. Davis is, like Elliott, long dead. He was not, on the face of it, a limelight seeker himself, so why he should want to take credit if some of it was really attributable to Elliott is not obvious. The most likely explanation is that each of them, and indeed others, played a role, sometimes in tandem, sometimes separately, in a tense and difficult sequence of operations. Remembering thirty years later, they may each have succumbed to the mind's rather natural tendency to place its owner in the centre of memory's gravity.

Back in Sofia, tensions rose. In the Legation, Rendel worried that key individuals, or even the building itself, might be the target for a surprise German attack. He had already sent Alexander Ross and the SIS Station Chief out of Sofia ahead of the main party, and on 8 March he cabled Whitehall to report that in the light of 'confidential information that a German plot was afoot to kidnap and do away with' Elliott and Aidan

Crawley, he had immediately booked them on the Orient Express leaving that afternoon for Belgrade; he had also taken the added precaution of asking the still non-belligerent US mission to send one of its people along as an escort. On 10 March, diplomatic ties formally severed, the sixty-strong Legation party left Sofia by special train, without King Boris at the controls. Bulgarian Foreign Ministry officials and the King's frock-coated emissaries murmured oily adieux and assurances of safe conduct. 'We shall look forward to renewing our professional and personal ties when this temporary problem is resolved,' purred the Head of Protocol but, when the party reached the exotic neutrality of Istanbul next evening, the secret war erupted.

Most of the Legation staff were lodged in the plush gilt comfort of the Pera Palace Hotel. At 9.45 p.m., as they were unpacking, bathing, sipping a restorative Gordon's gin and wondering idly about a late dinner in that nice Armenian place Johnny found last year on the edge of the Bosphorus, the ground floor of the hotel exploded. Walls and windows disappeared, javelins of flying mirror glass slicing through the dust and smoke. A huge hole gaped in the floor like a giant's yawn and five or six people plunged into the rubble of the cellars. The lift, providentially empty, smashed into the concrete well as its cables snapped. Just seconds earlier the background noise in the lounge had been the self-assured bleating of the English guests calling for waiters and greeting their friends. In an instant there were only screams, bewildered survivors lurching through the smoke and mouthing at each other silently like goldfish; it was many minutes before their hearing recovered from the deafening blast. It was a scene, as Rendel reported to the Foreign Office, 'of desolation and disaster. The victims, some of them with their legs blown off, lay about the darkened and shattered hall.' Blood dripped from the banisters. Two women on the Legation staff and two Turkish policemen on guard outside the front door had been killed. Many were maimed and all were shell-shocked.

The British blamed the Germans, but Goebbels's alert propaganda machine convinced the Turkish press (washleather bags of gold coins were a powerful persuader) to scream in banner headlines that the explosion had been caused by an 'infernal device' shipped by British secret agents in the diplomatic bags from Sofia, in violation of diplomatic protocol and of Turkish neutrality. It had exploded by accident, the German story claimed, when the case in which it was concealed was dropped by a luckless porter. This sly spin diverted attention from the Germans, set the Turks against the British (from whom the Istanbul authorities were angrily demanding compensation), and sounded a canny warning to Balkan recipients of British explosives that these might not be as safe as their spymasters claimed.

Beneath the springtime cherry blossoms of far-away Washington DC, the British Ambassador Lord Halifax quoted an 'authentic source' as claiming that the bomb had been planted by the Russians, in a bid to discredit both the Germans and the Bulgarians; 'Ingenious, but I doubt it!' a Foreign Office hand scribbled on the cable. British investigators soon determined that two small suitcases had been surreptitiously added to the mound of battered but impressively labelled Swaine Adeney Brigg's luggage, wicker hampers, guncases (Bulgaria was renowned for its excellent snipe-shooting), fishing-rod holders and hat boxes that made up the Legation's baggage, lying like the detritus of empire in the main hall of Sofia's railway station. Rendel reported darkly that two uniformed German officers had been seen picking their way through the peasants on the platform shortly before the luggage was loaded. Wherever the cases came from, there had been some complacency, negligence even, on the British side. The investigators reported to Rendel that as the train rattled down to Turkey, a vigilant clerk had deduced from the luggage manifest that the two cases had no known owner. At his insistence, they were opened, and each was found to contain what looked like dry-cell radio batteries wrapped in waxed paper closed with red seals, on which, the report said, there had been 'some writing in Serbo-Croat'. The first case also contained two silver-topped scent bottles. The second might reasonably have been expected to arouse the suspicion even of an unworldly country vicar inspecting offerings for a church bring-and-buy sale. Like some Balkan version of Kim's Game, the contents were listed in Rendel's subsequent report to the Foreign Secretary, Anthony Eden, as including, in addition to a second supposed 'battery', two or three pairs of dirty woollen socks, a back-number of *République*, a French-language newspaper published in Istanbul, and one soiled shirt with a Bulgarian tag. With a massive display of professional incuriosity about these bizarre, malodorous belongings or their owner, the British officials simply refastened the suitcases and took them on to Istanbul without further enquiry. For reasons for ever unexplained, one of the cases was sent to the Pera Palace, while the second turned up at The Excelsior, where the rest of the Legation group was billeted. According to the official version of events, one of the clerks who had looked into the suitcases, and who had taken the second one to The Excelsior, had the belated presence of mind to connect it to the blast he heard from the Pera Palace rolling ominously over Istanbul. He walked gingerly out of the hotel with the second case and laid it carefully on an adjacent lawn before sprinting for safety. When the Istanbul police arrived, they were shocked to find that the second 'battery' was another bomb, though not primed to explode.

The British investigation of the incident takes up many pages of the Foreign Office files, but, as with all such probes, carefully avoids any discomfiting conclusions. One worldly Foreign Office apologist noted that radio batteries were far cheaper in Bulgaria than Turkey, so there would be good reason to ship them from Sofia. But Whitehall was prepared to concede privately that the failure not to suspect that the so-called batteries actually contained a meaningful quantity of TNT was something in the nature of a professional oversight, all the more since the cases had been opened by the assistants to Elliott and Aidan Crawley. Given their professional training, they might have been a touch more sceptical about what they were looking at.

Some of the files remain concealed from public scrutiny even now, but there is no trace on the available record of any further debate on whether the bombs, as the Germans alleged, had actually belonged to SOE. Elliott's notes reveal that some version of the Goebbels story reached him in Yugoslavia, but, as he heard it, the accusation that the bombs were SOE's came not from the German propaganda machine but from Rendel himself. Elliott claims that, when he heard this, he fired off an angry telegram of denial to London, 'making it very clear that in fact we had distributed all our bombs to our agents before we left', but a senior SOE officer, summoned from its Baker Street headquarters to an urgent Whitehall meeting on the incident, recorded, 'it would be an understatement to say that suspicion was cast on [SOE] and I had a very unpleasant quarter of an hour'.

Over in Hungary, the nervous professional diplomats also believed the worst of SOE. Basil Davidson, representing SOE's interests under the increasingly threadbare umbrella of the Britanova news agency, was hauled like an errant schoolboy to the Budapest Legation to be told by a po-faced Second Secretary that the Legation had taken steps to dump into the Danube – fishermen and people downstream be damned – the small store of plastic explosives Davidson had left for safekeeping in their basement. In those far-off days of Satow's Rules of Diplomacy, homburg hats and pin-striped trousers, storage of sabotage materials on diplomatic premises was felt by the more righteous members of the Legation to be a serious breach of protocol. More to the point, perhaps, in the light of what the Istanbul explosion had suggested about the unstable nature of these devices, the risk of the Legation being literally hoist on SOE's petard was felt to be disagreeably high. The Bulgarian files recount the whole incident in detail and conclude that, while there was no definitive proof, there was 'indirect evidence' pointing rather clearly in the direction of the Abwehr's Bureau Delius and one of its local legmen, a Bulgarian named Asen Savov, recorded in the Abwehr's books as Mr Gochev. Picked up by the Bulgarian police a few weeks later breaking into the Egyptian Legation on the Abwehr's behalf, he confessed, either as a result of, or in anticipation of, their rather robust methods of interrogation, to having planted the cases in the pile at Sofia Station. But his and other collateral allegations were stoutly denied on the German side and the matter was left to drift on the backwaters of history. Savov's fate is unrecorded. Dogmeat, probably, but Elliott had left his mark in Bulgaria none the less.

Just after Dimitrov's escape, the indefatigable men of Section B uncovered two caches of British explosives and incendiaries in Sofia; in April, another treasure-trove of radios, explosives and 'large amounts of money' came to light, and eleven Bulgarians ended twitching at the end of a rope.

Aidan Crawley, who reached Britain and joined the RAF, was shot down in North Africa in 1942. Flown to Greece, he was put on a prisoner-of-war train for a hot and jolting journey up through the Balkans to a German prison camp. If Crawley's reminiscences are accurate, perhaps a few bombs and bombers made at least some impact: 'As we trundled across Bulgaria, I counted over a couple of days fourteen oil tanker trains along the way, derailed either because their bogies had been blown off, or because the track itself had been smashed beneath them. I said to myself that most of the explosive had come from Kavan before he left, and he had trained most of the saboteurs. A very fine leaving present.'

# 9

# Bulgarian Epilogue

According to the Bulgarian files, when the British circus left town, Smith-Ross instructed his agents to work to the US Legation, whose own espionage efforts were officially evaluated by the Bulgarians as 'minuscule'. The Bulgarians simply trailed 'many of the US personnel', and, 'after deciding the time had come for the final blow', arrested the 'five most important SIS agents' and rolled up the networks. Section B commented in its report that when all the agents were identified, it was established that, unlike Yugoslavia, where the British had recruited many 'high-ranking officers and officials' among the forty or fifty SIS agents uncovered by the Germans in Belgrade, the British 'fortunately' had not penetrated so deeply in Bulgaria.

King Boris abdicated to celestial authority in 1943, no doubt a'babbling of green railway engines. Elliott's leonine recruit Gemeto Dimitrov remarked sadly of King Boris that he 'laboured for Bulgaria all his life, but died for Germany'. Some said he died because of Germany, having been poisoned by the Gestapo or from a heart attack cunningly brought about when, on a flight back from Germany, Hitler's pilot Hans Bauer – so recently encountered – deliberately kept the aircraft at a very high altitude to add unbearable strain to Boris's already weak heart. When a jar allegedly containing that very heart, bobbing in formaldehyde like the soused fruit in a bottle of vintage Poire William, was dug up recently in the grounds of the former royal palace in Sofia, tests for traces of evil-doing showed nothing untoward. Dimitrov himself scrambled out of Yugoslavia to the comparative safety of Cairo and the tangled, rather more dangerous, Balkan conspiracies of SOE. Therein, according to the Bulgarian files, may lie another connection which could have led to Elliott being selected for his next mission, into Yugoslavia. The Royalist resistance leader in Yugoslavia, Draža Mihailovic, had served as Yugoslav Military Attaché in Bulgaria before the war, where he got to know Dimitrov well; whether his path crossed with Elliott's we do not know, but it seems clear that he struck up even then a potentially valuable relationship with SIS. Bulgarian historians are convinced, perhaps boosted by a touch of post-war revisionism, that part of SOE's grand design was to bring Serbia and Bulgaria together in a new Balkan Federation 'dominated by Britain' as a bulwark against Soviet Communism, even then seen as the next threat. To that end Dimitrov and Mihailovic had been encouraged to maintain close contact, and in exile Dimitrov continued those links through contacts in Bulgaria, Yugoslavia itself and the respective missions in London. He too, it was later claimed in Bulgaria, was used as a conduit to funnel the ubiquitous British gold sovereigns to Mihailovic for supplies and arms. He also wrote for the Free Independent Bulgaria radio station, which SOE had organised and which, although in fact based in Palestine, claimed to be operating clandestinely deep in the Bulgarian countryside.

A year or so later, Bulgaria followed the example of Romania (not a course generally to be recommended in politics or indeed anything else) by switching from the German side to the Soviet. Its forces then fought alongside the Red Army through the Balkans and Hungary as far as Vienna; 30,000 men died in the process. When the war ended, Bulgaria took a faltering step towards democracy with the first Fatherland Front Government, six of whose members, including the Prime Minister, came from the loose opposition formed by Dimitrov with SOE encouragement back in 1941. Dimitrov himself was then invited back to Bulgaria and hopes on all sides were high, but it is a sadly frequent failing of high-minded liberals to underestimate the ruthlessness of their totalitarian opponents. Dimitrov and the Bulgarian liberals were no exception, failing to appreciate Stalin's determination to take Bulgaria into the Soviet orbit. As elsewhere, their nationalistic aspirations had no chance, and duly crumbled under a Communist frontal assault. Backed by the menace of the omnipresent Soviet troops, the Communists engineered a 'popular' (i.e. highly unpopular) government, crushing any opposition and imposing the usual rule of terror by the secret police. By 1945 Dimitrov was a wanted man again, about to be hauled away into oblivion, this time by the Communist regime, for 'defeatism' and subversion. Under house arrest, the ever-resourceful Gemeto gave his guards the slip and sought protection in the apartment of a British diplomat. When the Legation's First Secretary consulted Whitehall after a late return from a heavy day shooting snipe in the Sofia hills, he was instructed coldly that Dimitrov was too hot to handle and would do better to try the US Chargé d'Affaires; notwithstanding Dimitrov's years of support for the British cause, the Foreign Office was reluctant to provoke Russian suspicion and anger by sheltering someone so obviously on the Moscow blacklist. Dimitrov was escorted by the SOE's ubiquitous Bill Bailey, who 'just happened' to be in Bulgaria, to the weekend house of Maynard Barnes, the US Chargé.

A sturdy Yankee, Barnes sheltered the harassed but unshaken Dimitrov for two months, refusing to hand him over even though the house was besieged twenty-four hours a day, as Barnes cabled to Washington, by 'gypsy-like Bulgarian police thugs', occasionally reinforced by a direct Soviet military presence when a special point was to be made. As the State Department cables show, Barnes stoutly resisted all forms of pressure, physical harassment and deceitful offers of compromise from the puppet Bulgarian Government. One reason for his obstinacy was the announcement that the Communist regime had rounded up and executed all 103 members of the wartime parliament, a clear enough example of the new regime's brisk attitude to the niceties of democracy. Another was what had by then become known about the fate of Dimitrov's secretary, Maria Racheva, who had been picked up by the police after they failed to get Dimitrov himself. A bland official statement a few days after her arrest claimed that she had committed suicide by jumping from a fourth-floor window of the main Sofia police station (a formula much in vogue in later years with the South African constabulary, when their victims proved unwilling or unable to be of sufficient help in their enquiries). However, Bulgarian friends who had collected Racheva's body for burial reported to Barnes that she had injuries which were a little hard to explain by a straightforward fall: she had been burned on the arms and legs, her limbs had been twisted from their sockets, there were two bullet holes in her chest and a knife wound on her neck. Bill Bailey's own report to London, which reached Churchill and Eden, prompting the latter to comment that in this case at least the Russians could not be blamed, spoke also of three fingers hacked off, an excised right breast and her tongue wrenched from her mouth. While the politics of Bulgaria had undergone a sea change, the medieval methods of its secret servants clearly had not. Invoking the assistance of Averell Harriman in Moscow to intercede with Foreign Minister Molotov, the tenacious Barnes eventually succeeded in negotiating a United Nations safe conduct for Dimitrov. He went into distinguished and finally peaceful exile in the United States. In 1991, as the world turned, Dimitrov's daughter, Anastasia, returned to post-Communist Bulgaria as secretary of her late father's Agrarian Union. A post-Soviet Government of former Communists re-badged as socialists led Bulgaria to the edge of an abyss of corruption, bankruptcy and rampant inflation. Their recent replacement by what appear to be genuine reformers may have been just in time or just too late. Little wonder that a confused and demoralised population gave their exiled King Simeon, Boris's son, a tumultuous welcome when he returned home on a 'private visit' not too long ago.

# 10

# Trains and Boats and Planes

When Elliott's train slid across the frontier in a hiss of steam in March 1941, German pressure on Yugoslavia was increasing by the hour. Hyenas yelping behind the German caravan, Hungary, Bulgaria, Italy and Albania were all poised to seize pieces of Yugoslav territory if it did not give in to Hitler's demand that it too should join the Axis. In London, Churchill told his War Cabinet colleagues whimsically that the attitude of the Regent, Prince Paul, 'looks like that of an unfortunate man in a cage with a tiger, hoping not to provoke him, while steadily dinner-time approaches'. The unfortunate Paul was more precisely pictured by his close friend, the feline diarist Chips Channon, as like 'me, only more so, with every conceivable quality I admire, except physical attraction. Distinguished, affable, entertaining, with sound judgment reinforced by a subtle Slav, almost feminine sense, which is unerring.' Channon, not for the first time, was wrong, at least about the 'sound judgment', though perhaps Paul had few real options. Inevitably Yugoslavia signed the Axis Pact in Vienna on 25 March 1941, but powerful forces were unleashed inside the country.

Unlike the Croats, Serbs felt capitulation to Germany to be an assault on their honour (not an attribute much in evidence in the 1990s) and mustachioed plotters turned their minds more actively to the downfall of the Regency. With Churchill's encouragement, the British mission in Belgrade under the Minister, Ronald Campbell, and his less visible SOE and SIS outriders, put its weight behind a coup led by former army and air-force officers. The Regency was deposed and the Prime Minister and the Minister of War were arrested. Nineteen-year-old King Peter was declared to have officially come of age and General Dusan Simovic, the retired Chief of Staff of the air force, became Prime Minister. Cables, many of them intercepted by Hermann Goering's *Forschungsamt*, or Research Bureau, en route, buzzed to and from London, the secrets of state reduced to a welter of dots and dashes. Diplomats, military men and secret agents scurried between secret and not-so-secret rendezvous. But while the coup was a consummation devoutly wished by the British clandestine services (SOE had for some time been subsidising the Agrarian Party, whose leader was a Simovic supporter, to the cheerful tune of £35,000 a month and had also been passing out worthwhile little earners to the press and what they called 'patriotic' elements in the armed forces), it was a spontaneous event not initiated by SOE, a gen-uine protest against the signing of the Pact and the dictatorial methods of the ousted regime.

SOE would have been less than human not to take credit for having been its prime mover and instigator, and Baker Street accepted Whitehall's congratulations with self-deprecating pride. Churchill was briefly encouraged, since the coup gave him hope of stiffening Yugoslav resistance. If active resistance developed, German troops capable of doing far more damage to the Allies elsewhere could be kept bogged down. Supporting sorties by Allied forces might then become a valuable reinforcement for Anglo-American efforts at strategic deception, forcing the Germans never to lose sight of the possibility of a major invasion thrust from the south-east. Simovic and his new administration gave little immediate sign of throwing their hats, brilliantine stains, tawdry gold braid and all, into the ring on the Allied side. Could Yugoslavia, they dithered, really be an effective fighting force for the Allies, given the faultline inherent in the perennial Serbian-Croat conflict? 'Gallant little Serbia', as it had been misleadingly styled by the propagandists of the British Harmsworth press in the First World War, had been firmly iden-tified as an ally of the West, but Croatia had only recently voted strongly in favour of the Axis Pact. How could they present a united front? Could conditions be introduced, they wondered, to limit the effect of their adherence to the Pact, without actually taking the risk of offending Hitler by abrogating it?

Not for the first time in the history of the 1940s, handwringing and vacillation were cut short by Hitler. Mottle-cheeked with fury at this threat to obstruct his Balkan plans, he ordered his generals to attack Yugoslavia and Greece on the night of 6 April. As Operation RETRIBU-TION smashed through their country, the Royal Yugoslav Government began its exile – first in Jerusalem, then Cairo, and later in London. It turned out to be permanent. In London, Prince Paul's relationship by marriage to the British royal family counted for nothing. Churchill, a fervent supporter of all royal houses, and even the ever courtly Eden, rebuked him for his weakness – tacit collaboration, some said – by treating him with 'scorn and disapproval'. Churchill mocked his trembling indecision by nicknaming him 'Palsy'.

In those final, confused days, Elliott arrived back in the familiar surroundings of Zagreb to represent SOE at a tax-free salary of £600 a year; he was probably never better off. Frustrated at being sidelined in the Consulate, which in three years had grown from a staff of under ten to something over forty, while the diplomats and his covert colleagues in Belgrade put as much steam as they could behind the coup, Elliott had little to do: 'I drove around a bit to see what I could see, and drew up some maps of potential bombing targets, which I sent to London. Then I gave out all the explosives we had left to the handful of locals who showed any glimmer of interest in resistance, and waited for the bell.' When it tolled, Elliott and the staff of the Zagreb mission, headed by the Consul, Terence Rapp, remembered by Elliott as a 'wise Yorkshireman', drove in nervous convoy down the 120 miles of dusty road, clogged with military traffic and terrified refugees, to the little Adriatic port of Boka Kotorska, where SOE had berthed one of its more exotic resources, the sixty-foot motor yacht *Jadzaica*, for their getaway.

Elliott reached Boka Kotorska on 23 April 1941 and, as he and the Consulate party drove into town, he saw an RAF Sunderland flying-boat lumbering heavily out of the harbour in a cloud of saltspray, but he had no idea until much later in the war that the Sunderland's passengers had been a rather special group, men and women from the Balkans whose close identification with British interests would compromise them terminally with the Germans. Among them, in one of the strange coincidences of those strange days, which brought people together and spun them apart like a drunken Arisaig reel, was Elliott's old friend Gemeto Dimitrov, the SOE's Dr Grigoriev papers in his battered brief-case.

The *Jadzaica* bobbed at the quayside in luxurious incongruity, surrounded by sandbags and the grey-green paraphernalia of war. A Yugoslav anti-aircraft gun pointed mutely into the sky, its crew muttering in confusion as they tried to decide who was friend and who was foe at that difficult turning-point. In the harbour, a German cargo ship lay broken-backed, victim of an SOE limpet mine.

Probably because it involved action, the incident stayed quite clearly in Elliott's mind. 'I went to pull the captain of the yacht out of a dockside bar,' he remembered. 'He had the balls to tell me that he wouldn't leave without his girlfriend, and that she wouldn't dream of going without all her things, which were still back at her flat. So we'd have to go up there and get her luggage. The sky was full of planes. The lads around the anti-aircraft gun were giving us very fishy looks, seeing that we might not be on the same side any more. Behind the town you could hear the rumble of German and Italian tanks and lorries. Time was running out and here was this little shit going on about some tart's luggage. I was close to deciding that the best thing to do was to shoot him and go. But I thought the Yugoslav soldiers on the dock would take a dim view, and anyway none of us in the group knew much about yachts, certainly not enough to get across the Adriatic. So I gritted my teeth. The girl came shimmy-ing out of the bar on her high heels, as if there wasn't a war going on around her. I pushed her into an Alfa Romeo that someone had aban-doned on the dockside, hot-wired the ignition and we shot up to her place. You can't imagine the amount of stuff she had.'

Even this brief diversion used up too much time. When Elliott swung the laden Alfa to a halt alongside the yacht, the Yugoslav gunners bustled up, under the command of a surprisingly determined officer who announced that he could not allow the yacht to leave. 'It's too risky for you out there,' he claimed. 'I'll have to take you somewhere safe until things sort themselves out.'

Deciding that urban discretion was better than maritime valour, the *Jadzaica*'s captain scuttled off, pulling his girlfriend with him, her lug-gage in an expensive heap on the wet cobbles. 'I've had enough of your British foolishness,' he yelled. The Yugoslav soldiers escorted the ner-vous British group back down the gangplank to a harbour-front hotel, where they learned with some relief that they would be Italian, rather than German, prisoners, the former having reached the coast ahead of their senior Axis partners. Uncharitable souls, noting this uncharacteristic display of military zeal, conjectured that the Italians were in fact retreating rather than advancing. The British were taken into what was politely called protective custody, first by an officer of the Axis puppet 'Independent State of Croatia' and a little later, to set a formal seal on things, by a tired but still indefatigably dapper Italian Bersaglieri officer. The shabby hotel was bursting with people, sleeping on sofas and stacked suitcases in the lobby, one man using as a blanket the dusty Union Jack which until a few days before had fluttered proudly outside the Zagreb Consulate. After three days of worry, rumour, stuffy heat, acrid slivovitz and tinned fish, the British were astonished to find themselves beginning an Odyssey, joined in Fiume in June by members of other British missions from Yugoslavia, that was to take them under an Italian safe-conduct on a rambling safari across Italy, the French Riviera and Spain, cocooned from the war in the wagons-lits railroad cars punctuated by stops in what Elliott recalled as 'quite decent' hotels. The US, still neutral, instructed its diplomats to keep a protective eye out, and progress reports were duly cabled back via Washington to Whitehall and SOE. After a few comfortable days in the Ritz Hotel in Madrid, it was back to the khaki reality of the guns and apes of Gibraltar, to await the journey back to England.

Elliott later speculated that their benign treatment was an attempt by the dexterous Count Ciano, the Italian Foreign Minister, to store up credit with the British against the inevitable day of Italy's defeat. Sir Alexander Glen, one of his train companions, and himself no stranger to the secret world, recalled, 'Even in those heady days when the Axis tide was running, the Italians weren't what you'd call stout-hearted. At one stage in Tuscany we were allowed out of our hotel a couple of times to shop for fruit and bread, but then the Italian officer in charge withdrew permission. "Spreading subversion," he said. We protested that we'd always been very discreet, and that when anyone in the village asked how the war was going, we took care to say that Mussolini and the Italian army were putting up a good fight, and that the war wouldn't be over in a hurry.

'"Exactly," he puffed, "that's what I mean by subversion. When you say that sort of thing it upsets them. They want the Allies to win next week so their boys can come home!"'

Elliott records little else of this strange interlude, except that pushing down the crowded train corridor on an early leg of the journey, he was startled to see the yacht captain's girlfriend, plumply comfortable in a corner seat flirting with a dapper duo of diplomats. Over their heads her suitcases, somehow miraculously transplanted from the wet Boka Kotorska quayside, loomed precariously in the luggage racks. 'I went back to look for her when we stopped next,' Elliott remembered, his interest in pretty girls always easily perked, 'but she was nowhere to be seen. Nor was her luggage. A born survivor.'

On Elliott's return to England in July 1941, the official summing up on his first spell of clandestine duty was positive. His personnel file recorded:

> Elliott is the man we recommend be attached to [SOE's] Middle
> East training school, if one is established. He worked with our
> Bulgarian friends right up to our departure, and did an exception-
> ally good job. He was particularly popular with Dimitrov and his
> men and by temperament and training seems very suitable for
> instructional duties.

The ensuing brief spell of domesticity, a second baby, watching my first faltering steps, dreams of a settled life after the war, if there was ever to be 'after the war' in those early nervous days, must have been pretty tame stuff for Elliott, with eighteen months of swashbuckling behind him and the challenge of more adventure just moments ahead, and his communication gap with my mother must have been compounded by the security barriers. What you had done, who you did it for, and what you and your playmates were planning next, were all off-limits for wives and families. None of the ritual bonding of 'Did you have a good day at the office, love?'. No wonder SIS prefers its officers to marry within the charmed circle. It reduces the strain and the need to lie (as well as providing an extra and unpaid pair of hands for the occasional errand, or to talent-spot for the Firm while running English-language classes for local foreigners).

Even the brief spell of domesticity was broken by several spells on underground warfare courses in some of the large country houses whose expropriation had led Claude Dansey of SIS to remark acidly that SOE's initials stood for 'Stately 'Omes of England'.

My mother had by then taken us to the cottage of a friend on the estuary of the River Wirral, in Cheshire, about 250 miles north-west of London. On one brief visit to the Wirral in September, coming back to the cottage from an early stroll collecting shrimps along the estuary mudflats, Elliott was hailed by a spotty youth on a bicycle, who handed him with a mix of pride and vicarious apprehension the small buff-coloured envelope used for telegrams, that now forgotten medium, which in time of war reeked ominously of death, injury and disappointment. In Elliott's case it contained a terse order telling him to report to the War Office in London the next morning. The name of the sender and the anonymous acronym of his office meant nothing to Elliott, but he caught the hint of action. The train jerked through the blacked-out countryside towards London, stopping often and seemingly interminably, sometimes when an air-raid siren sounded but usually for no apparent reason. The railway compartments and corridors were jam-packed with sweaty servicemen trussed with canvas webbing and hollow-cheeked civilians trying not to look guilty about their serge-suited safety, many of them grumbling sotto voce about Churchill and the war. By a frustrating trick of candle-power the tiny blue ceiling lights prescribed by the new blackout regulations were just not bright enough to read by, but just too bright to allow the passengers to sleep undisturbed. Those without tickets, unfortunates caught short by the ravages of wartime diet, and the occasional teenage couple consumed by pimply lust, jostled competitively for the ammoniacal sanctuary of the toilets.

In London at last, Elliott snatched a station breakfast of canary-yellow powdered egg and spam washed down by sweet tea. Grimy and frayed, despite an attempt to scrape the stubble off his chin with the cold water trickle in the washroom, its red-bordered posters ominously listing the addresses of the nearest hospitals specialising in social diseases, he went first to the War Office in Whitehall, where a taciturn staff sergeant checked a clipboard and told him to report to 64 Baker Street, 100 yards away from the fictional address of Sherlock Holmes, where behind a prosaic nameplate announcing the Inter-Service Liaison Department, there lurked SOE's headquarters. Two security checks, careful comparison of his identity card against a list of names, and finally he was shown into a featureless room. A uniformed colonel, who did not give his name, sat waiting behind a plain deal table, his ivory teeth flashing the false smile of an old Bechstein keyboard.

Elliott had been identified as the right man for an important mission in Yugoslavia, the colonel announced portentously. He would be parachuted in uniform, but there was a high risk of capture and if so the uniform might not save him. Even if the mission worked out, the colonel added, avoiding Elliott's eye, 'You know we don't give out medals in this game.' This was a business for volunteers, and Elliott was free to decline. But if he accepted, he would have to leave in forty-eight hours for training and briefing in Cairo. Elliott, who at this point had never even seen a parachute, volunteered in a second. It would have taken a brave man to refuse.

After a brief speech of encouragement, the colonel handed him a travel warrant, from which Elliott saw that he was to board a troopship leaving for South Africa from Liverpool, thirty miles down the road from the cottage where he had begun his tiresome journey the previous day, and to which he would now have to return, doubly weary, to collect his bags.

'I don't know whether you know, sir,' Elliott said, an edge to his military courtesy, 'I'm living right outside Liverpool at the moment. It might have been simpler if I could have been briefed up there and headed off directly.' The colonel tapped the side of his nose roguishly, his mahjong smile catching the light again: 'Confidential matters, dear boy. Left hand, right hand. You know what I mean.'

Gas mask over his shoulder in its canvas bag, Elliott took the next train north, collected his bags, patted the children absentmindedly on the head, pecked my mother's cheek, closed the door behind him and went off to board *The Empress of Australia*. In their hammocks on the lower decks, the army other ranks and junior NCOs sweltered, grumbled and worried about torpedoes as each rolling wave brought them nearer to Durban. The crew sneered at the landlubbers and toyed with each other in the chain lockers, continuing a seafaring tradition later described by the singer George Melly, paraphrasing Churchill, as 'On shore, wine, women and song. At sea, rum, bum and concertina.' On the upper decks, in the former first-class cabins and saloon, the officers had what Elliott remembered succinctly as 'a wild, wild time'. A chorus of gulls squawked a hymn to idleness and relaxation, and as the south approached, the noon sun burned daily brighter and the risks of U-boats receded, duty-free liquor and round-the-clock card games provoked beefy violence accompanied by the sound of shattering glass and splintering furniture. Elliott claimed that after the damage caused on this particular run, Whitehall had ordered that officers' alcohol was to be rationed. Another SOE traveller on this route, Sir Peter Wilkinson, recalls that gin was only sixpence a glass, making his bar bill of £30 for the voyage a tribute to his liver and his stamina.

The azure sky and relaxed atmosphere of Durban were a heady contrast to the edgy twilight threnody of the London air-raid sirens. An SOE officer in a crumpled tan suit slipped on board *The Empress* to meet Elliott. After some furtive eye contact, sideways shuffling and muttered exchanges across the throng of officers, 'for all the world like Seniors' Evening in a gay nightclub', as a watcher of strange encounters once observed, he took Elliott to a quiet corner of the deck and handed him his onward travel orders, which would take him by RAF flying boat to Cairo, droning endlessly through the centre of Africa, countless refuelling stops with little sleep, bad food and no interest in the wildlife scampering over the veldt below, the splendours of Lake Victoria or the dusty miseries of Khartoum. The arrival in Cairo, the plane circling the Pyramids before splashing down into the lethal waters of the Nile in front of the Semiramis Hotel, must have been the apex of every adventurer's dream.

Elliott was too tired to dream. Limp from the damp heat, brushing reflexively at the determined flies, he took a room in a boarding-house in Zamlek and reported back to SOE headquarters in Rustum Buildings, a block of apartments on Kasr al Aini Street widely known to Cairene taxi-drivers and also to the local German agents as 'The Secret House'.

For those stuck there and making the best of a good job, the gamey atmosphere of Cairo in 1941 was exotically appealing, given extra spice by the desert fighting sometimes so close to the city that, like the Duchess of Richmond's ball, dinner-parties were disturbed by the rumble of gunfire. A boozy bouillabaisse of fishy military men, merry widows, diplomats, spies, saboteurs and the shabby human flotsam washed on to the shores of Egypt by the tides of war, rubbing shoulders (and any other accessible body parts) with each other, in and around the court of the priapic King Farouk, who sweated over his world-class collection of erotic art and bibelots, while the uncountable, ignored poor sat dumbly waiting for bilharzia and the revolution. 'If only', as Oscar Wilde said more than once, 'the poor had profiles; the problems of poverty would be easily solved.'

SOE in Cairo was arguably neither very special nor operationally efficient, nor indeed all that hot at execution of its tasks, but the telling of Elliott's story thankfully does not require the parallel re-telling of the intrigues, coups and purges which periodically convulsed Rustum Buildings, simply because he was plunged rather quickly into preparation for action, and so avoided being enmeshed in the battles of the desk-bound warriors, fought with a venom and persistence which would have done credit to front-line troops.

Elliott became SOE's Agent D/H97, (D/H was the cryptonym for SOE's Yugoslav Section). Certainly, because he knew the country and its language, perhaps because he also knew Gemeto Dimitrov, and maybe because he had also actually met the object of his mission, he had been picked to head a team to re-establish Britain's fragile contact with the resistance leader Draža Mihailovic, then a colonel, but by the time Elliott's mission, codenamed DISCLAIM, went in, a general and Minister of War in the government-in-exile. The wider politics were outside Elliott's scope. It was unproductive for agents to know the nuances, the uncertainties, the ambiguities of their mission. They might worry, they might talk, so the picture of Yugoslavia and the aim of his mission painted for Elliott by his SOE briefers was in broad strokes and strong primary colours. It showed that after the German occupation, the map of wartime Yugoslavia had been redrawn by Berlin and its allies. Like a John Gotti shareout at the Ravenite Social Club on Mulberry Street in New York's Little Italy, the dons and *consiglieri* – Bulgaria, Hungary, Italy and Albania – each duly got a piece of the action for which they had clamoured before Yugoslavia was overrun. Living proof of the French adage that '*La merde surnage*', the Croat Fascists under the vicious Ante Pavelic had been transubstantiated into the government of a so-called Independent State of Croatia, technically a dependency of the Italian Crown. Serbia, redesignated the German Military Command Area, acquired its own puppet Prime Minister in the collaborationist General Nedic. These cosy arrangements looked good on paper, and provided those who had seized office with the nice uniforms, the big cars, the fawning private secretaries and the feel-good factor generated by the knowledge that you hold the power of life and death over your fellow men. As Elliott learned, almost from the start of the occupation the Axis forces and their allies had found themselves grappling with a deadly campaign of resistance. Since the end of the First World War, Yugoslavia had been bedevilled by roaming bands of deserters, refugees and brigands who had terrorised villages, held up travellers and robbed banks. Though mercilessly hunted down by the new federal police, these heavily armed gangs had been suppressed rather than eliminated and provoked the first green shoots of guerrilla war which sprang up overnight in the grey rocks, threatening vital German supply lines, tying down troops, and forcing the Germans (not that they ever needed much forcing into violence) into counter-action and reprisal, matched by the insurgents at each turn of the spiral in ferocity, if not in scale.

'Lead, kindly light, amid the encircling gloom,' the congregation bellowed on Sundays at Cairo's Anglican Cathedral, as the majors ogled the moist mock-modest maidens of the First Aid Nursing Yeomanry across the aisles. For SOE Cairo, and indeed for its London HQ, 'encircling gloom' hung over Yugoslavia like a pall. Peering through it in 1941, the planners, encouraged by the Yugoslav government-in-exile, were initially convinced that Mihailovic was the leader of the only significant resistance grouping, and they guessed, optimistically, that he might have as many as 50,000 Chetniks under his command.

A staunch Royalist, a detail fanatic, his dense beard and wire-rimmed glasses suggesting today a member of the Grateful Dead rather than a military man, Mihailovic had the legitimacy of being the designated senior representative of the government-in-exile in the occupied homeland. Other, rather ill-defined resistance forces were known to be in the field, but at that early stage of the war little concrete had emerged about the shadowy figure, known at various times in his underground career as 'Engineer Babic', 'Dr Kostanjic' or 'Engineer Tomasek', soon to become more familiar as Josef Broz Tito. But although less visible, in part because they had refrained from action during the false honeymoon of the Nazi-Soviet Pact, unlike the Chetniks, Tito's Communist Partisans were disciplined and dangerous.

A later British intelligence appraisal concluded with a measure of litotes that by September 1941 the resistance efforts had become 'a serious embarrassment' to the Germans. The Germans were far more than embarrassed. Their own assessments, found in the Wehrmacht records for Serbia, speak sombrely of countless attacks on soldiers, police posts and vehicles, of troop and freight trains raked by machine-gun fire, bridges blown up and telephone lines cut. Strikes and sabotage closed mines and factories. The whole infrastructure of the puppet Serbian state was destabilised to a degree that 'made orderly administration of the country impossible'. A post-war British evaluation thought that around this time 'an average of fourteen German divisions was held down' in Yugoslavia by resistance, suffering 'constant losses'.

The German response was predictable. From 1 September 1941 to 15 January 1942, the Wehrmacht command proudly tallied for their Berlin enemy losses of a nice, round 20,000, 'including those shot in reprisal measures'. For the month beginning 16 February 1942, Yugoslav losses were listed with the more typical Teutonic precision of a game book on a Junker's Pomeranian estate as 1,983 resistance fighters killed in battle and 1,557 in reprisals. The German Command was ordered to raze any house, any village, suspected of having been used by the resistance. 'Removal of the population to concentration camps can be useful', local commanders were advised succinctly. Behind the statistics lay the shrieking shock of the sudden firefights, the rumble of tanks and armoured cars, grey-uniformed ambushers lurking behind barns and the outcrops of rock, orange flame and black smoke on the snow. White-walled churches, often whole villages, were torched. The dry rattle of the German firing squads tumbled women and children into trenches they had first been forced to hack with difficulty in the frozen soil. Not everyone resisted. The Germans had a lot of help. According to a post-war study by the Yugoslav Jewish community, Pavelic's Croat administration, whose clerical Fascists were benignly viewed by the Vatican as the epitome of 'a pure Catholic state', killed 33,000 Jews, most of them starved or tortured to death with gusto by the Ustashe in local concentration camps. Not wanting to be thought unsupportive of the broader efforts towards the Final Solution, Pavelic also saw to it that 5,000 Jews were handed over directly to the Germans for deportation to Auschwitz, though this was a mere sideline compared to the breathtaking savagery with which his Ustashe, encouraged and sometimes led by senior prelates and wild-eyed priests with bloodstained hands, maimed, sliced, gouged and burned Serb and Moslem men, women and children. Those who were simply shot or stabbed out of hand were the lucky ones; the cruelty of Pavelic and his cohorts, most of whom escaped post-war justice with the Vatican's help, made even their German and Italian allies squeamish.

To give credit where little is due, this time at least, Serbian hands were less directly bloodied in the process of extermination and ethnic cleansing, although General Nedic's police, spurred by promises of cash rewards like bounty hunters in the Wild West, assisted the Germans enthusiastically in the round-up of Jews. Almost all the 14,000 Jews who died in Serbia were killed by the Germans themselves; some 5,000 men were shot in reprisals for Partisan attacks on the Germans; their widows and children were then gassed in a German concentration camp near Belgrade, about whose existence, like the good German burghers living around death camps like Ravensbrück, the local Serb inhabitants later claimed to have been blissfully unaware. Winter tightened its grip. In the self-pitying words of another German report with an uncanny resemblance to today's news bulletins, its soldiers faced

> violent cold and driving snow. We marched on wretched roads covered with ice and along mule tracks, and had to fight a malicious enemy, who could not be caught, in a wild and mountainous country. The guerrillas were everywhere and nowhere. It was possible to disperse them, but not to destroy them completely. They defended themselves in their positions on the rocks, and then quickly melted away again into their villages where they acted like 'peaceful' peasants in a 'friendly' manner towards our troops.

The British planners saw that the more that could be done to stoke the resistance fires with arms and supplies, the more the Germans and their allies would be harassed and diverted. But resources were scarce and before deciding how and where to allocate them, the planners needed better basic intelligence from snow level, to augment the tantalising but fragmentary scraps scooped out of the airwaves in the form of ULTRA signals intelligence and lower-level operational radio intercepts. It was also essential to have reliable men on the ground who could in due course help organise the supply drops and help guide the resistance to inflict the most effective damage on the enemy. SOE had the men who knew Yugoslavia and its languages, men who were bright and resilient. Men who, whether out of bravery or bravado, were unlikely to second-guess the considerable personal risks entailed in what they were being asked to do. Scrambling to justify a seat at the table in the strategic debate about its country's present, and more important its future, the exiled government ordered its intelligence staff to assist the effort by organising Operation BULLSEYE, in which two Yugoslav officers would be landed by submarine on the Adriatic coast to make contact with Mihailovic.

The Yugoslavs were soon made aware that their Whitehall hosts were very much their senior allies, and were not going to allow the government-in-exile any measure of independence or initiative in actions against their homeland. And as BULLSEYE took shape, the Foreign Office and SOE flexed their muscles, adding to the team Major (later Colonel) Bill Hudson, a tough engineer from the now familiar intelligence stable, the Trepca Mines. Hudson's reports began to throw up disturbing challenges to the prevailing view, highlighting, to London's surprise, the strong fight being put up by the Partisans, while 'numerous national elements (the Mihailovic Chetniks) are standing on one side and are waiting'.

In mid-October 1941, SOE instructed Hudson to contact Mihailovic in Serbia. This he did, although first meeting Tito en route and reporting again on the vigour of the Communist Partisans. Tito seems still to have been hoping, or pretending at least for Hudson's benefit to hope, that his Partisans could make common cause with Mihailovic. Hudson finally reached Mihailovic's mountainside headquarters at the end of October. Two days later, the two resistance leaders met warily, rival medieval barons, in what proved inevitably to be a futile attempt to cobble together a working co-operation. By mid-November, Hudson radioed to SOE that the two factions were at each other's throats; he urged London not to send supplies to Mihailovic unless he made another attempt to join forces with Tito, since arms dropped to the Chetniks would be turned first against the Partisans, not the Germans. Heavy German counter-attacks then scattered both factions of the resistance. Hudson was separated from Mihailovic and from his radio set. After two gruelling days scrambling through the mountains with Tito and his remaining forces, Hudson tried to rejoin Mihailovic, but the latter, suppurating with distrust over what he saw as Hudson's cosy relationship with Tito, refused to take him back, casting him out to wander, in almost biblical style, starving and frozen across the mountains for nearly three months with only a shepherd boy for company, before grudgingly accepting him back at his headquarters. With Hudson isolated, from early December 1941 London was again cut off behind a worrying wall of silence, aware now of the increasingly bloody intestine rivalries, but frustratingly unable to discern through the freezing fog who was doing what to whom. Such co-operation as there was, was grudging and intermittent; savage internecine skirmishes and betrayals were more characteristic. Behind the knives and bullets, the dead young men and women scattered in stiff silence across the snow were oblivious now of whether they had died for the King or for Communism. The two sides, already fighting less for the defeat of the Axis than for domination of Yugoslavia after the war, kept up a steady propaganda chorus via their puppet masters in Moscow and London's Lowndes Square, the government-in-exile's home (handily placed for lunchtime shopping 500 yards from Harrods).

From Mihailovic came claims that the Partisans' sabotage and pinprick attacks on the Axis occupiers had no strategic value, and only brought down reprisals on the heads of the luckless civil population. They also accused the Partisans of trafficking with the Germans when it suited them. For their part, the Partisans' partisan melody told those who heard it via the Kremlin and the Communist press that Mihailovic's policy of husbanding his resources, and 'waiting until the right time comes', was nothing more than a cloak for inertia, to put it at its most charitable. In fact, they shrilled, Mihailovic and his cohorts had actively collaborated with the Italians and the Quisling administration of General Nedic in a bid to keep the Chetnik forces out of the conflict so that they could be deployed against the Partisans.

The Balkans are the Balkans. There is some truth in all these allegations. Amid the bickering and the unknowing, SOE decided that, with Hudson's whereabouts and relations with Mihailovic uncertain, another push had to be made to find out what was going on. The files, the clubs, the messes and the bars were trawled for candidates who could be sent into the void. The first of these follow-up missions, HYDRA, was led by Terence Atherton, a journalist and an old acquaintance of Elliott's from Yugoslavia. It landed from the submarine *Thorn* on the Montenegrin coast on 4 February, but Atherton subsequently disappeared, probably murdered by a Chetnik for his gold sovereigns. A second mission, HENNA, consisting of two Yugoslav officers, was also landed by submarine and reached Mihailovic successfully.

HYDRA and HENNA were to be followed by DISCLAIM, Elliott's mission, and a fourth was planned with the singularly inappropriate codename DESIRABLE. These were to be inserted by air despite

Yugoslav protests in Cairo that parachuting blind into the mountains meant sending men to 'certain death'. (At their conception, the two later missions were rather prosaically styled 'BULLSEYE One and Two'. Why this was superseded by DISCLAIM and DESIRABLE we shall never know. Nor do we need to.)

# 11

# DISCLAIM

The briefing for Elliott's mission was signed on 21 January 1942 by Terence Airey, a former MI(R) officer in Ethiopia. Airey, who slightly unpatriotically for those times bred dachshunds, had just been appointed Director of SOE Operations in Cairo after yet another of the frequent purges of its senior ranks, this time amid a well-orchestrated arpeggio of accusations from SIS and the military that SOE was inefficient, grotesquely insecure, and that many of its people spent too much time partying around Cairo at taxpayers' expense (accusations not without foundation, though resonant with the gong-like echoes of the pot calling the kettle black).

Researchers, who claim to have established clear evidence of secret Communist manipulation within SOE Cairo as the real driving force behind the eventual dropping of Mihailovic in favour of Tito, have identified the late James Klugmann as Moscow's secret puppet-master. Klugmann, who never hid his strong Communist beliefs, came to SOE Cairo as a corporal. It was Airey, his old schoolfriend from Gresham's in Norfolk (where the pompous traitor Donald Maclean was another contemporary), who supported and rapidly promoted him to be Deputy Head of SOE's Yugoslav Section. There was, in fact, nothing underhand in Airey's enthusiasm. Klugmann was exceptionally bright (his name roughly translates from German as 'Clever Chap') and hard-working, slaving away on his own at the SOE cable traffic all hours of the day and night; no doubt he deserved promotion. Revisionist historians are probably right to smell something fishy in his role; but if their suspicions are correct, and if it is also true that when organisations go crooked, the fish rots from the head, who else was involved? It is difficult to see how in a solo burrowing act even the most talented mole can subtly edit two years of operational records and end up putting such a spin on the briefings based on those records as to subvert the policy of a government.

Many, but I suspect not all, of those interested in these matters had hoped that an officially commissioned history of SOE's role in Yugoslavia would have shed more light on these potentially disturbing undercurrents. All the more if it had been able to shed any light on the dealings between Mihailovic and Dimitrov. Sadly, it seems as though the history has been abandoned *in media res*.

The commander of DESIRABLE, G.A. Head, whose team trained alongside DISCLAIM, cabled testily to Baker Street about the 'considerable difficulty and procrastination' he and Elliott had encountered in getting the Yugoslav authorities in Cairo to nominate their own men for the two missions. Hardly surprising, since being hunted over the mountains by Croats and Nazis was not high on everyone's list of ways to spend the winter. Moreover, since, even in Cairo, Yugoslav intrigue and mutual suspicion were endemic, candidates acceptable to all factions were hard to find. Even as late as 21 January, the SOE briefers anticipated that Elliott would be accompanied by only one Yugoslav guide, Flight Sergeant Peter Miljkovic, a Serb.

In the final few days, a last-minute stroke of good fortune for the Yugoslav Intelligence Chief in Cairo, Colonel Popovic, or perhaps some more complex manœuvre, brought into the team a second Serb, Pilot Officer Pavel Crjnanski. DISCLAIM's radio operator was to be Robert Chapman, a diminutive twenty-five-year-old Royal Signals corporal from Barrow-in-Furness, who had joined the army from a chilly, bare-walled North Country orphanage and had been seconded to the Special Air Service to train in coaxing long-distance life out of the SOE's Vibrator wireless sets.

The mission's objectives were clear, at least as recorded in SOE's files. Establish communications with General Mihailovic and Hudson.

Report back. Prepare the ground for supply drops. Tell us, in short, just what the hell is going on out there. SOE's founding charter was supposed to keep it away from the task of intelligence-gathering. None the less, Airey set out many questions for Elliott, most of them indicative of how little was known of what was happening. The answers, Elliott was told, were to be sent back by radio to Cairo, Malta or via Atherton's group in Montenegro, whose fate was then still unknown. (Elliott was also told about a courier line running through Sofia to Istanbul, which could be used for messages, but no details of this seem to have survived.)

SOE wanted to know what areas were held by Mihailovic, the Germans, the Italians and the Bulgarians. They wanted information on 'any Yugoslav guerrilla activity, including their organisation and current operations against the Axis'. 'Who are the leaders?' Airey's brief asked, plaintively. 'Where is Hudson? How powerful is General Mihailovic's organisation? Where are its principal elements situated? Who are the principal local leaders? Who are the Partisan leaders? To what extent are they Communists? What is the relationship between General Mihailovic and the Partisans?' Although SOE also asked for information on the Axis forces, raw military intelligence does not appear as a central theme of their questions. They were more interested in the internal situation in Yugoslavia, from food and electricity supplies to the attitude of the key elements of the community – churches, political groups and paramilitary organisations – to each other and to the Germans and Italians. The brief makes no mention at all of sabotage, either as a strategy to be pursued or one from which Mihailovic should be dissuaded. In his own notes, Elliott completely ignores the strategic issues and does not begin to speculate on where DISCLAIM fitted into the much larger picture of the war itself. That is indeed how it was. The careful noting of dates, wise post-hoc reflections on strategy, the scoring of points, assessments of character, are for the historians and for the generals and leaders, not for the men and women who did the jumping.

On 25 December 1941, the men of DISCLAIM and DESIRABLE celebrated Christmas by beginning four days of parachute training at Al Shoufra, near Alexandria in Egypt, pulling ripcords rather than crackers. How DISCLAIM got off the ground, so to speak, is a story redolent of the muddle and fuzzy recollection so characteristic of SOE's workings, especially when, as here, they did not work. Whether lurking behind it all even in those early days were the first manifestations of the influence of the pro-Tito faction in SOE Cairo we have no evidence, and it may be safer to ascribe what did and did not happen to the operation of what the services termed Sod's Law, the age-old principle that if something can go wrong, it will, than to the plottings of a Communist cell scheming away in the dusty, shit-strewn shadows of the Sphinx. But at the least there was a lethal failure in communications between Baker Street and its obsessively independent barons in the Middle East, and when it came to getting the job done, the delays, difficulties and dead patches of silence stretch to the limit what might be explained away by the vagaries of war and the desperate shortage of equipment. The main puzzle is the timing. As noted already, SOE Cairo did not finalise the mission brief until 21 January, but in London, Eric van Maurik, an Air Liaison Officer with SOE despite or perhaps because of the fact that he was actually in the infantry, was detailed as early as mid-December to fly out to Malta on 26 December, the understanding in Baker Street being that the DISCLAIM team would arrive at the same time, or even a few days before, so that the mission could be parachuted in during the period of the full moon around the end of the month. As van Maurik flew out, Elliott and his team were only just beginning their parachute training in Egypt.

Sitting back today as the air hostess, a bouffant nanny *manquée*, stuffs you with pâté de foie gras in a neat reversal of the food chain followed to produce it, it is hard to imagine what flying meant back then. The multilingual van Maurik, whose job it was to act as a buffer between the phlegmatic aircrews and the sometimes volatile, often uncomprehending and incomprehensible foreign mission teams, to check the latter's parachute drills and to agree the dropping zone, first drove up to Stradishall, near Newmarket, which had lately become the base of the long-range Whitley bombers which ferried both SOE and SIS agents into the field. After a stop near Bournemouth to top up its long-range tanks, the Whitley, piloted by John Austin, thumped and bumped through the clouds over the Bay of Biscay, hour after endless hour as the cold, the noise and the fear of a Focke-Wulff fighter flashing out of the dusk fought with the fatigue and boredom, and the rubbery corpse breath of the oxygen masks. After a hair-raising landing low over a maze of masts and funnels in the harbour in Gibraltar, the Whitley flew on to Malta. With the land campaign in Libya turning against Rommel, the Luftwaffe had stepped up its efforts to smash the island out of its role as a supply base and naval and air staging-post, and it had become a very dangerous place to be. And a very foolish place indeed to park what grew to a flight of three scarce Whitleys waiting for agents who were not there, as scheduled, at the end of December, and whose existence, whereabouts and likely arrival time proved curiously difficult to ascertain via the Malta MI5 representative, officially the Defence Security Officer (DSO), who was van Maurik's designated contact and through whom all communications with SOE in London and Cairo ran. The weeks went by, the moon waxed and waned, and the frustrations grew. The official silence continued. The bombs fell. German bombs. Italian bombs. Regular bombs and, to ring the changes, machine-gun strafing attacks and bombs fitted with a screaming device designed to heighten the terror of those on the ground. Probably even more bombs than the Germans had planned, since once the bulky Whitleys had been spotted, the Luftwaffe's suspicions were aroused.

Inevitably first one, then two of the three Whitleys were put out of action. As a bizarre sidelight, John Austin also lost his crew, not to the Luftwaffe but to the grim grip of the military police. Alerted by a sudden irruption of gold coins in the bars and bordellos of 'the Gut', the Catholic island's ecumenical red-light strip, where greasy notes and worn florins were the usual currency, the police soon discovered that the crew, well aware of the sort of loads they were carrying, had painstakingly unscrewed one of the containers to be dropped with the DISCLAIM team and stolen a box of sovereigns intended for the resistance. 'Fell off the back of the plane, guv,' was not an excuse the subsequent court-martial accepted and the crew eventually spent several months in the army glasshouse under a harsh double-time regime that doubtless had them wishing they could have ended up instead in a comfortable prisoner-of-war camp in rural Germany.

Elliott's account deepens the mystery, though perhaps blurred memories and some obsession with security on the part of the DSO play their part too, since he recalls actually reaching Malta in January, only to have to return to Egypt in a rapid and dangerous round trip of which van Maurik was not aware. He and his team flew to the island from Alexandria. 'Funny, I thought it would be smaller. It's actually a bit like Egypt,' one of the Serbs, who had not seen Malta before, commented to Elliott when they landed after the two-hour flight. Their plane bounced to a halt outside a heavily camouflaged hangar, and, as he swung the door open, Elliott realised with bewilderment that it looked like Egypt because it was; they had returned to Alexandria. 'I was bloody mad, I can tell you.'

Like a tortoise, the pilot stretched his leather-covered head round the cockpit door. 'Sorry about that, the weather closed in and we had to turn around. We were a bit busy up front and I didn't have a chance to tell you.' He grinned and pulled back his head into the shell of the cockpit before Elliott could reply.

The next day the DISCLAIM team flew out again and this time reached Malta without diversion. They were driven to a safe-house tucked into the stone battlements of Grand Harbour to await the final long and dangerous leg into Yugoslavia the next evening. As Elliott remembered it, as they slid into their bunks, fortified by some of the jealously rationed stocks of whisky kept in the house for departing agents, they heard the wail of sirens and the crump of bombs. It was the raid recalled by van Maurik as having put the second Whitley out of action, and Elliott was told the next day, perhaps by the MI5 representative, that in the light of the problems the mission would have to return to Egypt and try again at the next moon period.

It is in fact perfectly feasible that the team's presence on the island could have been concealed from van Maurik as London's emissary, though one wonders quite why. He did not know any of them by sight, and was in no position to monitor all the flights in and out of the airfield. Nor did they know him; Elliott would presumably have been briefed that the DSO himself was the official SOE representative. To compound this particular puzzle, Elliott's service record shows that he spent a total of two months in Malta at some unspecified time, something his own reminiscences do not mention. Whether some great or petty game was being played out, and if so by whom on whom, we will never know. In any event, van Maurik stayed on in frustration and danger, and Elliott's team and the four men slated for DESIRABLE were sent into the mountains of Syria for a few days skiing, to keep them fit and to boost their understandably flagging morale. Elliott himself stayed in Cairo, laid low by the sinus problems which had plagued him for years and which were aggravated by flying in unpressurised aircraft.

When the moon began to show its bland face again, the DISCLAIM team re-grouped and rather wearily retraced their route across the Mediterranean to Malta, where at the beginning of February they finally met van Maurik and John Austin. Van Maurik recalls Elliott as 'a quiet and reliable looking man . . . in fighting trim'. One of the Yugoslavs impressed him less: 'A large bloke with a khaki sweater over his battle-dress trousers and a rather ample stomach.' John Austin, by contrast, made a deliberate effort not to remember anything about the Joes he was dropping or even to chat to them about personal details, on the sensible grounds that if he was shot down and captured, there was little or nothing he could tell the Germans about his charges.

The general area of the dropping zone having been fixed on the basis of what vague information the team and van Maurik had about where Mihailovic might be, the actual target was then selected on the rather charming if rudimentary basis that it was a spot Miljkovic thought he would recognise looking down from the plane's hatch when they got there. (For amusement, I once experimented by taking a KingAir turbo-jet over the wintry late afternoon skies of a hilly snow-mantled part of Vermont which I know well, to see how easy it actually is to spot a particular house, group of fields or configuration of woods on familiar ground from 1,000 feet. Not at all is the answer.) Van Maurik made sure that they knew how to use their parachutes, and it was time to load up and head out, an airborne party of pioneers, though heading east rather than west. Loading the Whitley was not easy. Most of its Spartan interior was taken up by the extra fuel tanks bolted along the sides, as a slender guarantee that the plane could make the long round trip with some margin of safety. The team's supplies were packed into empty 500 lb bomb casings, which in turn were slipped like Russian Matrioshka dolls inside six-foot-long steel outer tubes known as C containers. They had food for fourteen days, clothing, enough ammunition for a Los Angeles riot, Mills bombs (otherwise known as No. 36 grenades), blankets, sheepskin coats and medical supplies. Tucked in the containers were two German Mauser semi-automatics (the same model as the one Elliott brought home, years later, among his souvenirs) and 1,000 rounds of 0.763 mm ammunition. Why these German weapons, no doubt spoils of war on some other battlefield? Probably because in German-held territory, ammunition for a Mauser would be a tad easier to come by. Elliott had trained at Arisaig with a range of foreign handguns and machine pistols. To ease their way with the local peasants after landing, the team had packets of chocolate, salt, thread and matches, SOE's rather William Morris view of the kind of gifts that would melt crusty Yugoslav hearts. More usefully, in a separate pink-painted container there were four small but hefty waxed-paper packages of the kind filched from one of the other

planes by Austin's original crew, each holding 250 gold sovereigns, with
each team member also carrying another fifty sovereigns in his belt, as
well as 368 German Reichsmarks, a curiously precise figure. The two
cumbersome wireless sets, each with six-volt batteries, and spares were
packed separately, as were the team's wooden skis.

It would be nice to know, but the files make no mention of it, that the
team also carried some of the more exotic inventions of SOE's ingenious Devices Section at Station XV on the Barnet by-pass. The
exploding turd, a pat of imitation horse, cow or, in appropriate climates,
camel dung, stuffed with explosive, over which enemy vehicles would
run at their peril, was a nice combination of schoolboy humour and
lethal ingenuity. *Just William* joins the SAS.

As Elliott remembered it (though Austin, over fifty years and hundreds of dangerous flights later, does not recall any special element of
drama), the take-off of the Whitley, call-sign VZ5159, was entirely in
keeping with the mission's erratic progress. 'The pilot gunned the
engines on the runway, taking them up to almost maximum revs with his
foot on the brake. Then he shouted that we were carrying so much
extra weight with all that fuel, we all needed to be as close to the nose as
we could. The four of us jammed round the cockpit door. He released the
brake and the plane lurched forward. We rattled and roared about
halfway down the runway. We were up in the air for a second, then
bounced back down on the runway. The pilot throttled back and braked
hard. We taxied back to the hangar. I was scared shitless. We all were.
He said we still didn't have the weight right, so I pulled myself right into
the cockpit, where there was hardly any room to begin with, and jammed
in behind his radio operator. Chapman crawled half on top of me. Round
we went again. The crew's arms and elbows jabbing me in the face as
they struggled with the controls. We seemed to be glued to the runway.
Finally the nose came up very, very slowly and we just cleared the
perimeter fence. We limped out low over the waves like a brick with
wings.'

The Whitley droned unscathed across the Mediterranean, across the
heel of Italy, then over the Adriatic, reaching the Yugoslav coast near
Dubrovnik. Over Yugoslavia the seamless darkness of a pre-electric
peasant world was finally broken by the scattered clusters of lights that
marked Sarajevo. As the plane began to descend, the snowy February
hillsides were a grey pre-dawn blur, the thick clouds curtaining the

moonlight. The frozen ground threw back into the sky the rumble of the twin Rolls-Royce engines. After six hours battened inside the chill metal of the fuselage, the team were oblivious to the noise. In the bomb-hatch below, the supply containers rattled against their restraining clips. The Whitley banked, its starboard wingtip almost brushing the pines.

'I'm coming round one more time to make double sure, but I think we're there. The instruments are all frozen up and we'll have to do the last bit by the seat of our pants, but we've got enough visibility. No problem,' Austin's voice crackled laconically through the earphones. Elliott wondered how anyone could call an operation like this 'secret'. The aircraft noise and its lumbering turns over the last few minutes must have alerted every village, every watchful German and Croat patrol and every wary Yugoslav resistance group for miles around. He was right. Flying criss-cross patterns prior to a drop was intended as a security measure to confuse German tracking stations. While conceivably effective over a built-up area, over open country it had obvious risks.

'Cockpit again. Navigator reports he saw flashes down there about a mile or so from the dropping zone. He thinks it could have been rifle fire. We can pull out if you like.' Elliott leaned forward. Were they in the right place?

'Jump or go back, what do you think?' he yelled at the Serbs. Miljkovic shouted vehemently that whatever the others did, he was going to jump. It was the right place, he was sure of it. Crjnanski looked at him, smiled briefly, then gave Elliott the thumbs-up sign. Elliott pulled the helmet microphone close to his face: 'We're going in.' He balanced unsteadily on the bouncing metal deck, struggling against his parachute harness, the weight of his equipment and the thick bulk of his clothing. Each of them was wearing a leather jerkin over RAF coveralls with full battledress underneath and weighted down with a heavy knapsack, their Colts and the heavy-hilted Sykes-Fairbairn fighting knives that were standard issue for British special forces.

The crew member who was acting as jump master pulled at the two freezing steel buckles that held the parachute hatch in place. The first came undone without difficulty. As the Whitley slipped sickeningly sideways, his hands fumbled on the second. It refused to budge. Swearing savagely, he pulled himself back and kicked at it. The buckle clattered to the floor. He pulled the hatch handle. As though it had never been there, the cover disappeared, sucked into the night by the buffeting slipstream.

The ceiling light flashed red. 'Time to go. Good Luck!' Austin said quietly. Miljkovic clambered first to the black mouth of the hatchway, the Whitley now in a shallow dive from which it levelled out at 600 feet leaving little margin for error. As though cued by the long arm of British intelligence from the 'Secret House' in Cairo, the moon suddenly shrugged free of the clouds, and the clearing below blazed crisply white, the shadows of the pines etched black along its edges. Miljkovic tugged to check the cord clipped to a cable slung along the aircraft roof that would automatically pull open his parachute an instant after he jumped. The light flashed orange and then green. A clap on the shoulder from one of the crew. He braced himself and then tumbled into the mineshaft of the night. Chapman quickly pulled the two radios up the hatchway and pushed them out with his feet. Their ripcord lines tautened for an instant, then fluttered free. Austin throttled the 1,145 horsepower motors back another notch. The Whitley began its second circuit. Travelling so slowly over the ground, so close to it, Elliott felt he could simply have stepped out of the hatch into the branches of the nearest pine. The Whitley banked. 'Light in the DZ. Looks okay,' the dispatcher yelled as he saw the winking torch, indicating that Miljkovic was safely down. Then Chapman followed his radio sets into the icy night. The aircraft now lurching dangerously a hair's-breadth above its 110 mph stalling-point, Austin tripped the bomb-hatch switch. Free of its load, the Whitley bucked as the containers rumbled down, their parachutes brightly coloured so that they could be easily spotted against the snow. Crjnanski and Elliott scrambled forward through the narrow catwalk and squatted in turn at the edge of the hatch, legs dangling. Each of them pushed forward into the cold unknown. The Whitley climbed away in a full-throttle scramble for the shelter of the clouds. The navigator, Pilot Officer Lambert, told Austin that he thought he had seen another green light signal from the ground confirming that all four were down safely.

At 7.45 a.m. on 7 February, the Whitley landed back in the sticky red-flamed sunrise of Malta. The crew washed down an egg and bacon breakfast with mugs of sweet tea. But Sod's Law had not done with any of those involved. The flight back to England was as tortuous and risky a journey as the rest of the trip. In an echo of Dimitrov's cache of fruit, a crate of oranges being sent as a gift from the RAF commander in Malta to Buckingham Palace was jettisoned in Gibraltar to make space for SOE's French agent Peter Churchill. He, Austin, van Maurik and the sorely tried Whitley were in sight of the Cornish coast when the starboard engine failed. It took all of Austin's skill to juggle the plane on to a grass racetrack, at which point the port engine coughed twice and died in sympathy, a steeplechaser ready for the vet's mercy bullet after one jump too far.

We left Elliott in midair. He had dropped out of the Whitley's belly like a khaki egg, so close to the ground that the jerk of his parachute opening, the braking of his headlong fall and his landing were virtually simultaneous. 'I'd been trained to roll when I hit the ground. Cushions the shock. This was very different. The snow was so deep, there was really no impact as I plunged straight into it. It sucked you down and froze you. It felt like drowning in slow motion and I used up a lot of energy getting free of the parachute harness, and flailing around to get my feet on to solid ground. I couldn't see anyone. I heard the Whitley growling away. Lucky sods.' Elliott floundered to the edge of the clearing, buried his parachute and huddled in the bushes, shivering violently, stamping his feet and banging his hands together to keep his circulation going. Dawn began to backlight the trees.

'I heard three shots over to my left – our emergency contact signal. I fired one round to acknowledge, then moved off in that direction. It was hard going.'

The shots – whose strange choice of signal for a clandestine mission? – had been fired by Chapman, who had come across a farm building which he thought was deserted, but which he had not yet risked entering. Soon he and Elliott saw the two Serbs lumbering dejectedly towards them like survivors of a failed Polar expedition. Half-wading, half-swimming through the waist-deep snow, the four found one of their radio set packs, and then spotted the green parachute silk of the ski container, at that moment the most crucial part of their supplies. But the fates had decided to deal them another bad card. The container had smashed down hard on to one of the rock spurs that jutted like bears' teeth through the snow crust; the skis were matchwood. The drone of a light plane flying a regular up and down pattern above the crest of the hill added to their worry. Alerted by the Whitley's noise, the Germans had put up a Fiesler-Storch spotter plane to look for any signs of a parachute drop. The cold struck deep, like a sword. Elliott felt the numbness of frostbite in his right leg.

They burrowed deep into the snow like hunted foxes. Crammed

together in the freezing embrace of a deep drift, they pulled pine branches over their heads and shared their fast-ebbing body warmth. While in the distance, a German patrol glided past, skis hissing, grey-green toy soldiers silhouetted against the snow. Inexorably the cold began to win, driving the team in and out of the deceptively comfortable half-sleep from which the eventual exit was into unconsciousness and the stiffness of death. They broke cover, floundering towards the hut. Elliott, his leg now numb and useless, lay across Crjnanski's shoulders. The deserted building was freezing cold, but to men who had spent hours in the snow it was warmth and shelter. 'Just a shack,' Elliott remembered. 'There was a woman's shoe on the floor and bloodstains on the walls.' As night came to set the seal on their misfortunes, the four sank exhausted on the earthen floor, oblivious to the cold and the stinging bites of the bugs, excitedly awakened from their winter torpor by their warm bodies.

If it ever really began, the DISCLAIM mission ended abruptly at dawn, utterly and totally disclaimed by whoever is the patron saint of clandestine agents. The hut door crashed open. Yelling soldiers filled the room, prodding at the four dazed men with rifles, kicking them upright. A bleary, confused Elliott recognised that these were not Germans, but troops of the Croat Home Guard, or Domobran. 'Actually, I'd have felt a bit safer if they had been Germans. They looked like bandits and gypsies, some in scraps of uniform, some in blankets and peasant breeches. A few of them wore dirty fezzes. Perhaps because he saw that I couldn't walk, one mean bastard wanted to put me away there and then, waving one of those nasty curved knives the Moslems use for slitting sheep's throats, but an older chap stopped him.'

The four men were hustled out, Crjnanski and Miljkovic swearing and shouting in English in an attempt to conceal their nationality. Then as now, Croat militia were unlikely to take a long-term view of the fate of Serbian parachutists. Elliott was pushed down on to a horse-drawn sledge. 'We all tried to keep very calm, since our new chums were obviously trigger-happy, spitting and cursing at us. But when we got to the bottom of the hill and they told us to get into a truck they had there, I was a bit slow, and one of them pushed me. Without thinking, I took a swing at him and he went down on his back in the slush. Then a couple of them jumped Crjnanski, and things began to get out of hand. But one of the Domobran officers, very dapper, in a cockaded hat and a felt cloak, jumped out of the truck and started kicking and swearing at his own chaps to quieten them down, yelling that he had to get us to HQ safe and sound.'

Vilem Truhar was the officer's name, a reserve lieutenant of the 13th Domobran Regiment. In the strip of frozen mud that was the single street in the village of Mokro, Elliott was carried into the grimy lath-and-plaster police station, where he was questioned perfunctorily by a distracted Colonel Roman Domaniuk of the Croat Artillery, eager to pass him on to higher authority and get back to his hot lunch and the warm peasant girl who was serving it. 'I kept parroting that I was a British officer, and demanded the rights of a prisoner under the Geneva Convention.' In the station's outer room, Chapman, Crjnanski and Miljkovic kept up an English banter in the face of a milling audience of soldiers and some of the braver local children. Then Crjnanski's heart missed a beat. A Croat sergeant, who had bustled in to see what he called with a sneer 'the monkeys in a cage', did a double take. 'You're not British. I recognise you from that air rally a few years back in Rajlovac. You were a glider pilot, weren't you?' he said in Serbo-Croat. Crjnanski stared at him dumbly. 'Sorry, old boy, my name's Black. Don't understand your lingo,' he drawled. The sergeant stepped away muttering and scratching his head in bewilderment. He had, as it happened, been quite correct.

Freezing and bouncing in the back of the canvas-topped truck, the four men were driven down rutted tracks and half-paved highways from Mokro into Sarajevo, their guards eyeing them with trigger-happy hostility and blatant curiosity. Elliott remarked ironically to Chapman that they were 'back where it all started', where the shooting of Archduke Franz Ferdinand, another bloody milestone in the mindless marathon of Balkan political violence, had marked the start of the First World War. (No one could have known then that in the 1990s Sarajevo would become 'where it all ended', the vainglorious idea of a single Yugoslavia finally shattered.)

The Croat Domobran and police had done a methodical job of tracking and finding DISCLAIM, reporting their progress hour by hour to the German 718th Infantry Division and what their reports called 'the Gestapo Organs', those mighty Wurlitzers of the Reich. Their careful logs, which I found in Belgrade, suggest that Elliott had been right to worry about the Whitley's noise as it lumbered around the night sky trying to pick up its bearings. Separate reports of an unidentified aircraft were telephoned into the Sarajevo HQ of the 3rd Domobran Corps at 1.45, 1.50, 2.20, 2.45 and 3.15 a.m. The duty officer there, Captain Mardesic, heard the droning engines himself just before 2 a.m. At Rajlovac airport, about ten miles from Sarajevo, where both German and Croat units were stationed, radio-operators spun their tuning dials, scanning the frequencies in a vain attempt to contact the unknown plane. Was it a wandering German aircraft seeking to land? But by 3 a.m., the three nearest German air bases confirmed that no flights had taken off. The Whitley burbled away into the night. As the sky lightened from black to its daytime slate-grey, every military, police and Domobran unit was on the alert. So was most of the civilian population. Lieutenant Truhar had set out with Private Lucic and ten men towards the cluster of houses and a mosque that made up the village of Han Obodjas, over which the plane had reportedly spent most time. Within minutes an excited peasant, described in Truhar's later official report as a 'road-sweeper' (his task must have been Herculean in those months of incessant snow), rushed up to them to report proudly that he had seen parachutes, collapsed like 'pitched tents', in the fields north of the village, close by the school.

The teletypes clattered and buzzed as the Germans digested the news. The long arm of the fabled (little did they know) British Secret Service had struck again.

# 12

# Inquest into Failure

In Sarajevo, the Domobran began to sift through the team's possessions, and the piles of material gathered from the trampled snow of the dropping zone. The Domobran noted with glee that the parachutes bore the labels of their English manufacturers. They photographed much of what they found, and some of the photographs still survive in the Belgrade archives. Only one radio was captured. The second, which had fallen several hundred yards away from the main drop, was found by a Partisan patrol six weeks later and, no doubt, put to good use. Professionally the most surprising thing is that the Domobran found the team's codes, fifteen small sheets of paper in a waterproof pouch: an extraordinary trophy. No wonder copies were rushed by motorcycle courier, skidding and sliding through the snow, to the Croat General Staff, the Wehrmacht and the Gestapo, who must have found it hard to believe their good fortune. All the more curious that, at least as far as the files in the public domain indicate, the Germans made little or no attempt to exploit these treasures into an active 'radio game'. It has been argued that as word of DISCLAIM's failure reached London relatively soon, any mischievous use of the codes would have set off a five-bell alarm at the Radio Security Service listening stations in Britain. However, based on SOE's later misfortunes in Holland, as one example, this argument is optimistic in the extreme; vigilance and attention to procedural detail were not always hallmarks of SOE's listeners and their supervisors.

Not to have burned the sheets when capture seemed inevitable was another grave lapse of security. It is curious that in his own notes, Elliott specifically recalls that when the team first stumbled into the deserted farm hut, he had realised they were unlikely to get away and had burned the flimsy strips of paper giving the times and frequencies for the mission's radio reports to Malta. So why not burn the codes too? Did he forget? Did he ask Chapman to take care of it? And did Chapman forget? In yet another sign of SOE's lackadaisical approach, there had obviously been no proper security check before the mission set out. The two Yugoslavs were carrying material which was bound to stimulate questions even from a brain-dead country policeman: two postcards of Moscow and a Yugoslav identity card in the name of Aljoza Petrin. Crjnanski had his own driving licence, but on the back had written, the Croat investigators noted, 'a code number and a list of names'. He also had an identity card from the factory where he had worked before the war. Written on another piece of paper were names of contacts in Serbia and Bosnia, and 'an address in Ankara', the latter presumably an escapers' safe-house. The biggest conundrum is a memorandum, closely typed in Serbo-Croat. Unsigned and undated, it is headed simply 'Mission Attachment' and attracted a lot of attention when it was circulated among the various Croat intelligence units and passed on to their Italian and German counterparts. In turn, on 12 February it was sent by high-speed teleprinter from the Sicherheitsdienst (the Nazi security service) office in Sarajevo direct to Himmler's headquarters in Berlin's Prinz Albrechtstrasse, where, at war's end, American intelligence outriders found it in the cloacal archives.

The memorandum deserved the scrutiny it received. It sets out the mission's objectives in unambiguous detail. But which mission? Certainly not DISCLAIM as recorded in the files, since as we have seen, while SOE did list political and military intelligence topics on which Elliott should report, these were rather general; SOE's interest was far more in Yugoslav politics and internal attitudes. In sharp contrast, the 'Mission Attachment' is an intelligence brief pure and simple. The sort of tasking that would have been given to an SIS intelligence agent: troop and gun battery positions, especially on the islands off the Yugoslav coast; the morale of the German forces; identification of Yugoslav factories and businesses working for the 'enemy military machine'. Whoever drew up the questions had a very special interest in knowing about the strength and morale of the Croat Ustashe, their relations with the Germans and the identity of any Royalist officers who had thrown in their lot with Pavelic. The carrier was also ordered to tell 'the underground organisation' that, while it should begin to organise caches on the coast and in the mountains so that the 'weapons ammunition and food can be securely delivered', they were to take care not to act against the Germans in any way that would provoke 'too severe retaliation' and thus 'perhaps even block the entire underground cause'.

The initial German report on DISCLAIM says that the 'Attachment' was found on 'one of the Englishmen', but since for the first day or so while the team was still in Croat hands the Germans believed that all four men were British, this may not necessarily mean either Chapman or Elliott. Did someone on the team actually have two briefs, one for SOE and the other for SIS, of which this memorandum was the heart? Was Crjnanski, the last-minute addition, those mysterious scraps in his wallet, foisted on SOE by SIS or the Yugoslavs with other tasks in mind? SIS certainly recruited Yugoslav officers for its missions, but those in a position to know claim that given its jaundiced view of SOE, its almost invariable practice was to keep SIS missions very much separate from – indeed, usually undeclared to – its upstart, brass-knuckled brethren from Baker Street.

(Very little is known, by design, about these missions. However, anecdotal evidence suggests that around the time of DISCLAIM, SIS itself had inserted perhaps a dozen missions inside Yugoslavia [which it knew as Country 35], most of them headed by Yugoslav exiles recruited in Canada, but three or four directly under the command of British officers. They monitored military, naval and Luftwaffe dispositions, train and troop movements, and coastal traffic, and sent back regular weather reports. Reporting to Cairo until the SIS Yugoslav section moved to Bari in 1943, the SIS missions' codenames seem to have been picked with even less alphabetical consistency than SOE's, ranging from CIGAR through to ESQUIRE, JUDGE and PIPE.)

SIS may have had some furtive finger in the DISCLAIM pie. It is equally possible that the so-called 'Attachment' was some manifestation of one of the bent and incompetent manœuvres so characteristic of the Yugoslavs in exile. As vampires are sustained by blood and darkness, so

the waxy corpse of the Royalist government-in-exile was sustained by a
regular diet of intrigue. One especially fractious bout about the time
DISCLAIM was being briefed had bitterly divided the Yugoslav officer
corps in Cairo, and it is easy to see that one faction or the other would
have an interest in setting up a separate intelligence back channel to
Mihailovic. The memorandum was, after all, in Serbo-Croat. Long after
the war, Stefan Rapotec, one of the Royalist officers landed by submarine
on the HENNA mission, recounted how, before he left Cairo, Royalist
General Ilic had warned him of the duplicity of their British allies and,
after swearing him to secrecy, had given him a note for Mihailovic.
When, months after DISCLAIM's capture, Rapotec finally caught up with
the wandering Chetnik leadership and proudly handed over the secret
note, he was crestfallen to be told that it had already reached Mihailovic
from a secret Chetnik sympathiser in the Croat Domobran, who had in
turn copied it from a memorandum captured 'from another secret mission'. This is likely to have been DISCLAIM, indicating that the
mysterious 'Mission Attachment' was of Serb origin; whether or not it
had first been inspired by SIS is in the realm of conjecture.

   In Sarajevo on 7 February, Elliott was separated from Chapman and
the two Serbs. Leaning heavily on the shoulder of an escorting soldier,
he limped into the office of a German colonel, whom he remembers as
being 'extremely polite and friendly. Fascinated with all things British.'
The colonel spoke in halting but correct English, of which he was obviously quite proud, asking only perfunctory questions. 'He was rather
more interested in reminiscing about his time in London before the war.'
This amiable interlude ended abruptly when three Croat officers minced
in, the senior announcing with a proud smirk that as Elliott was a
Domobran prisoner, they had the right to interrogate him first. One of
the trio, Captain Ivcevic, serving an opening ace, recognised Elliott from
pre-war Zagreb. 'No need for English, Colonel,' Ivcevic crowed. 'We can
talk to him in our language or in German. He speaks them both as well
as we do.'

   After some routine Croat questioning, Elliott was helped downstairs.
Opening a storeroom with a flourish, the officers showed him the con-
tainers which the Domobran had found scattered in the snow after
DISCLAIM's capture, their contents spread out on the floor.
Conspicuously missing, Elliott noticed, were the packets of sovereigns,
which had vanished into the recesses of some lice-studded Domobran

apology for an undergarment on the way down the mountainside; the pink markings of SOE's gold containers had rapidly become well-known to every peasant pilferer out in the mountains. Elliott made what even he felt were 'fairly unconvincing' denials that the matériel had anything to do with him or his colleagues. Near collapse from the pain in his leg, he was relieved when the questioning was cut short and he was taken to a nearby German military hospital to be treated for frostbite. The Croats were keen to continue his interrogation, but the local German army headquarters, furious that they had been denied first crack at such an important trophy, insisted vehemently that the DISCLAIM team and its matériel should immediately be taken out of the amateurish hands of the Domobran, and sent for more professional scrutiny by the German security services in Belgrade, 'where we have the facilities to obtain proper answers'.

From the hospital, Elliott was taken under heavy escort to the station and bundled into a train bound for Belgrade, handcuffed to two burly lance-corporals of the Feldpolizei. Arriving there at about 11 p.m., he was locked in a cell in a civilian jail near the station – alone, unlike the local prisoners, who were crammed ten or twelve to each small cubicle. Hearing the clink of keys and slamming of doors that heralded a new arrival, the Yugoslavs began to clamour through the bars for cigarettes, for news of the war, to know why Elliott was there. Elliott did not respond directly, but in a technique he was to use again later (perhaps it was part of some drill on what to do if captured, learned at one of the country-house training schools), he began to make a nuisance of himself, banging on the cell door, demanding to see the prison governor. As light relief, he bellowed out several repetitions of *God Save the King*, disturbing the chill and stinking night, sparking curses from his sleepless fellow prisoners and yells from the infuriated warders, who rattled their truncheons menacingly along the cell bars but held back from giving Elliott a beating, no doubt because he was a 'special category' prisoner. It worked, more or less. When the warders changed shift at 7 a.m., Elliott was bundled roughly upstairs to the prison's German commandant, hoarse, tired, still limping but proud of himself. Blustering in officer-corps German that he had not been fed for two days, Elliott demanded something to eat. 'I don't know why you're worrying about food. It's seven o'clock now, we're going to shoot you at eight,' the commandant purred, looking pointedly at his gold Patek Philippe wristwatch, the perfect ellipse for the perfect Nordic wrist. 'In that case, can I just have some coffee,' Elliott retorted with a sang-froid he did not feel.

The commandant, impassive, picked up the telephone and ordered coffee for them both. As they sat looking at each other, the door opened. A fusillade of heel-clicking and an erectile flourish of Hitler salutes heralded the arrival of two German officers. Apprehension gave way to relief as Elliott understood from their staccato exchange with the commandant that rather than being taken down to face a firing squad, he was being transferred to Belgrade's central prison for what was leeringly referred to by the new arrivals as 'detailed interrogation'. An armed guard crammed in on either side of him, Elliott cruised across the familiar city in a Mercedes staff car, an orgasm of leather upholstery, gleaming black bodywork, huge chrome headlights and fluttering swastika pennants. One of the officers sat edgily in the front passenger seat. Two leather-coated motorcycle outriders revved self-importantly alongside. 'Damn odd to be a prisoner in a place you knew so well,' Elliott reflected.

'A lucky man, my dear Major,' a German prison officer told him sardonically in the dark prison courtyard. 'You're listed for solitary confinement, but all those cells are full. You'll have to go in our dentist's office for a day or two. He's on leave and our prisoners have more to worry about than a little pyorrhoea!' The dentist's office, its windows barred, had been stripped of its furniture and equipment; a rebarbative straw mattress had been slung in one corner for Elliott to sleep on. Left on his own, Elliott was astonished to find behind the window curtain an old upright Bakelite telephone, overlooked by the warders who had cleared the office. 'Before the war I used to spend a lot of time at the Majestic Hotel just up the road. I could still remember the number, so I just picked up the phone and dialled. When the desk clerk answered, I told him who I was. I asked if they had a room free because I wasn't very comfortable where I was!' Whenever Elliott's narrative comes anywhere near something of real intelligence significance, some innate discipline pulls him back. Nearly fifty years later, we are therefore left to guess whether, as he portrays it, the call to the Majestic (whose plain façade is today almost unchanged from the way Elliott knew it, although the trees seen outside in a 1930s' photograph are long gone) was just a Scarlet Pimpernel whimsy, to keep his spirits up and to tease his captors, or did it have a more professional purpose? Elliott was not a whimsical man.

The inside of a German jail is not a place for gestures, and I suspect that his real aim was to alert a British contact on the Majestic's staff that he had been captured, and to say where he was. Perhaps someone at the Majestic had been identified in the verbal SOE briefing on how Elliott was to set up his courier lines. Perhaps Elliott simply had a contact there from his pre-war work. Whatever he was up to, 'there was a moment's silence at the other end, and the phone went dead. A few minutes later the Germans heard what had happened from one of their eavesdroppers at the exchange. They came bursting into the dentist's office, yanked the phone out of the wall, and gave me a good smacking.'

The chronology of Elliott's narrative is not clear, but the call was probably made around 11 or 12 February. A Polish intelligence report from an agent in Istanbul, which reached SOE in London on 16 February, said that the DISCLAIM party had been 'seen in Belgrade on 12 February', and may thus be linked to Elliott's telephone alert. Berlin radio trumpeted the official news of their capture on 18 February. In Belgrade, meanwhile, things turned nasty. There was no toilet in the dentist's office and the guard outside was stubbornly deaf to Elliott's calls to be taken to the bathroom down the corridor. In a mix of desperation and petulance, he used his wooden coffee bowl instead. Next morning, when two German orderlies clattered to his door with the urn of tepid acorn coffee, they laughed when they saw how Elliott had used his bowl. They grabbed his arms. A guard called in from the corridor to join in the fun topped up the foul-smelling bowl with coffee. Pinching Elliott's nostrils, they forced him to swallow. 'I was very cross and very sick.' The episode produced the first signs of a bout of dysentery which sapped his strength over the weeks ahead. Later that day, Elliott was brought together again with Chapman, Crjnanski and Miljkovic. Surrounded by a circle of barking interrogators they were shown a selection of the compromising items found in the container, which no amount of dissimulation could explain away. In the middle of the hail of questions and the brandishing of incriminating pieces of evidence, a German officer took Elliott by the arm and steered him out of the room. 'We can talk as friends. You speak such good German.' He professed oily praise for DISCLAIM's 'highly dangerous' mission, which he described as 'the act of a hero which, speaking as one officer to another, I greatly admire. All we need to know, my dear Major Elliott, is the background. Who sent you? Where were you going? What were you doing? Just tell me, in confidence, what this is all about. You can then go off quietly to a decent sort of camp. Who knows? Perhaps we can even get you repatriated. We are straightforward military people, and so are you.'

'I told him to sod off,' remarked Elliott. As the questioning unfolded, Elliott, by his account, conceded a series of relatively undeniable facts, but maintained a veil of fatigued imprecision over detail; SOE's briefers stressed the need to avoid telling outright lies to a hostile interrogator 'as it usually defeats its own object'. After several fruitless sessions, the friendly officer told Elliott, 'I'm afraid I have some very bad news for you.'

'Now you really are going to shoot me?'

'No, but since you clearly don't want to co-operate with us, I have to hand you over to the Gestapo. We have, I hope, treated you like gentlemen. But I can assure you they won't,' he said ponderously, as if auditioning for a minor part in some low-budget post-war movie. Escorted this time by dour leather-coated Gestapo agents, Elliott travelled in a grey van to the thick-walled cellars in the basement of the Skuptsina, the green-domed Parliament building, which in a triumphant demonstration of the priorities of the New Order the Gestapo had taken over as its headquarters. Over the next two days Elliott was deprived of sleep, punched and kicked, and left without food under a blinding ceiling light. 'But they still got nowhere at all.'

DISCLAIM was a tiny piece in the jigsaw of wartime Yugoslavia. To have even Elliott's jottings, fitfully illuminating a few personalised highpoints of what actually happened, is interesting as far as it goes. Remarkably, though, we have quite a lot more. German, Yugoslav and British archives, US microfiches, the two Yugoslavs' own stories told first in interrogation records and, years later, in Belgrade newspaper articles, combine to provide some unusual extra insights. But none of the records can capture the fear, the self-doubt, of the four men. Human nature being what it is, frustration and anger too, the feeling that you had been badly let down by the desk-bound planners, now safely swapping secrets and gossip at a well-lubricated Cairo cocktail party before going on to dinner and a quick goodnight fumble in the back of a horse-drawn hackney carriage. All the more if in your heart of hearts you were tempted somehow to blame yourself for the fact that it had all gone so badly wrong. And all the more again if you now faced the certainty of hostile interrogation and imprisonment, and even the possibility of ending up blinking in terror at a bullet-pocked cellar wall waiting for the sledgehammer crash of an executioner's bullet in the nape of your neck.

Although Elliott was trained in resisting interrogation, the other three were not, and the Germans had little difficulty in extracting a broad picture of what DISCLAIM was supposed to be about. But they got little of substance on SOE itself, about the use of Malta as a base, or on Britain's understanding about Yugoslav affairs. The 'Mission Attachment', though it aroused much initial interest, was for some reason not given a great deal of further attention; to the Germans, long-since avid believers in the myths of the British Secret Service, it must have appeared only natural that a mission dropped from the sky at dead of night would have a list of espionage aims as long as the Kurfürstendamm.

The four men had agreed with their SOE briefers that the two Serbs should try to maintain for as long as possible the façade that they were only along as guides, who knew the Yugoslav terrain, and that they had no idea what Elliott was really up to. For some hours they did better than this, and were able to maintain the pretence that they were English. Only when a second, thorough, German search found their blue-backed RAF AB64 identity books, which gave their names and nationalities, were they forced to concede who they were. But the two Serbs were thankful for small mercies. First, they had avoided being tagged as Serbs until they had put a safe distance between them and the kneejerk savagery of the Croat troops. Second, while the AB64s gave the game away, they were at the same time proof of their service bona fides, making it difficult for the Germans to claim, at least by the rules being followed at that early stage in the war, that they were spies. The initial interrogation record has survived the last half-century quite well. Typed like Truhar's report on a greyish paper that, while cheap, seems to have had long-lasting qualities, it shows that when questioned by the Croats in Sarajevo on 7 February, Elliott gave factual half-answers to a series of what seemed to be rather general, almost pro forma questions, identifying himself with comprehensive, although safely unchallengeable, economy as 'a Reserve Captain, a Clerical Officer in the Information Section of the British General Staff in Cairo, and a Protestant'; quite what prompted this fairly late and otherwise unexplained conversion to the Church of England, we can only guess. He said his mission, for which he claimed to have been briefed by the Royalist General Ilic – not a whisper of SOE – was to 'find out what was happening in Bosnia. We simply didn't have any information.'

Probably the only point on which he could seriously have been challenged was his blunt denial that the team had any written codes. 'We kept them in our heads,' he told his interrogators. That he was not jumped on from a great height at this point suggests that the Croats either had not finished sifting through what they had found on the snowy fields or had not worked out what the pouch full of flimsy sheets actually was. It also suggests that Elliott had no idea the codes had fallen into enemy hands. He went on to deny (here with some confidence, since he had burned the schedules himself) that there were any fixed times or frequencies for communications back to base. Snuffling through archives always produces surprises: in Elliott's case, a photograph of the actual interrogation. I imagine it was taken for its propaganda value – English Terrorist Tells All. It has a strange, stagey feel to it. A cloth-covered table. Elliott on a brocaded sofa, the collar of his uniform blouse unbuttoned. Haggard, shadows round the eyes, but composed. The three Croat officers are attentive, rather than aggressive. On the table there are a pack of cigarettes and coffee cups. No stainless steel impedimenta of torture. No whips, no scorpions, but a tough spot to be in. Interrogated the same day, off camera, Crjnanski stuck to the line agreed for the Serbs. Only Elliott knew the real tasks, he told the Germans. 'The British were very mistrustful of us.' The two Yugoslavs would therefore have only been given full details once the mission was safely bedded down inside Yugoslavia. 'We were to familiarise ourselves with the situation, find out how many troops of what kind were in Yugoslavia, and to make contact with the peasants in the area to achieve all this. . . . My impression was that the British knew very little about conditions in Croatian territory, and Bosnia in particular, so we were given the mission of reconnoitring and collecting information which we were to send back to Egypt. I don't know whether there was any other purpose.'

Crjnanski said nothing about SOE, or about Mihailovic, but he told the Germans he had been instructed by General Ilic that 'if the Englishmen were to make any attempt at sabotage on our arrival, I was to exert my influence to stop them since this was not the time for such things'. Like Elliott, Crjnanski left the impression that the mission had come direct from Alexandria, making no mention of Malta. Miljkovic's version was recorded only in January 1945. After his interrogation, he had been sent to a German prisoner-of-war camp. Escaping in December 1944, he wandered lonely as a cloud through the collapsing Reich for over a month before falling into the beefy arms of the US infantry. He told the Americans that while locked up together in Sarajevo for four days, he and Chapman had carefully gone over what they would say (either they were confident that the Germans had no microphones hidden in the cell, or they were lucky), agreeing to stick as long as possible to the line that they were just non-coms, technicians who knew nothing about DISCLAIM's real tasks.

The two of them then spent fifteen days in Belgrade, spells in the jail punctuated by unpleasant interrogations in the Parliament building. All four men had then met again briefly at a Luftwaffe prisoner-of-war camp outside Frankfurt. Miljkovic told the Americans that in nearly three weeks there he had seen Elliott when the two of them were in the camp hospital for a short time. He had also glimpsed Chapman in the prison yard under heavy guard. The two Serbs were then taken to Berlin, separated and slammed behind the doors of a Gestapo jail in Leitnersstrasse. Miljkovic stuck to his 'I know nothing' story, despite being told in another elephantine ploy that both Elliott and Chapman had 'confessed everything' and had each been paid 30,000 Reichsmarks by the Gestapo as a reward. What did Chapman say? What are you expected to say, wet behind the ears, an orphan, from a Lancashire shipbuilding town, with zero intelligence experience, or indeed any experience of life that would help you to cope? In one of those odd eddies, a translation of the report of his interrogation was found in April 1944 in a file in Rome, from where it was eventually repatriated to the archives in London. In punctilious observance of the niceties of Axis co-operation, it had been sent to the Italian military by the Wehrmacht. Dated April 1942, it was written during the spell in the Luftwaffe camp near Frankfurt recalled by Miljkovic. From scanty family reminiscences we know that Chapman, who died in 1971, was badly treated by the Germans, including a spell in chains. In the circumstances, he did a creditable job of filling the Germans' notebooks with a coherent chain of facts and narrative that must have seemed pay dirt to the questioners, but which on closer scrutiny really give little of substance away. In particular, what he is quoted as saying about the mission's sabotage aims, and the proposed follow-up by transport planes with men and supplies, is actually so far at odds with the mission's brief and a radio-operator's likely knowledge of it as to be more likely the regurgitation of half-digested Naafi gossip, perhaps embroidered by an ambitious Luftwaffe interrogator.

The Germans reported that Chapman began by telling them about 'the Parachute Corps', composed of two completely independent formations:

> PARACHUTISTS – small units of real parachutists composed of recruits who have volunteered for that job, and of RAF personnel. Such units are to be found in England and have not yet been used.

> COMMANDOS – sabotage troops composed of small units of the army and of the police . . . ; these have already been used in Norway, at Taranto, in the Dodecanese and in Libya. They are also called LAYFORCE from the name of the general who organised them: LAYCOCK [then Colonel, later Major-General Sir Robert Laycock] . . . . Their training consists of a series of jumps with and without matériel, of strenuous physical exercises and of specific theoretical instructions necessary for their work. In three days each man [on DISCLAIM] had to make 4 jumps from the hole in the base of the fuselage of a WHITLEY aeroplane, from heights varying from 1,800 to 180 metres. They were also given a demonstration of the dropping of various containers from 800 metres. Each action was prepared for by training suited to the actual zone of operations. The captured saboteurs, four including source (Chapman), had completed one week's instruction – in an area near Cairo – in skiing and in practice jumps, in which matériel was also dropped. Concerning the present operation, source states that after a sufficiently careful preparation, his group had to organise, on Yugoslav territory, a collaboration between the Chetnik detachments under the command of the Serb General ILIC in Egypt.

> The Serbian Partisans, in all about 30,000 men, in collaboration with and under the direction of the English saboteur troops, were to destroy, in the Belgrade–Sarajevo area, lines of communications, railway installations, bridges, power stations and other military objectives.

> For this initial action a group composed of the following military personnel was to be dropped in the neighbourhood of Sarajevo (Romanija mountains): OC, ELLIOTT, Major, English

army; Corporal (English army) CHAPMAN, radio expert; and two Serbian pilots who knew the language and the country.

These four men were to establish immediate contact with the Partisans and to communicate, through the very-short-wave radio transmitter ( a new and secret apparatus somewhat different from that normally used by the army), information on the situation, on the possibility of help from the Partisans, and on objectives pre-selected for sabotage. This information was to be transmitted to Egypt. Consequent upon this information 3–4 transport planes, each carrying 10–12 parachutists, were to come from Egypt to the pre-selected zone bringing the necessary matériel – explosive, arms, etc.

The Partisan organisation itself would have informed Egypt of preparations made, the landing ground chosen, its whereabouts, the presence of Partisans in the area, etc. The date of the operation had been fixed by this organisation for 29 January.

For reasons not known, this operation – viz. the dropping of the group of four – was postponed for about seven days.

Of the aeroplane, source has specified that it was a WHITLEY with a circular opening in the base of the fuselage. The fuselage was completely filled by the reserve petrol tanks which were attached to it. The actual crew of the plane consisted of four men.

As to the equipment and clothing of this group source has stated that all four wore the uniform of the British army with airforce overalls, and parachutist helmets with a protection of rubber at the neck. In addition, each was given a pair of shoes with thick rubber soles and a pair of ski shoes. Each man was supplied with a Colt automatic pistol, a Fighting Knife and a pocket torch. The materials necessary to this operation were stored in a container and in another container composed of three smaller ones; in addition, there were another six small containers. These containers were affixed to parachutes of varied colours.

The plane, after everything had been dropped and everyone had jumped, turned back towards Alexandria. Whilst the plane was manœuvring – CHAPMAN declares that it was done extraordinarily badly – one of the doors came off and fell to the ground. It was a beautiful moonlight night; the snow was thigh deep . . . .

Chapman then went on to give an account of the landing, the freezing
hours in hiding and their capture, which even through the plodding pen
of the German interrogator, and after translation from English into
German, into Italian and then back into English, reads far more vividly
than Elliott's flattened prose, though he tells the same story. Neither the
codes nor the 'Mission Attachment' are mentioned. The German report
continues:

> In the event of the failure of the mission it had been foreseen that
> both the Serbs should escape into the surrounding country using
> the civilian clothes brought for that purpose, whilst the
> Englishmen were to attempt to escape to 'friendly' Turkey.
> No other information relative to the operation has emerged from
> the interrogation of Major ELLIOTT which was subsequently
> made by the German authorities.

Chapman went into captivity, escaping, by his family's account, three
times during his spell as a prisoner-of-war, surviving in part by selling
bits and pieces of clothing. The last time, as the war drew to its messy
close, he ran into a scouting party of Red Army Cossacks and rode back
with them in triumph as they liberated his prison camp.

A stone thrown blindly into a night-time pond. Silence. A soft splash in
the distance. A few ripples. As a Yugoslav historian wrote coolly, 'In time
DISCLAIM fell into oblivion.' When Elliott and his team were carted
away in handcuffs, wondering whether they were going to be shot out of
hand, little could be done by way of a postmortem in London or Cairo.
'Regrettable, but we are all professionals, and we understand that these
things happen,' would have been the pragmatic view in Baker Street.
DISCLAIM's target, Mihailovic himself, was in fact about a hundred
miles away from where the team dropped: in that weather, over that terrain, a journey of several days. He heard about DISCLAIM from the
Chetnik commander on Romanija, who sent a relay of messengers
scrambling through the snow with the news. The commander added
ruefully that DISCLAIM's failure must have been partly due 'to our own
sloppiness and the poor communications with London, who were not
informed in time that [the area] was no longer under our control'. A
secret Tito supporter, Colonel Suleiman Filipovic of the Croat

Domobran, sent word of the mission's capture to the senior Partisan leader, Svetozar Vukmanovic Tempo, on 10 February. He added that 'Elliott had refused to say anything when questioned'. Tempo passed the information by courier to Tito on 12 February. The Partisans' initial reactions to DISCLAIM reflected in equal measure their understandable confusion and inherent suspicion. Mirroring Mihailovic's constant requests to his government in London, Tito had been importuning his Comintern masters in Moscow for arms and matériel, and his response to the first, hazy reports of DISCLAIM was to wonder whether it really had been a British mission. Might it, he speculated, have been Russian, a follow-up to a message received from Moscow on 12 January 1941 telling the Partisans of 'the possibility that in the very near future we will send people to you'?

Even when it became clear that the mission had indeed been British, Tito worried that the landing markers and secret light signals by the Partisans for the possible Russian drop had somehow passed from the Comintern into British hands and been used by DISCLAIM. He warned Moscow, via a clandestine Partisan radio in Zagreb, not to pass such information on to the British again. For Tito, the British attempt to send DISCLAIM to Mihailovic on the heels of HYDRA and HENNA, and in the wake of Hudson, was yet more proof that, at the bidding of the government-in-exile, Whitehall was still bent on stepping up efforts to support the despised Chetniks, relegating the Partisans to a sideline role. Mistrust aside, the eventual Partisan view of DISCLAIM echoed that of Mihailovic's commander on Romania: 'It came at a most inopportune time, just when the enemy was in control of the area.'

What did London think had gone wrong? Some wondered whether DISCLAIM had been lured into a German trap. Towards the end of 1941, there had been suspicions – there were always suspicions about something – in London and Cairo that the Germans had captured one of Mihailovic's or Hudson's radios and two or three codes, which were being used to send false traffic – playing the radio game. These suspicions had not been resolved before DISCLAIM was sent in. It was not until 17 February that the matter was more or less laid to rest, when Mihailovic replied to a test question from SOE Cairo, phrased in terms to which only he could have answered, telegraphing via Malta to his Royalist colleagues, that 'the name of the Butcher's dog is Gadza. Does he know his master?', a message that must have baffled the German monitoring stations. In any event, as Elliott later recollected, he was told before he set out that 'transmitters had been dropped to Mihailovic by the British, but SOE in Cairo were not certain whether Mihailovic had the transmitters or whether the Germans had captured them and were using them for false messages'. With this level of awareness, the likelihood of DISCLAIM having fallen victim to a German trap is remote, even for SOE at its most cowboyish extreme of enthusiastic inefficiency. So where else, short of a malign plot for which no evidence exists, can the reason for failure be found? In a perfect world, SOE's London headquarters and its Cairo centre, which was directly responsible for organising and briefing DISCLAIM, would have shared the same degree of knowledge. But no world is perfect. All the more a world at war, and an organisation, like SOE, that was also at war with itself and its partners. In Cairo, Terence Airey told Elliott in his briefing that SOE believed that 'Patriot forces reported to be operating in Serbia are under [the] command [of] General Mihailovic. They were in [the] area Suvobor-Ravno Gora [about 100 miles from Romanija] on 8 December. Since that date communication with General Mihailovic has been intermittent, and his exact whereabouts are not known, but it is believed he has retired with his forces into Bosnia.' The brief then identifies Romanija as the dropping zone. Cairo's information on German activity in the area seems to have been both sparse and woefully out of date, referring to nothing more recent then a 'German punitive expedition' advancing on 30 November down the valley of the western Morava.

By contrast, London probably knew too much, in the sense of being overloaded with blurred, often contradictory, ever-changing information. Indeed, reading some of the files of SOE recalls Voltaire's dismissal of London two centuries earlier as 'the city where they purvey the most inaccurate news and produce the worst possible arguments based on information which is entirely false'. Just how much data gleaned from the German and Italian ULTRA decrypts went back out from London to Cairo for SOE remains to be fully explored by historians. It has been suggested that apart from that 'celebrated, underrated, overblowing warrior' Brigadier Keble, imposed on SOE by the Army as its Cairo Chief of Staff and who was on the ULTRA distribution list as an accidental overhang from a previous post, SOE did not receive this highly secret material on an organised basis until well after DISCLAIM's time. Nevertheless, unofficial back channels in the form of discreet 'personal messages' from the Director of Military Intelligence in London to his representative in Cairo, Brigadier John Shearer, were used to pass on for both military and SOE use the gist of some key ULTRA decrypts available in London.

London also seems to have had a more comprehensive and up-to-date flow of German operational signals intercepts. On 10 December, for example, an intelligence summary told Whitehall planners that, in the face of a German assault in Western Serbia, there had been 'heavy insurgent losses'. On 13 December, they reported that in the Sarajevo area 'the insurgents still seem to maintain the initiative. In the hills to the north the Croats have been forced on the defensive . . . .' A report dated 5 February records the arrival of fresh Croat troops to strengthen garrisons around Sarajevo, with 'insurgents still active east of Sarajevo'. Another indication of what the London planners believed can be seen in two Most Secret maps of Axis dispositions in Yugoslavia prepared by Military Intelligence Department 3(b) in late January from information dated 24 December (probably again intercepted operational signals). Reflecting the then prevailing perceptions of the resistance, the section of the MI3(b) map showing the rough boundaries of the area where the insurgents were active is lettered simply MIHAILOVIC. Only in a footnote is this expanded to 'Mihailovic and Partisans'. Also shown are the sites of several recent 'guerrilla' attacks. On the Romanija plateau is a note: 'Mihailovic HQ apparently here.' A nearby arrow pointing away from Sarajevo has the legend 'Attack expected'. Right or wrong, all of this was far more up-to-date than the 30 November intelligence used by SOE in Cairo.

On 27 January, a request from Churchill for a briefing on Yugoslavia produced a memorandum from SIS to its masters in the Foreign Office stating that 'our only information is from most secret sources [ULTRA intercepts]. During this past month extremely little information has been received from them . . . . The occupying troops in the Sarajevo area have not yet succeeded in rounding up the insurgents.' The subsequent Foreign Office report to Churchill contained the additional phrase, apparently taken from a briefing note of 26 January, that Mihailovic 'is believed to have shifted his HQ in NW Serbia further west to the neighbourhood of Sarajevo'. In the best mandarin tradition of political infighting, in responding to Churchill the orthodox diplomats added the provocative caveat that the situation described in their memorandum was 'so far as is known to the Foreign Office . . . however, the Foreign

Office is not being kept regularly informed by the departments [SOE and SIS] involved'. 'Surely we ought to be,' Anthony Eden scribbled petulantly, rising to the bait. So London was better informed than Cairo. In reality, no one actually knew what was happening, which is why DIS-CLAIM was sent in. Even if Cairo had access to all London's data, it is doubtful that they would have delayed DISCLAIM, or dropped Elliott somewhere else. Forget the contradiction and complications. The real reason for the mission's failure lies less in where Mihailovic was or was not; no one could seriously have expected a degree of precision that would have dropped DISCLAIM like a laser-guided bomb down the stovepipe of Mihailovic's bivouac. And even if the curious delays and Elliott's unannounced presence in Malta did have their origins in some pro-Tito manœuvres in Cairo, it is difficult to see how, in the event, they had any direct bearing on the débâcle.

The root cause of DISCLAIM's failure was the fact that Elliott was being parachuted into a maelstrom of intense Axis activity against the insurgents, with the situation on the ground changing more rapidly than even the speediest intelligence could track, with far greater likelihood of running headlong into Germans, Italians and Croats than insurgents of whatever stripe. The German initiative had its origins some two months earlier. In December 1941, as their difficulties on the Russian front increased, the General Staff in Berlin had decided to pull some of their forces out of Yugoslavia, filling the gap with their less reliable but much more expendable Bulgarian and Italian allies. The lickspittle Marshal Dido Kvaternik, the Croat commander, argued vehemently that since this would inevitably lead to a lessening of pressure on the insurgents, any Wehrmacht withdrawal must be preceded by a vigorous 'mopping up' operation under German leadership. Kvaternik, an enthusiastic signatory of mass execution orders, came from a family whose members were traditionally revolting, in both senses of the word, a tradition he passed on by appointing his son, Engon Dido, as head of the Ustashe secret police and concentration camp network.

The Germans did their best to oblige. On 24 December, their commanders in Bosnia were ordered to 'suppress the revolt' using Croat troops selectively reinforced by army and SS forces, which would remain at Kvaternik's disposal until the end of January. After an interval for the maudlin chanting of *Stille Nacht*, the swilling of beer and the execution of a few prisoners to keep the gunmen's eye in, the operations moved powerfully into gear, Weather conditions, the same into which DIS-CLAIM was to be dropped – another element under-appreciated by the planners – were described by the Germans as 'terrible', with temperatures of twenty to thirty degrees below freezing. Ahead of the German and Croat patrols advancing over a broad front in trucks, trains and armoured cars, the Chetnik and Partisan resistance units followed their well-tested technique of dissolving – slipping away into the snow, the ravines, the village cellars. *Reculer pour mieux sauter*, to regroup when the Nazi storm had passed. Behind the attacking shock waves, 'special' German units went implacably about their work of murdering civilians in a bloody pavane of round-up, grave-digging and machine-gunning. With their usual feeling for leaden euphemism, the Germans reported the operation to Berlin as 'strenuous'. The first wave rolled across Romanija on 15 January, and Sokolac (smashed again by the Serbs almost fifty years later) six days later. The army reported that the insurgents had been dispersed but not destroyed; their officers complained that when their quarry slipped away southwards into the Italian area of occupation, Mussolini's men were far less robust in their response.

In the end, DISCLAIM should probably go down in the books as a well-intentioned but ill-conceived cock-up, a mission which had little chance because its planners knew so little about what was happening on the ground; a story of insufficient, poorly co-ordinated intelligence, and an underestimation of the risks. Would it have made much difference if Elliott had reached Mihailovic and Hudson? In the long run, probably not. Was it worth the gamble? Probably. But failure being ever an orphan, it was a mission soon forgotten as the far larger process of war unfolded. Its funeral rites in London were few, although as a matter of prudence the planned DESIRABLE mission was swiftly aborted.

On 12 February, the Permanent Under-Secretary of the Foreign Office, Sir Orme Sergeant, called a meeting of representatives from the War Office, the Air Ministry and SOE. In a blaze of good, if by now rather frayed, tailoring, canvas gas-mask cases at their feet, those present sipped their tea in ritual foreplay as they glanced at each other, and around the room. A light patch on the panelled wall marked the removal of Gainsborough's portrait of William Pitt, shipped for safety to the bowels of a Welsh slate quarry. Two notes of the meeting survive, one by a Foreign Office official, the other by Lord Glenconner of SOE. The only substantive difference between them is SOE's coy use of code letters to identify the other organisations – ZP for the Foreign Office, ZA the Air Ministry and ZM the War Office. The meeting's purpose was to review the latest pressing Yugoslav request for material assistance and, above all, the government-in-exile's renewed demand to take control of communications with Mihailovic. Glenconner told the meeting in pass-ing that DISCLAIM had landed and had reported its safe arrival. This incorrect report may have been the distant echo of the message from the Whitley's crew that they believed they had seen a 'safe landing' signal after the drop. More likely, it was crossed wires or just sloppiness. Glenconner also made what stands out as, for its time, quite a frank assessment that Mihailovic might not be as strong as everyone then thought. When contact with him was in the end re-established, he said, the news might be 'to the effect that he no longer exists as a force and that his followers have been dispersed. On the other hand the reports may be of a positive nature,' but he agreed with the meeting's consensus view that until the facts were clear, it made no sense to consider dropping supplies. Nor was there to be any question of the squabbling zealots in the government-in-exile taking over the reins of communication. Two days later, Glenconner wrote to the Foreign Office to correct what he had said; no message had in fact been received from DISCLAIM. Curiously, even at that point Glenconner believed that the team had con-sisted of 'two British officers and one Yugoslav officer', an error which, as well as implying the ex-post facto promotion of Corporal Chapman, left out the last-minute Yugoslav addition. On 17 February, Glenconner wrote twice more to the Foreign Office, the first time saying that there was 'a strong presumption' DISCLAIM had been captured, and later in the day that SOE had finally received a report confirming this. He made no mention of the supposed circumstances of their capture. As recalled by Erik van Maurik, Colin Gubbins, soon to become head of SOE, told him that the team had actually set out to walk into Sarajevo. Only when they realised that they were walking on the pavement alongside German soldiers had it dawned on them that they might be in the wrong place. Trying to slip away, they had been spotted and arrested. As van Maurik also recalls, Gubbins had expressed considerable vexation and some suspicion about the role of SOE Cairo in the inexplicable delays in Malta.

On 18 February, the *Daily Telegraph*, quoting Berlin Radio, got it more nearly right, except for the date, when they reported that 'an English major, two Yugoslav officers and a radio operator' had been arrested the previous day in Sarajevo, for sabotage. The major 'led riots against the Germans', the broadcast was quoted as saying, perhaps reflecting Elliott's attempts to disturb the night-time tranquillity of Belgrade.

In March, Victor Cavendish-Bentinck, head of the Joint Intelligence Committee, reported to Eden in the prissy Mrs Miniver tones of a *Country Life* book review that DISCLAIM had 'descended without any precise knowledge as to General Mihailovic's whereabouts. The result was that they were captured. SOE consequently wish to avoid a repetition of the misfortune. They hope to obtain communication with General Mihailovic through the Poles.' This reference, and Polish intelligence reports via SIS to SOE a week or so later that they had received two messages about DISCLAIM from an agent in Belgrade, lead us down yet another fog-shrouded byway.

These are not the only references in the literature and on the files to intelligence received from an underground Polish radio set operating in Yugoslavia. The Sixth Bureau of Polish Intelligence was resourceful, and at one stage itself sent a Russian-speaking officer to try to reach Mihailovic, but he fell in a skirmish with the Germans. They worked hard and well not only by radio but through courier lines, and there can be little doubt that Roman Belinski – or Bilinski – and his French mistress, Clare Darie, were important elements in their structure. Their story was told after the war by two Yugoslav journalists, in rather *Boys' Own* style. Anticipating by forty years Clint Eastwood's arrival in a remote mining village from the hostile distances of the windswept plain, Belinski drifted into Sarajevo from nowhere in particular – rumour had it, Istanbul – in 1935, and took up a bedroom and adjacent parlour at the down-at-heel Hotel Poste. In a few months, he had set up in business as a portrait photographer, moving to a studio in the Villa Paloma on the city's leafy outskirts. He rapidly became known as much for his redoubtable social life as his professional prowess, twinkling at the ladies of Sarajevo over a neatly trimmed moustache, and outfitted, by some accounts, with the fastest set of fly buttons in town, notwithstanding the hovering presence of the pert Mlle Darie.

However, behind the suggestively thrusting bellows of his Thornton Pickard camera, Belinski was in fact a Polish agent, whose intelligence was shared without reserve with SIS. Darie ran his radio. As foreigners with no verifiable background, they had for some time been on the watch list of Hugo Herdes, who combined the formal duties of German Consul in Sarajevo with the less visible but increasingly important post of the local Abwehr counter-intelligence chief. Immediately after the Germans took control of the city, Herdes had the pair of them brought in for questioning, based partly on hunch and partly on the fact that Belinski had given temporary shelter to one of the British service attachés as the latter scrambled for neutral territory. Under German browbeating, Clare Darie quickly confessed to working for the Poles and thus also for London. Armed with her story, the Germans were able to make short work of Belinski. But in 'confessing', he also made Herdes an offer that was too tempting to refuse. He would go on running his network of sources, but now there would be a different chain of communication. All the information he collected would be given to the Abwehr. They could decide what, if anything, to pass on, plus anything in the way of disinformation they chose to add. Darie, who would not be let into the secret, would radio the resulting concoction back for the delectation and eventual confusion of SIS. Herdes weighed up the offer and decided to accept it, rather than have Belinski shot out of hand. In fact, so the Yugoslav story claims, Herdes was conned. Belinski was playing the most dangerous game of all, the double double, and gave up to the Germans only half his agents. Totally unknown to the Abwehr, he had a second set of sources and informants, known as the B network, and a second hidden radio. At the same time, Darie, in her first German-controlled message to the SIS listening-post on Malta, used the prearranged dropped letter sequence that should have alerted the British operators that she was transmitting under duress, but there is no way of knowing now whether or not this was spotted.

The loyal Darie was now virtually a German prisoner. Belinski, ever a randy opportunist, turned his smooth charms to the seduction of Eva Bartel, a Yugoslav national of stolid German stock who had been Herdes's secretary and had recently been promoted to work for Dr Alfred Heinrich, head of the Sarajevo Gestapo. Belinski persuaded her to act as courier to his second network. All very interesting, not to say confusing, and even implausible in the re-telling, but what has it got to do with DISCLAIM? Like everything else in this twilight zone, it is very hard to make a watertight connection, but towards the end of 1941, in a message via the 'safe' radio, behind the Abwehr's back, Belinski told London that the Partisans had laid out a rough airstrip on the Romanija plateau. He suggested that this might be a suitable dropping zone for matériel or even a landing ground for secret British flights. This can be corroborated by detailed references to the airstrip both in a British intelligence summary, based on intercepts, in December 1941, and in Partisan records. The Partisans had been keeping the strip clear, principally for a Soviet airdrop, but they also thought the strip could be useful in case, as the German offensive unrolled, Croat or Serbian pilots could be induced to bring their planes over to the Partisan side. The little airstrip, a five-pointed star painted on the frozen ground at one end, at the other an arrow of wood planks, would have been a good target at which the Whitley could aim in dropping DISCLAIM. The mission report by the Whitley's pilot John Austin refers to finding 'the pinpoint' from which another bearing enabled him to pick out the dropping zone 'in the clearing in the woods'. It would be stretching things to read much significance into the use of 'the' rather than 'a', but someone in Malta must have figured out, presumably for good reason, some specific aiming point for the flight and a small, cleared strip would serve well.

Belinski's story also claims that he had been well aware from his German contacts and his own observations of the ferocity of the German offensive – so much underestimated in London – but had been unable to get the message through to SIS because, in those vital days, the second, still undiscovered, radio lacked a vital component. Who knows?

# 13

# Spangenberg Castle

Fifteen days of questioning in Belgrade 'got us nowhere', in Elliott's well-worn phrase which covers a multitude of unpleasantnesses. 'Then one morning the Germans told me they were sending me to Berlin where "other people" wanted to talk to me!' Vans, trains and a spell in a hut under the walls of a French officers' camp near Mainz, where the Gestapo produced a folder of pre-war photographs of Elliott in Sofia and Zagreb, mostly in civilian clothes, hammering at him that he was a spy, not a soldier. Another train, and a *mauvaise quart d'heure* in the main hall of Frankfurt Station, where his guards bellowed at passing commuters to come and show what they thought of English 'terrorists' by spitting in Elliott's face. The British air offensive against the Ruhr had begun on 8 March, when over 200 bombers struck against Essen, to little obvious effect. Stumbling through the city streets, pulled like a dog on a chain, held by the guards, Elliott went to Frankfurt jail. The next day, there was a jolting meander by train through Erfurt and Kassel, the journey frequently broken, indicative of the pounding the German railways had received. The Germans told Elliott that they had not reported him to the International Red Cross as a prisoner. 'They kept on about how they could prove I was a civilian, and not entitled to the protection of the Geneva Convention. I took no notice. Then they made a balls-up somewhere along the line . . . .' Looking for a secure place to dump Elliott overnight (the previous day he had broken out of a military police cell on a railway station and got halfway to the street before being spotted), a short-sighted clerk thought of the RAF officers' prisoner-of-war camp at Sagan. 'As soon as I got there, I identified myself to the senior officer, Wing Commander Day. Day went off straight away to register me officially with the camp authorities and the Swiss protecting power, and the Germans' bluff was called. They gave up threatening me with what they were fond of calling "the punishment we mete out to spies and saboteurs", and decided to make the best of a bad job by shipping me off to PoW camp.' Off, in fact, to Oflag (short for Offizier Lager, or officers' camp) IX/AH, Spangenberg Castle, twenty miles south-east of Kassel; in the prep-school idiom which infused their world, many of its inmates referred to it for years after the war as 'Spangers'.

Elliott arrived there in late April 1942, after a stop, not mentioned in his notes, in an interrogation centre in Frankfurt on 16 April. SOE Cairo was told by London that he had sent my mother a postcard from Spangenberg 'in April'. Spangenberg Castle (it took its name from the curious geographical markings – like 'bracelets' or 'Spange' – on the hillside rocks) was not a lot of fun, but neither was it a place of savagery and squalor. A report in July 1941 by a Swiss inspection team in their capacity as the Protecting Power could have been the promotional brochure for a Teutonic Fawlty Towers:

> This camp is in a seven-hundred-year-old castle, picturesquely situated on the top of a high hill reached by a winding road. The castle is entered over a bridge. Before the war it was used as a forestry school and its interior has been thoroughly modernised with central heating and electric light, although traces of its former magnificence may be seen in the wood carvings and monumental fireplaces in its interior. Every window, as well as the walk running part way around the castle between the walls and the moat, affords a fine view of beautifully wooded semi-mountainous countryside,

the Swiss inspector gushed with the objectivity of a man who would be back in the bland neutrality of Zurich by the weekend. There were two camps in one, actually: the Castle itself and, 600 yards away down in the

village, the Lower Camp, a seventy-five-yard square of barbed wire,
watchtowers at each corner and two barracks for the prisoners. The
main problem, already endemic throughout the German camp system,
was overcrowding. The Germans had never believed that they would
have so many Allied officers and men in their hands. Lower
Spangenberg bulged at the seams with over 220 officers, many of them
badly wounded. By the summer of 1942, the Castle had a further 236, as
well as a supporting cast of orderlies – without whom, as the British files
so often complain, no officer can survive. As the three-car steam train
from Erfurt puffed self-importantly round the curve into Spangenberg,
one of Elliott's guards poked him in the ribs and gestured up at the
Castle silhouetted against the sunset like an engraving from Grimm's
Fairy Tales. 'Have a good look, Englander,' he sniggered. 'That's where
you're going to spend the rest of your life.'

'That's what you think, chum,' Elliott said laconically. 'In the station
yard, I felt vastly tired and done in. The escorts fixed their bayonets and
began to prod me, yelling at me to shift my arse up the hill. My temper
snapped. I stopped and began to curse at the guards, their mothers and
their sisters. If the gates hadn't swung open then, there would have been
real trouble.' Elliott was shooed inside like an enraged sheep.

Lieutenant-Colonel Swinburne, the British Security Officer, came
down to the narrow, cobbled courtyard to cast an appraising eye over the
new arrival. All newcomers were treated with scepticism, Elliott especially. Nearly all the officers had been inside since the early days of the
war. Some had been taken at Dunkirk and although a more recent contingent had arrived not long before Elliott, captured in the Commando
raid on the U-boat pens in St Nazaire, 'not many of them had heard
about parachute drops into Yugoslavia, and they were a bit wary because
I'd been heard swearing and yelling at the guards in German. They obviously wondered if I was a plant.' Elliott was taken into 'The Big Room',
home to over forty officers, a cube of pinewood double bunks about
eighteen inches apart. On its heavy wooden doors were carved the
names of some of the 350 French prisoners locked up in Spangenberg
during the Franco-Prussian War of 1870. Elliott sat quietly at a table, a
rock-crystal wall of silence around him. While they pondered, the wheel
of fortune spun again; it has its own secret system. No one could have
predicted that as the name of this intriguing newcomer was passed
around the Castle's prisoners, like that of some exotic new boy arriving

by dark-windowed Rolls-Royce at a Highland preparatory school, it would be recognised. That would have been less surprising if Elliott had had a conventional upbringing and had come across some old school chum, or a colleague from the office. In this case it has to be quite a coincidence that among the prisoners in the camp was Elliott's friend Antony Terry, last seen when both were ersatz officers at Aldershot. Terry too had been earmarked for espionage, but, blatantly disregarding the trustworthy adage 'never volunteer', he had put himself forward as a military intelligence officer for Operation CHARIOT, the Commando raid on the strategically vital dry docks of St Nazaire on the Atlantic coast. His bravery in face of the mission's impossible odds earned him his Military Cross. The invisible wall dissolved, and a group of officers led by Terry came up to Elliott to shake his hand. 'I was taken into the family. They gave me a little food, allocated me a bunk in Room 18 and gave me some cigarettes.' It looked out, frustratingly, on the bridge which was the only way in and out of the Castle. 'So I became a prisoner.'

Prisoner-of-war camps have proved fruitful for the confection of literary and celluloid folklore; one TV channel or another seems to run *The Great Escape* about every four or five weeks through the year, and escapees' memoirs are regularly and profitably reprinted. Mainly, though, the stories are about camps for officers; those for other ranks were not written about, and very seldom put on the screen, probably because in the 1950s the British studios at Elstree and Pinewood, where the genre had its roots, found it easier to cast the roles of public schoolboys teasing and outwitting the thick-necked, small-brained German guards. At the same time, it was somehow also easier for audiences and readers in those days to accept an upper-, or at least an upper-middle-class hero. Working-class men were typecast, if cast at all, as batmen or cookhouse orderlies, cheerful, cockney scroungers; for occasional light relief, there were senior NCOs in the Harry Andrews' mould, whose bluff and stupid exterior turned out, in the folklore, to conceal a heart of gold. Fantasy and reality blurred in the tales of daring escapes under the earth, over the wire, or through the gate disguised as priests, German officers or Swiss inspectors. On the screen, the cast was usually drawn from the same pool of stereotyped talent; Anton Diffring as the arrogant German officer backed up by someone like the charming but weasel-faced Vladek Sheybal. Digging for Britain, the team had Eric Portman, Trevor Howard or some other headmaster figure being given a hard time by Bryan Forbes, Michael Medwin or the young Richard Attenborough as cheeky, sometimes slightly shifty characters, the whole edifice supported by a phalanx of cleft-chinned, wavy-haired B-picture pooves in polo-necks and duffel coats.

'Beethoven,' muses the German officer one day, when he hears a gramophone playing in the barracks hut, masking the scratchings of the tunnelling moles beneath the floor, 'he was a good German.' 'Yaas,' comes the drawled response from a lower bunk, 'he's dead.' Ho, ho. Escapers' sweaty journeys in trains crowded with hostile and suspicious German commuters, beetle-browed Gestapo men in leather coats just about to begin a check of identification papers at the other end of the carriage. The brave face put on failure. The occasional understated sense of victory over the beastly Hun when one of our heroes actually makes it into Switzerland or Sweden. The parallels with the mythical portrayals of British public-school life are everywhere evident, Tom Brown's schooldays played out in khaki drag.

Back in the realm of reality, the official British post-war report on Spangenberg noted with scrupulous restraint that under the brisk but fair German commandant, Graf Wedel,

> discipline in both camps was strict but in accordance with the accepted standards. Food was plentiful and good, the only complaint being that menus were not sufficiently varied. Owing, however, to the number of Red Cross parcels which were coming into the camp in 1942, the usual food ration issued by the German authorities was cut down, but this made no difference as the parcels contained sufficient food to feed prisoners comfortably. The infirmary at Oflag IX A/Z was used for sick men, those who were seriously ill were sent to hospitals much further afield. Religious services were held regularly in both Upper and Lower Camps. The library appears to have been well stocked, but the canteen was practically permanently empty. Prisoners were allowed to play football on parole, a sports ground having been built in 1942, and in summer swimming was permitted. Walks, parole having been given first, were also allowed. In winter, curling took place on the ice which formed on the moat round the Castle. In August 1944, twenty officers volunteered and were allowed to work in the neighbouring woods. Mail became rather

delayed in the early years due to the fact that letters were cen-
sored elsewhere. This practice ceased, however, after complaints
had been made and was carried out in the village of Spangenberg
instead. Parcels took a long time to arrive from England, the
average time being from three to four months. The morale at IX
A/H seems to have been good throughout . . . .

It is not clear from the report whether its author had actually been in
Spangenberg. There are probably not many Spangenberg survivors alive
now (an advertisement I placed prominently in a British weekly aimed
squarely at the elderly middle classes produced not one reply), but they
would doubtless disagree vehemently with this bland portrait. But there
were certainly far worse places and one of the inmates, the journalist
Terence Prittie, an inveterate escaper who had seen the inside of several
German prisons, described Spangenberg as 'one of the most comfortable
camps in Germany'.

I myself have only ever been locked up as part of a training exercise,
in which the aggression, the slamming doors and the darkness were
inevitably stagey because you knew it would end in laughter and a gin
and tonic; the key elements of fear, deprivation and above all uncertainty
cannot be stage-managed. Even for the Germans the weakness, and for
their prisoners the substantial strength, of an officers' camp like
Spangenberg was that it was all too gentlemanly. The 'free association' in
the dormitories and courtyards, the punctilio of the Geneva Convention
which meant that prisoners could not be forced to work, and the fact that
the guards were, for the most part, German reservists keen on a quiet
life and the plump, flaxen-haired diversions of the village, meant that life
was not that stressful, once the prisoners had come to terms with the
fundamental fact of being prisoners. There was culture: study groups
sprung up for almost every European language, and several Arabic and
Oriental tongues, as well as for subjects as diverse as architecture and
wildlife preservation. In the Castle, there were sports, rather bizarrely
adapted to the confines of the moat, while the Lower Camp had its own
sizeable playing field. There were groups devoted to poetry, to drama
and to art. There were men who wrote, men who grumbled, men who
loafed, many men who plotted escape and revenge, and men who went
slightly mad. I came across a little album of watercolour sketches by officers in the Lower Camp. Rural bliss, a mythical, now far away German

scene of half-timbered houses, ox-drawn carts, white kerchiefed peasant women with pitchforks, huge bales of hay, geese strutting through the hot dust like caricature Pomeranian grenadiers. The church tower. Somewhere unseen a gramophone scratches out 'The Moonlight Sonata'. All is orderly. And at the same time, the reality obtrudes. The barbed wire and watchtowers, the deep-down Nazism of those nice apple-cheeked old ladies, the grey-green menace of the scout car squatting by the roadside.

Elliott moved without difficulty – he had only the clothes he wore – into a small room lit by two low-wattage bulbs, with six double bunks, a small cramped cupboard for each man, two tables, a microclimate in which personal space was delicately protected and respected. Clothes hung from wires and pipes. The air hung grey with tobacco smoke and the smell of bodies. God knows what tensions crackled, the mounting, overwhelming irritation at your neighbours' way of acting, talking, farting or playing a hand of bridge. Quarrels, icy silences, permanent hostilities. Even, perhaps, sexual passion and jealousy. The taking of sides, teasing sliding quickly into taunting. And the long wet days brooding about the love left behind in Worplesdon or Winchester. Will it last? Are her bright words true? Is there someone else? And about the war itself; were we really going to win? It is amazing that there seems to have been almost no physical violence and negligible nervous collapse. Instead, as one of Elliott's more perceptive if prolix fellow prisoners wrote, 'I learned at least two important things [in Spangenberg]. The first was to respect and often to appreciate points of view hitherto completely foreign to my way of thinking. The second was to recognise, if only dimly, the vast amount of diverse skill, of painstaking thought, of hard competent craftsmanship which goes to form the basis of our whole industrial, commercial and social order.' But perhaps the wounds lay suppurating under the skin until later.

Spangenberg was about as escape-proof as a camp can get. The Lower Camp was in the middle of the town, while the Castle sat on its rocky hilltop girdled by a moat thirty feet wide which the prisoners managed to cross by rope only once; the two officers who scrambled across were soon recaptured. In a spirit more of optimism than confidence, another group even set about trying to tunnel out of the Castle through the rocks, but the project was betrayed to the Germans by a British NCO stoolpigeon. Antony Terry told me that Elliott was under strict orders from London not to escape, and even to avoid any obvious connection with escape work, since if anything went wrong, he risked having his SOE background subjected to fresh Gestapo scrutiny. Accordingly, he took on the role of camp interpreter. This may sound like a small part for Kenneth Williams in one of the early British *Carry On* films, but Elliott recalled it as 'a difficult job jammed literally between the British and the Germans. Translation was the least part of it. I was really a sort of intermediary, a negotiator taking messages to and fro on all sorts of things, some minor, some important. The messenger always gets it in the neck if one side or the other doesn't like the message. So quite often either the Germans or my own side got very cross when they felt I'd failed to get the right response.'

Antony Terry remembered that over and above his fluency in German,

Kavan also had the advantage of a smart appearance in both dress and bearing. In present-day terms this may sound trivial, but in dealing with the Germans it was important. It also contributed to the esteem in which Kavan was held by the often rather stuffy regular British army officers in this Senior Officer camp. Kavan was liable to be called on at a moment's notice to interpret for the Senior British Officer at any hour of the day or night when the Germans descended on the camp in a raid to search for escaping equipment or illegal radios or escape tunnels, and so he had to be smartly on parade whenever needed, either to intervene when some aggressive and interfering Gestapo official was wanting to turn everything upside down, to accompany the Senior Officer to the German Commandant's office to register a complaint, or to hear one from the Germans. After some of these sessions we used to retire up one of the winding stone staircases of the Castle to brew tea or cook an egg, chicken leg or potato (illegally purchased from a German guard, with cigarettes) on a device known as a 'Patent Roddam Cooker' made out of Red Cross milk tins and invented by another prisoner, a Yorkshire lawyer.

I got to know Kavan really well in Spangenberg and I found his unconventional approach to life a joy. He had a wonderful sense of humour and his irreverence under extremely difficult circumstances was a much-needed tonic. He and I worked as a team, together with another volunteer, for making the camp newspaper which was in fact a translation of the German newspapers, the Nazi Party journal *Völkischer Beobachter*, the *Kasseler Post* (Kassel was our nearest town), the *Deutsche Allgemeine Zeitung*, Goebbels's *Das Reich* – a weekly the size of *The Times* – and so on. Kavan and I used to sit in a draughty spot on the stairs taking down from the radio the *Langsame Wiederholung des Wehrmachts Berichts*, the dictation speed repeat of the German High Command communiqué which, when bereft of its propaganda overtones, often gave an accurate idea of the real position of the front in the East (and also later in the West) when the details were applied to the giant wall-covering map I had put up in the camp library. The Germans themselves used to come and study this map after we had been locked up for the night, as it gave them a more realistic picture of the war situation as it really was. We three, Kavan, Major Richard Vining and myself, then went to the tiny 'office' high up in the turret of the Castle, where we wrote it out legibly for the camp inmates. Kavan's writing was excellent for this, as it was so clear. The result, on quarto sheets of paper, was then pinned to the notice-board in the library, where it attracted a lot of attention, as, apart from the nightly clandestine BBC reports which I later ran also (at some considerable risk from discovery by the Germans), people at the camp were news-starved. Our aim in the newspaper was not only to inform, but also to raise morale, which at times was low owing to Allied losses. Heralded by a great blare of trumpets these were blasted into the camp by the Germans every day by loudspeaker, often as a gloating recital of shipping and aircraft losses, some of it true, some not. The effect on the prisoners was not unnaturally somewhat depressive, and it was this that we tried to counteract by showing the Russian front as it really was. Later we could show similar advances after the landings in the West. But before this time, in the darker days of 1942, 1943 (up to Stalingrad) and then El Alamein, the only hope was on the Russian front – with our own news often pretty grim. It was this which our little newspaper set out to counteract, by taking the mickey out of the Germans in the words of Goebbels's own propaganda, which when you translated it verbatim from German into English could be made to sound ridiculous. A cheap gimmick in a way, but it worked. When one is in that situation, it is a case of anything for a laugh. The camp consisted largely, until we got there, of older Territorial and regular army officers who had been there since 1940 and they were getting pretty camp-weary. You can understand why Kavan's brand of irreverence was a tonic in those grim days.

Terry made this last comment in an early letter, when I think he had not decided how much to tell me, and wanted, humanely, to err on the side of generosity. When I later spoke to him about it in order to understand just what he meant by 'irreverence', he hesitated, then asked me what Elliott had died of. When I said natural causes, which seemed a fair description of the effects of booze, cigarettes and disillusion, Terry seemed relieved. Becoming more forthcoming, he told me, 'You know, his seeing the joke in something unpleasant or untoward, his irreverence, had another side to it. When he felt down, he could show a streak of real Black Irish melancholy. I always wondered at the time and afterwards that he might end up taking his own life.' When his moods were grey rather than black, Elliott was to be heard chanting to Haydn's melody for *Deutschland Über Alles* and the irritation of the guards,

> 'Life Presents a Dismal Picture
> Dark and Dreary as the Tomb,
> Father's got a Penile Stricture,
> Mother's got a Fallen Womb,
> Sister Nelly's Been Aborted
> For the Forty-Second Time,
> And Brother Bobby's Been Deported,
> For a Homosexual Crime.'

Camp life went on. So did the plotting of escapes, supported by formidable logistical and supply efforts. The British post-war report on Spangenberg quoted earlier notes, for instance, that parcels, sometimes ostensibly from officers' families, but usually from cover organisations such as the Licensed Victuallers Association and the charmingly styled Local Ladies Comfort Society, infiltrated into the two camps over the course of the war 3 wireless sets, 148 compasses, 3 suitcases, 44 hacksaws, 2 wirecutters, 2 draughtsman's sets for forging documents, 19 pre-forged passes, no less than 109 general maps and 61 'special Maps and Plans'. The Germans did sometimes uncover the contraband, but for the most part the 'Special Parcels' were simply stolen from the store before being opened by the Germans, via a door in the rear, which had been double-locked by the Germans for the duration of the war but to which a British craftsman had promptly made a key. Spangenberg had a well-organised intelligence function, and for that low-tech era was in surprisingly close touch with the outside world. Its intelligence officer had a wide brief: 'News. Communication with home. Communication with other camps. Security. Letters. Wireless and Special Messages. German [news] from Press. British [news] from wireless.' Keeping in touch with home kept several officers rather busy. The main medium was letters in a code which had been memorised by a small number of officers on special courses before the war, then passed on in great secrecy to others in the camp. Incoming or outgoing letters, on the face of it perfectly ordinary correspondence, were identified as containing a coded message by the date, which was written as '22/4/43' in contrast to '22nd April 1943' format reserved for ordinary letters, and if the signature was under-lined. The first two words of text then provided the key to unravelling the message buried in the domestic banalities. The volume was surprising. Over the years, twenty-two officers in the two Spangenberg camps were indoctrinated into the code; 500 coded letters were sent and 227 received. What on earth were they writing about? Though the value of the effort must have been as much psychological as real, the prisoners did pick up military information from a wide range of sources, as a later report revealed:

From prison guards, who were not staunch Nazis.

From British Officers who were sent to PoW Hospitals when sick, and gathered information there from other sick men and sometimes, perhaps, from an Officer stationed in the hospital (possibly a doctor) who took it upon himself to collect and dis-tribute information.

By allowing British Other Ranks to act as drivers of German vehi-cles. These men during the course of their driving picked up a lot of information some of which, when sifted, did prove useful.

From new prisoners to the Camp.

From other Officers at the Holiday Camp [*sic*]. [As late as 1944, handfuls of lucky officers selected from those who had served the longest periods of imprisonment were sent to the Bavarian Alps for a short spell of fresh air, a remarkably civilised minor feature of a remarkably uncivilised major war.]

When an officer or other rank arrived at the Upper Camp, he was treated with suspicion until such time as he had proved to be a genuine PoW and not a 'stool pigeon'. When it was known he was a genuine case, and having been issued with clothes and food, he was interrogated by the officer i/c Intelligence.

Officers returning from Hospital were also interrogated by the Intelligence Officer, who, having sifted the information, reported it to the Senior British Officer. Valuable information was eventually despatched to the UK.

Recaptured escapers produced a lot of information about difficulties encountered during their escape, and action to be taken when certain occasions arose.

The letter system was supplemented by radio. The Castle received its first set, as part of the A network set up by the MI9 escape organisation, as a series of components hidden in the recesses of several YMCA parcels sent from Switzerland, all adroitly opened and resealed in the store before they were examined by the Germans. But the completed set was soon uncovered by a random German search and the Castle was cut off from outside news until a nimble-fingered major, who had worked before the war for Marconi, stole four valves from a piece of unattended German cinema equipment and built a new set hidden inside a gramophone.

As well as the news broadcasts, scribbled down by Antony Terry, a single earphone pressed to his head, BBC transmissions also contained messages, and replies to coded letters, often buried in the homespun sanctity of the weekly talks by the Reverend Selby Wright, the Radio Padre. Wright, a straightforward muscular Christian, to judge from his photograph, knew only that if his scripts were prefaced by the greeting 'Good Evening, Forces', as distinct from 'Hello', or 'Good Evening', they had been skilfully doctored to weave in coded messages without altering the wholesomely uplifting sense of the text. But like every ideal cut-out or go-between, he remained unaware of the contents of the messages themselves.

In Spangenberg, sadly, his words fell not so much on deaf ears, but on ears that had difficulty taking down with any precision over the crackly ether the Padre's rather rapid delivery. The official report noted: 'If one piece of the message was lost or misunderstood, it was difficult to make any sense of the rest. Only on a very few occasions were messages picked up successfully.'

In July 1942, Spangenberg began to transmit as well as receive. This time tins of Players pipe tobacco brought in the components of a Morse keying set. Precariously plugged into the mains with metal paperclips and matchsticks, the aerial wire looped over the attic beams, it was a slow, risky but reasonably reliable way to send brief soundbites of information. Elliott sent several messages back to SOE on his capture and interrogation. Only one survives, from December 1942. He told Baker Street: 'Interrogated about Sofia, Zegrad [?Zagreb] and much on British Council. No persons seek Ross; Norman Slade.'

'Ross' is presumably Elliott's Sofia boss, the crafty brigadier, and an unknown SOE hand minuted on Elliott's message that if the rather convoluted phrase (probably a result of the coding process) really meant that Elliott had not been questioned about him, it was 'somewhat surprising'. Whoever Norman Slade might have been, he is not now to be found either in SOE records or the files of the British Council.

Back in England life went on. We moved at some point, 1943 or 1944, from Eynsham up to Westmoreland, to take us further out of the reach of German raids. Puny memories. The large grey house in a park where we had rented the top floor. Its owner, the frozen-faced Mrs Gatson Wandy, sank valiantly to the occasion, making clear her patrician distaste for outsiders. A long walk over wet fields to the nearest village. The burned-out carcass – so much for being out of range – of a German bomber at the edge of a wood. Crunched metal, wires and a smell of rubber, the black Iron Cross insignia looking far less menacing when framed by swaying corn stalks and bright green weeds. A sunny day in a rowing boat with my grandfather on Lake Windermere. There was no sense of missing my father. Like thousands of other children of that age, we had not had time to know what having a father was like.

Elliott's own recollections of Spangenberg are neither literary nor introspective. Others who were there remembered him with respect or affection, tinged by the feeling that he was something of a mystery. One day was probably very much like the next and most of his memories are of minor incidents – annoyances, grievances, tricks played on the Germans – which seem trivial today, though they were felt intensely at the time. But he was clearly much struck by one episode, perhaps because it touched some wellspring of Britishness, the school playground delights of 'goon-baiting' and the hearty rituals of military camaraderie so redolent of the changing-rooms he had never known, all that mythic sense of England which turned to dross when he actually tried to live the English life. The British officers normally paraded twice a day to be counted by the Germans, and took perverse pride in teasing their captors by being deliberately unmilitary. Elliott wrote: 'Everybody shuffled and lounged about, cigarettes dangling, talking, changing places all the time, and absolutely scruffy. Buttons undone, no ties, a real shambles. Sometimes, just to get a rise out of them, one or two people would fail to turn up, the Germans would then have to search the Castle, and the whole thing would waste hours. We had nowhere else to go. The Germans wanted to get off duty and back to the beer, cards and the local women.' As interpreter, one of Elliott's duties was to march up to the German Commandant, Graf Wedel, when the parade was finally in some semblance of order, to report that the British officers were ready for counting. 'And I never, ever, wore my cap, because without it, I couldn't salute them.'

In early April 1944, Elliott was sent to ask for permission for the Castle officers to parade in honour of the eighteenth birthday of the then Princess Elizabeth, on 21 April. 'After several days of to-ing and fro-ing, the Germans said grudgingly – they already had a sense where the war was heading – that we could, provided it was done as part of their normal counting parade, and we didn't make any noise – especially cheering – that could be heard down in the village. Frankly it was about the most impressive thing I've seen in my life. Everybody was turned out as though they were on the Aldershot parade-ground. Buttons polished, uniforms pressed under our straw mattresses, shoes cleaned, neat haircuts. And for once we'd all shaved. Although he didn't normally appear before the count, this time General Fortune, the senior British officer, took the parade from the start. A parade in absolutely 100 per cent British style. It was perfect. Everything was by the book, for the first and last time. Crisp orders and everyone moving very sharply and smartly indeed. The parade was in order of seniority. We had full colonels, lieutenant-colonels, majors, captains, lieutenants, second lieutenants, a couple of hundred all told. The German officers were waiting in their usual position at the courtyard entrance. General Fortune told me crisply, "Major Elliott, please tell the Germans that we are ready for them to count." It was the one and only day in the camp I had put on my cap. I turned, saluted General Fortune punctiliously – longest way up, shortest way down – and marched smartly up to the Commandant and his two officers. This is a thing I shall never forget. One of them was the security fellow, with whom I had a wary mutual respect. I saluted them too, absolutely smartly, and said in German, "We are ready to count." And to my amazement, the Germans were so taken aback that they said, "We are not going to count today." They just couldn't face it, so I stamped back to General Fortune, saluted him again and said, "Sir, the Germans do not wish to count today." Flouting the Germans' orders, he called for three cheers for Princess Elizabeth. We yelled as loudly as we could, and then he dismissed the parade. We turned to the right, paused for a count of two, then doubled away. Fortune had been a prisoner since the St Valery raid. Commander of the 51st Highland Division. As he faced me when I saluted him, the tears were streaming down his face. The Germans just turned on their heels and walked away.'

Elliott recorded little of the war's final days. Guards and prisoners were equally jumpy, as the thud of distant artillery rolled over the hills and American fighter planes droned unscathed overhead. But on both sides four years of giving and taking orders, of the power of the trigger, were hard to discard. So when the British officers were ordered to parade in the courtyard with all their gear, ready to march off to God knows where, they obeyed. But as they trudged, down the dusty, poplar-lined roads, the fir plantations a green mat on the distant hillsides, discipline soon eroded. The guards – there were already strangely few German officers attached to the shabby column; most had melted away into the nearby villages to scramble out of uniform and hope for the best – became tolerant and resigned, and after fifteen miles of this bizarre procession, many British prisoners had also slipped away into the woods. As Elliott remembered, 'It was a funny thing, being out. Because you weren't really free, and with the fighting rolling nearer (you could see villages burning in the distance), we realised we were as much at risk from our own side as from the Germans.' Suddenly, as another of the group recalled, 'We saw this group of young men in khaki, a few fields away walking with a swing and swagger, a looseness so unlike the Germans' rather stoop-shouldered shuffle.' They were Americans. It was over.

In the war's closing days, desperate displaced persons washed up from God knows what smouldering lice-infested corners of Europe scrambled into Spangenberg for shelter. Seeing the lights and the movement, nearby SS troops, misinformed, malicious, or simply by this stage yelping red-eyed mad, turned their guns on the Castle, reducing it to rubble and the refugees to pulp. Spangenberg Castle is now rebuilt and serves as a youth hostel. In the early 1960s, a misplaced Teutonic sense of letting bygones be bygones, *Das ist alles vergangen und vergessen*, or perhaps just an entrepreneurial travel agent, brought invitations to the wartime prisoners to join their former gaolers for an 'old boys' reunion'. 'One or two of the fellows went,' Antony Terry told me, 'but not as many as the Germans hoped. Scarcely surprising. Damned if I was going to spend good money having a happy holiday at my old prison.'

# 14

# The Major and the Menshevik

Yugoslavia is as dead as my father, roiled in a bloody orgy of dismemberment, keeping abreast of which requires a computer programme. Whether things would have turned out differently if Mihailovic and the Royalists had led post-war Yugoslavia rather than Tito is a fruitless speculation. They didn't, and really never had a hope of it. When peace, that wonderful moment for settling scores, came to post-war Yugoslavia, Mihailovic was repaid for his considerable contribution to his country, for doing his duty, staring back at a firing squad in the improbably bourgeois setting of a golf course outside Belgrade.

In the dismissive, equivocal epitaph provided by the official history of British diplomacy,

> it is possible to hold, as the Foreign Office was inclined to think, that on balance neither General Mihailovic nor Tito was of very great military value to the Allies since each, while wanting the defeat of Germany and Italy, was concerned at least as much with internal political feuds and preoccupied with securing a dominant position in the control of Yugoslavia after the war.

I doubt that Elliott ever gave the matter a moment's thought. Nor, I would bet, did he give much time then or later to ruminating whether

SOE in Yugoslavia, or in the wider context, made an effective contribution to the war effort. Though the clarion calls to resistance made some strategic sense, and were a brave rallying cry, there may have been a fundamental miscalculation in the vision of SOE as an incendiary force. Did the occupied people of Europe have a real appetite for insurrection? Defeat was traumatic. Occupation by the Nazis was oppressive and demeaning. But it was not always bloody and cruel, and indeed often brought in its train more jobs and more business for legitimate, if collaborationist, manufacturers and traders. It brought the delicious opportunity to settle old scores. But when resistance did emerge, whether in France, Czechoslovakia and indeed Yugoslavia, the German response was the epitome of ruthless efficiency. Those who resisted with or without SOE's direct support were gallant beyond measure, but they were few, and paid a high price. SOE is dead too, though, Dracula-like, it lingered on in various guises rather longer than post-war British governments cared to admit. Even now, some of its basic skills are still to be found, when needed by Whitehall, mainly in the Special Air Service (SAS). An indigent Britain could not in fact afford to lug into peacetime the cost of a clandestine paramilitary force on the scale really needed to deal with the crumbling of an empire. That was probably just as well; America could, and created the vast and so often uncontrollable juggernaut of the CIA's Office of Policy Co-ordination. The CIA carried some battle honours off the field in terms of unfriendly regimes toppled and US interests maintained against the odds, but its record overall – from a conspicuous failure to create real destabilisation in Communist Europe, through Laos, Vietnam and, above all, the fatal fiasco of Cuba – is hard to promote as a shining example of value for taxpayers' money.

SIS in contrast goes on for ever, Whitehall's Tennysonian brook. Though not yet as far out of the closet as his recent counterpart at the new feminist MI5, now presented to the world as a uniquely British blend of St Trinians and the Spanish Inquisition, the Chief of SIS goes so far as to give discreet press briefings in his riverside dining-room, though avoiding the photographers and the temptation to deliver public lectures. The Service has even acquired a legal basis in the statute books, all of which probably signals the need for some latter-day Claude Dansey to ride to the rescue by recreating something private and flexible, 'off balance sheet', discreet, disavowable satellites for use when the bureaucratic behemoth stumbles.

Croatia, where the loathsome Ante Pavelic is still venerated, has adopted a central part of the wartime state's emblem for its national flag, and now uses the Pavelic 'kuna' as its new currency. Ageing Ustashe diehards still appear in prominent official positions, and life goes on under seventy-five year old President Tudjman, self-proclaimed 'Father of His People', strutting around in a self-designed uniform more appropriate to the Head Commissionaire of the Zagreb Palais de Danse. Obviously a believer in the adage that charity begins at home, Tudjman has been described by an Austrian newspaper as 'the richest man in Central Europe'. Death also continues. And in late-twentieth-century Serbia demagogues, whose sharp twentieth-century suits and designer haircuts made them seem men of this century but who in reality were as bloody and bloody-minded as their forebears, 'ethnically cleansed' their Moslem fellow countrymen, repeating history in a style the Wehrmacht and General Kvaternik would have applauded. One of this new breed was Zelijko Raznatovic, known as Arkan (or by some journalists, tritely but accurately, as 'The Beast of Belgrade'), whose Tiger Brigades went to work in a tragically familiar way. As a contemporary commentator wrote, 'The well-oiled cleansing machine provides clear evidence to an operation that was organised and directed from Belgrade. First Yugoslav and Serb army regulars surrounded and shelled the village they wanted to "liberate". After that Serb paramilitaries like Arkan's Tigers would swarm down, terrorising the local population with beatings, rapes and massacres, burning churches and looting homes and businesses in the process.' The same commentator noted, as a sign of the country's tragic history repeating itself yet again, that another paramilitary leader, Vojislav Seselj, in private life a law professor no less, was used 'to whip up World War II vintage animosities and preach Serb authority'. When he moved from words to deeds, Seselj even called his own paramilitary brigades 'Chetniks'. And like President Tudjman, Serbia's President Milosevic and his family have not neglected the material side of life, accumulating villas in Greece, yachts and making sure their offspring are put in the way of 'nice little earners'.

What of some of our other characters? The pernicious Dr Franz Six, mastermind of the original Gestapo 'Wanted List – UK' and later Eichmann's mentor on matters of Nazi philosophy, fell firmly on his well-shod feet. Sentenced to twenty years' imprisonment at Nuremberg,

Six was released under a general amnesty in 1962 and promptly appeared on the staff of General Reinhard Gehlen's new and thriving West German intelligence service, receiving no doubt a boozy and convivial welcome from his many Gestapo and SS colleagues already on the payroll. With a cover job as publicity manager for Porsche Diesel, his real task was recruiting agents from among Soviet prisoners of war for infiltration back into Russia.

At his trial in Jerusalem in 1961, with a hint of sour grapes perhaps justified by the disparities in their respective positions by that stage, Eichmann turned on his sleekly successful and chastely deNazified former teacher as the man who of all of them had descended lowest from the pedestal of a self-proclaimed 'intellectual' to the depravity of mass murder only to 'bounce back again after the war as the confidant and advisor of both the American and (West) German Governments'.

Selby Wright, the Radio Padre, became a school chaplain and later Moderator of the Church of Scotland, and was thankfully long dead when a newspaper sought to attack his reputation based on unsubstantiated allegations about his sexual preferences.

After a brave career as chauffeur to so many agents good, bad and indifferent, professional bandits and courageous rather ordinary men and women nervously clutching cheap cardboard suitcases, Elliott's pilot John Austin gave up flying after the war in favour of the rather straighter grain of the timber importing business.

Eric van Maurik, who despatched Elliott from Malta, became a key player in transporting agents of SOE's French Section into occupied territory. After 1945 he began a new career in the state's service, where he found himself among friends.

Too little seems to be known about another of our cast, the larger than life Brigadier Keble. Allegedly commandant of a military prison in Malaya before transferring to the Middle East, Keble figures as the sweaty conniving *éminence grise* of many SOE memoirs. He has been traduced as the source of an SOE Cairo campaign to sabotage Fitzroy Maclean's mission to Tito by spreading rumours that he was a homosexual, and when that failed arranging for him to be supplied with a faulty parachute. Keble even appeared in one post-war novel in barely fictional guise as the instigator of a plot to assassinate a suspected but innocent German agent. He is probably due for a biography of his own.

Terence Airey, who briefed Elliott for DISCLAIM, went on to a distinguished military career. Towards the end of the war he represented the UK in Allan Dulles's secret negotiations for the surrender of German forces in Italy, acquiring in the process from the German team yet another dachshund, this one named Fritzel.

One Yugoslav source reported sighting the mysterious photographer Belinski just after the German collapse dressed in a US Army officer's fur-collared jacket and peaked cap sitting self-importantly in the back of a jeep as it drove at high speed through a displaced persons' camp in upper Austria.

James Klugmann died as he had lived, a staunch Communist, much in demand as a polemicist as the exigencies of post-war history required the Comintern to undertake a sweeping revision of its recent past. In a minor *tour de force* of its kind, he argued in a slim volume launched in 1949 as part of Stalin's anti-Tito campaign that the real backers of the Partisans were not Moscow – or by implication Klugmann and his accomplices in Cairo – but the British themselves. Tito, he now asserted with a straight face, had been an SIS pawn all along. Yes, progressive elements including some 'in the British army' – this perhaps an oblique reference to Klugmann himself – had grown disenchanted with Mihailovic's Nazi collaboration. But in truth they had been duped by the fiendish cunning of British intelligence into believing that Tito was a real alternative, only to discover later that he was no more than a pawn of Broadway Buildings and Foggy Bottom and, worse than that, a Trotskyite.

Johnny (or rather Kavan, Clian or Balkan Joe) came marching home again around the end of April 1945. Home in inverted commas. At some point that year we had rattled back from Westmoreland with boxes, toys and a treadle sewing-machine. We were billeted, pending its sale, in the apartment of a lately dead great-aunt in Vernon Court, a mock-Tudor building, now much favoured by taxi-drivers as a logistically convenient and socially adequate residence. Standing proudly at the start of the Hendon Way, one of the main arteries out of London to the north, it is just on the wrong side of the as yet unmarked border where chic intellectual Hampstead slides self-consciously downhill into racially cosmopolitan Golders Green, Central Europe condensed on to a postage stamp, four square on the Northern Line of the Underground.

In those days, before the German, Austrian and Russian refugees had been overtaken by Indians, then the earnest, giggling Japanese, and moved onwards and upwards to Mill Hill or Grosvenor Square, Golders Green could boast, in no special order, the site of a particularly nasty post-war murder, a crematorium, a variety theatre, three cinemas, several warmly spicy bakers' shops (names such as Appenrodt and Grodzinski struck a marked contrast with the Cake Shoppes and Aerated Bread Company stores in other suburbs), and a white-tiled Sainsbury's, where butter was measured and served by aproned assistants with ribbed wooden spatulas, and large Cheddar cheeses cut with wire. The Macfisheries shop down Golders Green Road, just by the railway bridge, knew its clientele; it made up for meagre sales of kippers by selling large quantities of olives and pickled cucumbers from the briny depths of an oak barrel on the pavement.

There I once dissolved into tears of utter desolation when I lost my mother in the crowd of shoppers; not much of Elliott's stiff upper lip there. The search for her was prolonged by my sobbing insistence to the worried shopgirls that my mother was 'tall with golden hair'. Since neither attribute existed outside my imagination, and indeed in that neck of the woods tall, blonde ladies were rather few and far between, gefilte fish out of water, it took some time to track her down as she searched for me along the pavement in the opposite direction.

There was no party, no celebration, no fatted calf – not even Woolton Pie – when Elliott came back. Nothing much of anything at all. No build-up of expectations, no lump in the throat as the familiar footsteps are heard in the hall. No popping of corks and tears of joy as the kitbag is dumped in the hall and the loved ones group in an awkward but warm embrace straight off the cover of the *Saturday Evening Post*. As always, Elliott's arrivals and departures were unheralded and unremarked. Suddenly he was there, with a small black Scots terrier which lasted about a week before dashing defiantly to destruction under the wheels of a truck. Life didn't change noticeably. In fact, my only memory of the great victory over the Hun is of the head teacher at the Edwardian red-brick primary school down the hill at Wessex Road solemnly handing out to his puzzled, rickety pupils cyclostyled letters from King George VI thanking God – a necessarily broad concept in the NW11 postal district – for our deliverance.

After a little while you got used to the gaps in the rows of houses, the sandbags, the cabalistic white direction signs painted on the walls by air-raid wardens, the grit and grime. Those were thin-lipped times, times of queues, string bags, shortages and ration cards. I would stand like a Central American beggar on the grass verge of the main road, which ran past the school, yelling, 'Got any gum, chum?', at the US army trucks. Huge black faces, white-toothed grins. A foil packet of Wrigley's would often come whizzing my way. There was one special treat. Elliott took us to the Bertram Mills circus, a totally new experience, to be followed soon after by my first banana (a strange letdown, that, after the wartime years of seeing enticing pictures of clusters of Fyffes yellow fingers stuck to greengrocers' windows). My abiding memory of the circus visit is of a man apart. Elliott took us, bought the tickets, sat with us, but didn't say much and was somehow not there at all. After the show was over, we went to the funfair. The stomach-wrenching spin in a vast wooden drum, whose rattling floor receded as the drum spun faster and faster, leaving the awed punters glued to the varnished wall by centrifugal force, was curiously sterile. No excited yelling, no nervous clutching of hands. My sisters and I in mid-air on one side. Across from us, frozen like a movie still, Elliott, his blue overcoat flung flat on the wall. Expressionless. The spy in aspic. We went home in the dark.

Then he was gone again. According to the War Office records, he returned to Germany on 28 June 1945, only a few weeks after getting back. Back from a war that had been difficult, but hardly any worse than the time others had spent fighting in the desert, the jungles, or as prisoners of the poisonous Japanese. But still a war which would have entitled him to say, if asked to go on, 'enough is enough'. But off he went. No peace for the initiated.

The children of failed marriages often, I gather, silently assume the guilt for their parents' separation. That I never remember crossing my mind. In fact, Elliott had been around so little that his going off again was not a matter for much discussion, let alone concern. What turned him away? The most obvious problem, hardly unusual in those years of enforced absence and strain, would have been if my mother had become involved with someone else. She was a pretty, vivacious soul. But dusty though my memory is, try as I might, I can think of no trace, no hint, that this might have happened. We lived on top of one another, and her family lived, for the most part, right on top of us. She had three small children to look after. Unexplained absences and star-struck romances, clandestine meetings at the Strand Palace Hotel or brief encounters at the roadside coffee stall, searchlights playing in the background while sirens wailed, would have been almost impossible to pull off. Had there been someone else in the picture, some memory must surely have stuck with me or my sisters, of the *faux-bonhomme* Uncle Sid on the sofa trying awkwardly to ingratiate himself with the children, doling out bags of sweeties and black-market toys, sidling nervously out of the bathroom in the morning with a shame-filled sponge bag. Girls are more acute, more furtively aware, than boys of this sort of torrid undercurrent, but my sisters remember nothing. And, even if there had been something going on, surely there would have been tears, recriminations, the slamming of doors. Instead, there was virtually nothing said at all. Perhaps it was just drearily inevitable, given my father's complex make-up and his solitary cussedness, and on my mother's side, the forlorn hope that somehow it would all come right if she said and did nothing, made no waves, uttered no threats. Elliott was a stranger, moulded in alien lands.

He had spent the most interesting part of his life wrapped in the sheepskin myths of the Balkans and the mischief of Spangenberg Castle, freed from his past. In London, the reality was the cloying demands of domesticity, back to an office in a government-issue demob suit in the grey dawn of the welfare state. A wife and three children represented a new, uncharted landscape, on to which he ventured with the hesitant lumbering steps of an early astronaut. We children were unknown, and, no doubt, awkward and uncomprehending. We might as well have been hired for his homecoming from Rent-a-Kid. My mother and her family, always closely knit, wrapped in their own strengths and their carapace of language, had closed ranks still more tightly during the war. All of this must have been a hard nut for Elliott to crack even if he had a mind to do so. The family had coped quite well without him, and he was not a man to reach out and touch someone. Equally, what an ordeal it must have been for my mother to try to get back into real contact with a man who was emotionally about as reachable as the driver of a Sherman tank.

For years he had lived inside his head, keeping the secrets, tight-mouthed, bottling up emotions, screwing down the lid on his past. Safe inside Spangenberg, he had finally joined a man's world, an appealing mix of Gordonstoun and Dotheboys Hall; an Englishman's world, a world of 1930s' Bulldog Drummond values, in which he was admired as

'Balkan Joe', a man of secrets, not a world run by lefties, intellectuals and organisation men. In his early dabblings in the secret world and in the camp, he had been respected for his bravery, his talents and his mystery, and he had played a useful part in prison camp life. He had been accepted, popular, yet nothing had been required of him emotionally, except a contribution to the common cause of treating the German captors with contempt.

We could become badly diverted in defining what you, I or anyone else believes 'love' means, so I have no idea whether on my terms or his Elliott loved my mother. On his rather flexible, pragmatic terms, he probably did, until he didn't. Having met Kati and other women who knew him later in life, I would say that, for him, her main attractions were prettiness, bubbling cheerfulness, a slightly scatty charm and, in large part, her foreignness. After I had met at least some of the others, it struck me that while Elliott himself looked good, had an appealing air of toughness and mystery, and was a prodigious spender, the brighter, more perceptive women tended to be cautious, to see inside the outer man and to keep their distance sexually.

Whether in some furtive little box at the back of his mind, Elliott had the idea that by marrying my mother he was plugging into a family that were, by his standards, comfortably off and ran a business which would employ him, or at least generate some useful income for his wife, there is no evidence, nor could there be. But in later years, he was much given, when boozing with Terry and others, to bitter attacks on David Redstone, contrasting his supposed wealth (non-existent by any sensible measure; he was only a small shareholder in a business controlled by his brother) with his meanness (a grotesque distortion of the truth; after Elliott took to his heels, my grandfather stoically bore the burden of providing for my mother and her children).

Redstone and Elliott's mutual dislike was palpable. And yet behind the acid-etched contrasts there was, as I later discovered, a curious affinity, of which each was totally unaware. If ever, after Hungary, they had been able to talk about their lives and secret times, it would probably have come too late to make any difference. The contrasts began at the physical level, and went on from there. Elliott was a tall, slim, part Irish, part God knows what, illegitimate rover, who chose exile, adventure and secrets for their own sake. Curiously for a man to whom anywhere abroad was better than anywhere in England, he was well imbued with that knee-jerk 'wogs begin at Calais' spirit, which, I was about to say, was typical of his generation, until I realised that things aren't much different today. With it (again not much has changed) went a non-vicious but none the less deeply conditioned set of stereotyped anti-Semitic attitudes. A bed-hopping, bar-hopping spendthrift, he messed up more than his fair share of lives, his own, as we shall see, among them. I really have no idea whether he read much and, if so, what. All I can recall seeing scattered around on his brief stopovers were books of the macabre cartoons of Charles Addams and Don Marquis's free-form poems of the life of Mehitabel the cat, with a 'wild hobohemian strain in her blood'.

In the opposing corner, David Redstone was a small, portly, uxorious Ukrainian with a silver beard and a strong accent, whose revolutionary and Jewish roots had been moulded by my grandmother's fanatical adherence to her Russian Orthodox beliefs and rituals, and the tranquillising power of her cooking, into a mellow, pantheistic, *Manchester Guardian* liberalism. Redstone had been chased into exile rather than chosen it, but had managed by hard work to build for himself and his family, in the shade of the tall monkey-puzzle tree in his North London garden, a comfortable émigré life. His tipple was lemon tea sipped from a saucer. Unlike Elliott, he was a genuinely friendly soul. Even today, no really English club, except perhaps the Turf or the Special Forces, would admit someone so quintessentially foreign into its membership, but he was at heart a clubbable man, unlike Elliott, to whom a club was something with which you bashed Germans on the head. Redstone embraced English middle-class virtues with the passion of a convert. He read voraciously. Whether he read Byron I don't know, though he did have a book of the poet's letters. If he had read up on the subject, he might have found Caroline Lamb's dismissal of Byron as 'mad, bad and dangerous to know' rather appropriate for his son-in-law.

It was curiosity and chance, those longtime helpers, which led me one rainy afternoon to the Bodleian Library, and to the stacks which housed the *Greater Soviet Encyclopedia*, that Orwellian compendium of lies, damned lies and statistics. Redstone had, I knew, been exiled to Siberia before he was twenty. But when he talked about his experiences, he tended to highlight, because that is what children are interested in, the unbelievable severity of the climate, and the exiles' primitive life sandwiched in the snows between the Tsar's police and the stone-age Yakut tribesmen. He never really explained why he had been sent there, and what had happened, beyond vague references to some sort of trouble.

I remembered that he had been in Yakutsk and was able to find a brief paragraph in the *Encyclopedia* eulogising the seminal proto-revolutionary significance of something called the Yakutsk Uprising in 1904. A cross-reference, and the diligence of the Librarians, produced what was, for Redstone's life, as significant a find as Bill Deakin's cache of Elliott memorabilia: a diary kept by one of the rebels who took part in the Uprising, complete with grainy photographs and the police dossiers of all the participants; it had been privately printed in St Petersburg in 1906. There, with the same eerie frisson as looking at Elliott's portrait photograph of 1945, I found David Redstone, in a high-necked Russian blouse, posed rather formally among his fellow revolutionaries, their lawyers and a dog, Igolkin, who put a paw print in history by serving as a clandestine courier. Rather like the Joe/Kavan, Elliott/Burnley transformation, my grandfather's Roitenstern became Redstone, in his case at the insistence of a harassed immigration clerk in the echoing Customs Hall on Harwich dockside many years later.

I cannot tell you what Redstone's early life was about, who his parents were, or what they did, except that he had a brother who got out of Odessa to England ahead of him. Since the two of them ended up in a decent way of business in the London tobacco trade, there may have been some family background in wheeling and dealing in the then much prized, now so despised, fragrant orange-brown leaves. Nor do we know how the spores of revolution drifted into his conscience; a friend, a teacher, a brush with the gendarmerie, unpleasant encounters with the sour breath of anti-Semitism? However it happened, he was committed well before he struggled into the prickly serge straitjacket of his artillery uniform. And seriously committed, since once under martial law dissent became a capital offence. But while the flame was there, it was then and for the rest of his life the slightly softer Magicoal glow of Menshevik liberalism, of Soviet democracy, rather than the laser intensity of the Bolsheviks. He believed passionately in the power of the ballot over the bullet. He never seemed obviously cast down by the fact that for his entire life history seemed to prove him wrong.

The military police had dragged Redstone out of a barracks in his home town of Odessa, that polyglot port with the pram-challenging steps, charging him with distributing seditious pamphlets. He spent fifteen months in Moscow's Butirki jail before being shipped out to Siberia. Neither Lenin nor Stalin can claim credit for inventing the exile system. They simply applied modern techniques of transportation and the creative use of cruelty to develop the slave labour industry of the Gulag Archipelago, that sea of frozen, broken bodies and crushed minds, a long-standing centrepiece of the Russian penal structure. Exile had become a growth industry in the mid-eighteenth century, when, by some quirk of the Age of Enlightenment, the death penalty was abolished. Pragmatic officials soon saw that shipping criminals off to Siberia instead offered the double benefit of ridding the cities and villages of undesirables while providing cheap human shovel fodder to exploit the mineral treasures of the East. And once the system was working, it was easy enough to stretch the definition of 'criminal' to include anyone the regime did not care for. Before the Trans-Siberian railway, last grandiose gasp of a faltering regime, was completed at the turn of the nineteenth century, all the hundreds of thousands of exiles reached Siberia the same way: they walked, for months, in the snow, in the dust, in the mud, across Mother Russia, past the sad boundary posts at Perm that marked the limits of the homeland and the start of the hostile indifference of Siberia. But by the time the Romanovka group's turn came, the railway was in steady operation clattering across the Steppes from its regular appointments in Samara down to Irkutsk, close by the black, bottomless waters of Lake Baikal and the aromatic mysteries of the Mongolian border. Redstone and his fellow exiles travelled like Jim Crow at the rear of the train in a now familiar fug of body odour and tobacco, jam-packed on wooden benches, their possessions and food stacked in boxes and bundles around them, doors locked and windows fastened with iron brackets. At the end of each compartment squatted a burbling metal samovar and a pair of watchful armed guards. As the eternity of Russia rolled past the windows, the exiles were sustained by their endless talk, dreaming dreams, spinning ideas, mapping out their vision of the world to come; flirting, quarrelling, plotting, worrying about what lay ahead after their sixteen-day journey.

In the train's front carriages, the paying passengers got rather more in return for the 75 roubles (about $600 in present values) they had laid out for a first-class ticket from St Petersburg to Irkutsk. Cosseted in tassels and brocade, they ate fine food off fine china. Moiré silk sofas sat plumply in the private compartments; the Pourthault linen sheets were changed every three days by bewhiskered, gold-braided stewards, straight from the set of *War and Peace*. The mahogany-panelled library car offered deep armchairs, breakfront bookcases, even chess tables fitted with silver tea-glass holders specially made for the railway by the gnome-like craftsmen of Moscow's '1st Artel'. For the devout, or for sleeping-car sinners seeking quick repentance, one carriage had been lavishly converted into an exquisite miniature Orthodox church complete with Bokhara rugs, red-and-gold icons, blue-and-gold blessing crosses, silver censers, and a ceiling of polished wood and brass. The rectangular carriage windows had been rebuilt as elegantly curving ogees, their panes replaced by stained glass. On the roof, the stubby metal ventilator shafts had been camouflaged by a scaled-down onion-domed bell-tower. In the dining-car, French and Russian wines supplied by Denker of St Petersburg, chocolates by Messrs Konradi and the highly prized mineral waters of Keller & Co. complemented the fish and game picked up daily at major stops. After dinner, the air grew comfortably blue from the smoke of the best Havana cigars, and the scented aroma of Laferme & Co.'s Frou Frou cigarettes. Portraits of the Tsar and Tsarina (that sad marriage of the ineffectual and the unpopular) swayed on the velvet-lined walls to the motion of the train. In the marble en-suite bathrooms of the luxury suites, cut-glass bottles of Brocade's Triple Strength Eau de Cologne were on hand to mask the tiresome soot and sweat odours of travel. Ladies could wash that muzhik right out of their hair with the rather unromantic sounding Petrol Soap. 'A great strengthener in case of falling off', the wrapper claimed, in proud, if ambiguous, English.

At Irkutsk, where varnished carriages with plumed horses and fawning staff awaited the nobility and gentry, their hair washed, their souls cleansed, Redstone and his dishevelled companions were held under guard until the station had been cleared, then crammed into horse-drawn carts, each holding three prisoners and two green-uniformed guards, for a bumpy forty miles through the hills north of Irkutsk, to the new Exile Transfer Jail, a larger version of the wooden stockaded *étapes*, or prison waystations, which punctuated the post roads all the way across Russia. Two days later, deloused, paperwork checked and rechecked, they bounced on another 200-mile cart trek to the first navigable stretch of the Lena, where they shuffled on board prison barges to be towed down river by one of the paddle-steamers, which, like NASA shuttles, tied together the edge of the known world with the outer space of Siberia. Modelled by a Russian penal expert on English convict 'hulks', the 150-foot barges had separate compartments below deck for men and women. The mesh-enclosed deck was for sitting, reading, brooding, talking. The escorting soldiers were housed in a raised cabin at the rear; two smaller cabins, built in a little superstructure on the bow, could be rented by exiles with money or influence. Were it not for the hovering guards, and the menacing sense that at the end of the endless caravanserai, lay a freezing, dangerous place from which many might not return, the voyage down the Lena in those far-off years would have been a never-ending delight: clear water, starry nights, towering cliffs of sandstone and basalt, the infinite forest stretching on either side, a million subtle tones of green and silver. Unseen in the woods, red-eyed wolves howled eerily as the boats glided past. The excitement on reaching a settlement carved out of the woods on the river bank, where earlier exiles, some of them old acquaintances, could be hugged, sobbed over, gossiped with. Where fresh sturgeon and game could be bought out of communal funds from the incomprehensible natives gliding alongside in their birch-bark canoes. Singing the sad songs of the exiles, passed down from generation to generation; lamenting the loved ones they had left behind and might never see again: 'My lad, your father is long laid in his grave, under the damp soil of the motherland'; or entreating Bukhaga, the Stone Age deity who ruled over Lake Baikal, to bring the prison hulks safe to the distant shore.

The journey's end was 200 miles from the Arctic Circle, closer to the United States than to Moscow. Yakutsk today is home – a word deserving heavy quotation marks – to 155,000 people, a socialist sprawl of prefabricated concrete buildings with blistered stucco fronts, wallpapered with the smells of food, sweat and diesel fumes. A last-chance saloon for former Gulag prisoners with nowhere else to go, drifters, drunks and the sharp-eyed, gold-chained Mafiosi trading over their portable telephones in missiles, low-mileage tanks, drugs and illicit diamonds. The newer buildings, intermingled with a few wooden houses from the past, rest on iron piles steam-blasted into the frozen soil. (For centuries the Siberian soil has been perpetually frozen – the so-called Permafrost. It is ironic, and perhaps a reflection not just of changing climates but of changing times, that in today's Yakutsk the soil is now beginning to melt, endangering the city's structures to a point where the

Mayor has declared a State of Emergency.) Nevertheless, visitors are still shown with some pride the last remaining timber tower of the battlements built by the Cossacks in the seventeenth century. If pressed, the local guides might also mention as worth a visit the two-storey wooden villa known as The Romanovka, the key setting for David Redstone's part of the story. Today it is a museum, but it does not honour the two young men who died in what has gone down in a couple of paragraphs of Russian revolutionary history as the Romanovka Uprising. They had the misfortune to be serving the Tsar, whose memorials are now only to be found in grainy Pathe newsreels of white-tunicked officers and their parasolled ladies, moving in autistic double time, in television documentaries claiming to shed new light on his murder, and in the Fabergé Easter eggs and diamond-eyed lapis lazuli frogs which trickle in diminishing quantities through the Geneva auction rooms. Instead the Romanovka, as long as it stands, is a monument to Redstone and his fellow revolutionaries.

There was no real hope of escape. North, beyond the deathtrap Verkhoyansk mountains, lay the nothingness of the Arctic. All around, more effective than barbed wire, dogs and minefields, were thousands of miles of uncharted oceans of larch, spruce, cedars and silver birch trees, broken by vast areas of boggy, featureless taiga, roamed by wild life, and patrolled by the unfriendly Yakut and Tunguz tribesmen, always anxious to curry favour with the police by turning in an exile. Fifteen hundred miles to the west, the tide of turn-of-the-century European comfort was already lapping around Irkutsk, which boasted a theatre, a museum, grand houses, expensive private schools, a congregation of churches catering for a catholicity of faiths, sputtering gas lights on the main street and even half-a-dozen primitive telephones. But Yakutsk had nothing. It brushed the outside world only with its fingertips. Important news sputtered along the telegraph wire, if snow and wind had not smashed the poles. When the river was open, the paddle-steamers splashed and hooted their way along the Lena once a week, bringing people, supplies, mail and news. There was a so-called post road, little more than a cleared strip through the forest, which worked well enough in winter when sledges could glide over the snow with some approximation of smoothness. But in the wheel-swallowing mud of the brief spring, and the rutted dry earth of summer, when squadrons of mosquitoes remembered by one scarred exile as 'the size of small grapes' would dive-bomb the bouncing traveller, the road journey was a nightmare even for those prepared to run the gauntlet of marauding bands of escaped convicts and time-expired prisoners.

When the Uprising took place, in February 1904, Russia was already racked by the political cancer which would lead inexorably through cycles of repression, concession, vacillation and indecision to the downfall of the Tsar. As one of the Tsar's ministers characterised that bitter and tumultuous period, 'The paralytics in the Government are struggling feebly, indecisively, as if unwillingly, with the epileptics of the revolution.' The Tsar himself commented spitefully to his mother that 'ninety per cent of our revolutionaries are Yids', but as it happens only about half of the fifty-one men and seven women who took part in the Uprising were Jewish. Most were in their mid-twenties. All were well armed.

The Uprising was, or more accurately was contrived as, a protest against a series of long-standing grievances about the exiles' treatment, ranging from restrictions on their movement through forced resettlement in remote tribal communities to censorship of their mail – grievances which became more pronounced under the harsh regime of Eastern Siberia's tough new Governor, Count Kutaisov. The exiles barricaded themselves in the house of a local merchant, Nicolai Romanov (at the time no one seems to have found anything odd in the fact that he shared the name of the much reviled Tsar), and proclaimed with gusto to the small snowy world around them that they would stay there until their grievances were resolved. Clearly they were deliberately courting confrontation, and after nearly a week of stand-off and provocative exchanges with the Town Governor and the Chief of Police, whose Cossack troops encircled the building, someone inside fired. Two soldiers died in the snow. The Cossacks retaliated, as the protesters wanted them to, by spraying the Romanovka with bullets. One of the protesters died. The group had its token martyr and two days later they surrendered. What followed, a saga of swingeing prison sentences, appeals, courtroom dramas, a daring tunnel escape from jail and an eventual free pardon from a tottering regime in a fit of weakness, is a story all of its own, the telling of which would divert us too far from Elliott's story. But the tailpiece does bring us back, first to my mother and then to Elliott himself. Having narrowly avoided death or a long spell in prison, you might have thought that David Redstone would have called it quits. But revolutionaries, even soft-centred Mensheviks, never do, and a few months later Redstone and several other Romanovka veterans reappeared 400 miles to the east in Chita.

Though the revolution came first, Redstone at least had the excuse of having fallen in love with a girl from the Chita region, who wanted to move back towards home after working as a nurse in Irkutsk, where she had looked after him while he was in the prison hospital with typhoid. She was one of the twelve children of a Cossack merchant in Nerchinsky, on the Argun River, 200 miles west of Chita. As she told us many years later, 'If you rolled out of our house down the river bank, you'd land in Mongolia.' Papa Flegontov must have been in a reasonable way of business. She remembered a household of twelve servants, 'one for each child', but out there that was less likely to have been some grand *Upstairs, Downstairs* establishment than a sprawling extended family of serfs, peasant girls and distant, simple-minded cousins with recessive genes doubling as wetnurses and nannies. Flegontov traded fox, marten and squirrel pelts and bearskins from the Buryat tribesmen in exchange for bolts of cloth, tools and glass ornaments. If his luck was in (and the animals' out), he was sometimes able to get the highly prized furs of the sable, tracked through the mountains by the tribesmen and their dogs. Two or three times a year, he would travel, in winter with laden sledges, in summer leading a train of horses, to the great trading fairs, teeming with men and animals from Chita, Mongolia, Siberia and Russia itself. At the summer fairs in Arginskaya, near Chita, and Spaso Preobrazhenie, there would be camel trains, thousands of tons of tea and spices, piles of precious furs, and bundles of the yellowing deer antlers much prized by the Chinese as an aphrodisiac, and felicitously known in the local dialect as 'panty'. In the winter, the traders gathered round braziers at the fair in Verkhneudinsk (whose two hotels, the *Railway Gazetteer* warned fastidiously, 'are under the management of Jews').

Chita was altogether much less of a raw frontier outpost and more like a real town, given life by the daily tooting transfusions of the Trans-Siberian railway. Once a clutch of dirty peasant hovels, it had been transformed in 1825 by the arrival of the princely families exiled after the Decembrist revolution and, as the century opened, it had 11,000 inhabitants, two hotels (with 'very bad' accommodation) and a vast stone cathedral commemorating the Tsar's visit in 1891. More to the point, Chita held real attractions and challenges for the revolutionaries as the headquarters of the Tsarist regional administration and of two Cossack regiments. Disgruntled workers could be found in plenty at the town's tanneries, the soap factory and the mills. In the surrounding countryside, credulous iron-ore miners and peasants could easily be brought to believe by sharp-minded orators that they harboured justifiable grievances against the Tsar, capitalist owners and landlords. As the plotters realised, even a temporary disruption of life and routine would deal a heavy blow to the vital railway lifeline between Russia and its troops fighting in the Far East. Redstone intrigued, wrote polemical, but irredeemably intellectual, pieces for the *Transbaikal Worker* underground news-sheet, and helped operate a basement press producing subversive pamphlets, which he and his friends distributed around the town by night. By October 1905, the revolutionary cells in the town were ready for action. It began when another of the Romanovka group, Kostya Kalyuzhanich, led a group of workers in a raid on the railway's armoury, stealing, according to the official report, nearly 800 rifles. Telegraph lines were cut. Printing works were taken over to roll out still more revolutionary broadsheets. The first local revolutionary 'Soviet', or Council of Cossacks and soldiers, proclaimed its shaky existence. In December, the local police were disarmed by the revolutionaries. The streets filled with demonstrators, many armed with the railway's rifles. But the troops who had backed the Soviet began to wobble, and in January 1906 the short-lived 'Chita Republic' was snuffed out by two punitive expeditions, which retook control of the city without much resistance. The Soviet dissolved in sad recrimination.

In 1907, my grandparents and their first daughter made their way, somehow (the trail is forever blurred), to Harwich, on England's east coast. David Redstone joined his brother in a small cigarette manufacturing business, financed by a blind Greek tobacco merchant who 'liked the sound of our voices'. He must have had a little money by 1908, since, when Maria became pregnant again, he arranged for her to have a private bed and doctor at the London Hospital in Whitechapel Road. When the birth pains came, David was away. Maria took a horse-drawn cab to the hospital, across the street from The Blind Beggar pub (which in the 1960s became, for the unlamented Kray brothers and their hangers-on, the sort of in-crowd watering-hole that White's provided in wartime for SOE and SIS). In an émigré nightmare, unable to speak more than the odd word of very odd English, she found herself totally unable to explain to the forbidding, overworked duty nurses that a bed had been booked and arrangements made with a doctor whose name she could not have pronounced even had she remembered it. In a babble of mutual incomprehension, the nurses hustled her to the public ward. For the rest of her life she remembered the straw on the floor, the gaslights, the dirt and the feeling of being very far from home. When a chastened David Redstone came to see her and the baby the next day, she told him she had had enough. She and the children (she named the new baby Sonia) were going back to Russia. If he wanted to come too, so much the better, but they were going anyway. And back they went, dropping almost out of sight in Chita until 1917. Though there is no evidence on the point, it is quite likely that Redstone's return to Russia was promoted less by Maria's unhappiness than by the groundswell of feeling among Russian exiles at all points on the revolutionary spectrum that now was the time for all good men to come to the aid of the Party. From Lenin and Trotsky down to the humble foot soldiers such as Redstone, they went back to pull down the last bricks of the tottering edifice.

The only evidence left from those missing years is a pair of studio photographs of Redstone's two daughters taken in 1915 by Konovalov of Chita: middle-class girls, in matching dark smocks and lace collars; a gravity even then, a sense of caution in their steady gaze, reflecting an adult awareness of the fragility of their lives and times. As 1917 began, the wartime shortages in Moscow and St Petersburg brought strikes, disorder and the abdication of the Tsar. The self-appointed Provisional Government of the charismatic but ineffective wordsmith Aleksandr Kerensky promised reform, not revolution.

In far-away Chita, as Redstone's elder daughter Nina recalled in a BBC television programme in the 1980s, 'Life was very dull. To the peasants the Tsar was still the Little Father, and whatever had gone wrong, they didn't blame him, though they hated the Tsarina . . . . We were liberal. I was brought up to believe in the freedom of the individual, the right to express yourself.' Kerensky's Government was doomed to fail; a commitment to keep Russia in the war and a stonewalling of law reform were hardly vote-winning platforms against the simple ferocity of Lenin and the Bolsheviks, whose punchy promise was 'Bread, Peace, Land,' and who did not put much faith in votes anyway. Kerensky drowned in his own rhetoric, but in those early months of 1917, and in Nina Redstone's eleven-year-old world, 'we shouted revolutionary slogans, had parties, everyone congratulating each other that the revolution was here at last. At school we sang revolutionary songs . . . though I didn't know what all the words meant. Everything was absolutely marvellous . . . for about six months.' The Redstones sniffed the wind and scented real trouble ahead. It was time to go; this time for ever.

As the war fronts crumbled, hundreds of thousands of peasant soldiers began to melt away confused, badly led, egged on by rabble-rousers who urged them to get back to their villages to share in the much-rumoured carve-up of the great estates. The so-called Soviets or 'Councils' began to take the reins of government out of the hands of the Tsar's officials. Redstone left first, ahead of his family, warned that in the uncomradely settling of scores that was beginning to unfold, Social Democrats and Mensheviks such as he were a high-priority target for elimination by their Bolshevik opponents, far more determined and ruthless than the Tsar's police had ever been. He went to Harbin, that artificial Russian enclave in the north of Manchuria, a Slav oasis in a yellow desert of Chinese created to service the extension of the Trans-Siberian railway. As if trapped on a slowly-sinking *Titanic*, the bands of Harbin played on while remnants of Tsarist society clung desperately to the old forms of life. Operas, theatres, genteel finishing schools, bowing, scraping, bearded lips brushing ladies' pale fingers, from which, as the months went by, the rings steadily disappeared into the hands of pawn-brokers and money-lenders. Maria and the children followed a week or so later, with what little money they had tucked into baby Valentin's thick swaddling clothes, taking the risk that the surly border guards would never dream of searching an obviously ailing infant. Thousands were trying to make the same journey: deserting soldiers, families, mothers, grandmothers, businessmen, sweating officials. Chita's station, low built, in a vaguely classical style, was an opened anthill: scurrying, pushing, yelling people clutching boxes, cases and cloth-wrapped bundles. Sometimes the trains came. If they didn't, or you could not get on, you squatted and waited, moving closer to the rails and the trains' deadly wheels; the Trans-Siberian's engineers seem not to have believed in the raised platforms beloved of British railway designers. Desperate passengers filled compartments until they overflowed. Then ten more would push their way in. People cursed, fought, bribed and suffocated. Maria saw a flimsy iron service ladder leading to the carriage roof. Valentin under her arm, she shooed Nina and Sonia up, and passed first the baby, then their rope-wrapped cases, up to Nina, whose eleven-year-old arms suddenly developed strength and sinews born of sheer terror. They all scrambled to take a precarious hold on the soot-covered, slatted walkway running along the roof. Nina recalls, 'There were hundreds of thousands of deserting soldiers . . . the train moved off and we were on the roof for what seemed like for ever, although it was probably only a few hours. I was so petrified I don't remember how long. We lay there with our mother sort of spread-eagled over us. Eventually some people in the carriages made room and began to haul us in through the windows.'

In England, Redstone helped his brother Shia build the business, which they named Balkan Sobranie. He criss-crossed England by rail and bus selling the product while his brother ran the factory and worried about the money. He knew practically every high-class tobac-conist – that soon-to-be-extinct breed, those Angel Botibols, Weingotts and Sullivan Powells of long ago – up and down the British Isles and he was in turn known by those courtly retailers (who today would be vili-fied as merchants of death) as Uncle David. As he opened his suitcase of samples, the heady aromas would fill the shop. Plump Turkish ciga-rettes, sold by the hundred in porcelain boxes which are now collectors' pieces. Oval Egyptian. Long cigarettes in the style of Russian *papirosi*, whose cardboard mouthpieces had been originally designed to cool the smoke for the sensitive throat of the singer Chaliapin; he gave Redstone a signed photograph wishing 'all success to your superb business'. The Black Russian brand, whose gold-leaf tips left a more elegant stain on the fingers than nicotine, and whose dark tobacco provided its own remedy against excessive consumption; more than two in succession had a markedly laxative effect on the system. On the box, where today some futile health warning would be printed, was a heavily embossed Tsarist double-headed eagle. For many years the cigarettes were hand-rolled in a City Road factory by cheery, aproned and kerchiefed ladies from the East End, later partly replaced by an impersonal but more efficient Molins machine. The business then had some success with a line of 'Cocktail' Virginia cigarettes wrapped in a variety of bright-hued papers. Aimed principally at ladies who wanted what they smoked to match their dresses, they also enjoyed a certain *éclat* among the male theatrical community.

The Redstone home was cramped, comfortable and carcinogenic, a nicotine necropolis. David wreathed in a blue Turkish haze, Maria puffing at whatever came to hand. If Nina was there, she would add to the fug by chain-smoking Players Weights, loading and re-loading from the cheap white packets with the reflex precision of Burt Lancaster fighting off the Clantons at the OK Corral. Visitors smoked. Teenagers smoked; we were encouraged to help ourselves from a suitcase in the spare bedroom full of samples of every current and past Sobranie brand. Had the Redstones been a pet family, the cats and canaries would surely have smoked too. The curtains and the moquette upholstery were cured like best bacon and on a clear day the nicotine pall around the house was probably a landmark for aircraft approaching Heathrow. What the hell, it was after all the family business. The case full of cigarettes lay next to a paper-wrapped box tied with several strands of heavy white string containing the now worthless Tsarist banknotes and coins they had brought out of Russia. Behind the smoke, Redstone the revolutionary mellowed into the man of family. Nina, a terrier with ferocious energy, went off to work as a secretary, married her boss and lived happily ever after. Towards the end of her life she was much in demand as a Russian-speaking caller, telephoning psychiatric hospitals and prisons across the Soviet Union to let the commandants know that Amnesty International had its beady eye on them and their prisoners. Sonia was far less focused. She trained as a beautician, learned how to make hats, and was twenty-five when, in 1933, Elliott's lanky shadow fell across her path. The circle was closed. Balkan Sobranie met Balkan Joe.

# 15

# His Bonnet in Germany

Whatever Elliott found, didn't find, thought he had found, or thought he had lost when he came back from 'Spangers' in 1945, he didn't enjoy the experience. Nor is it a surprise, then, that when Antony Terry suggested a way of returning to the despised 'Goonland' as a minor form of conquering hero, he jumped at the chance as rapidly, and with as little forethought, as when he had jumped out of the Whitley in 1942. Terry was already back in Germany, helping root out for the Nuremberg Trials the evidence to be used against those Nazis already in custody, and the clues to the whereabouts of the nervous majority of middle-ranking thugs and villains who, apprehensive but unrepentant, had slipped furtively back into an equally unrepentant and uncommunicative community.

Whatever job he offered to Elliott would have come as a marked improvement on the snivelling children and the voluble tea-swilling, chain-smoking Slav in-laws carrying on with the voluble verve of a Ukrainian town meeting. So it was an easy choice: back to state secrets and duty-free State Express, back with the lads and, as always, a clutch of adoring, compliant lasses. Psychologically reinvigorated by reinstatement in his wartime rank as a major in the Intelligence Corps, Elliott was part of the British element of the Allied Control Commission in Germany. In the lunar landscape of defeat, the Commission had a huge task. Britain alone sent 25,000 civil servants, lawyers, administrators, businessmen, engineers and intelligence agents, and the US 7,000, into a shattered Germany to do it. The country had to be pulled back together from the ruins from which weeds, bones and broken pipes sprouted in surreal profusion. Food. Fuel. Clothing. Schools. Hospitals. Transport. Each was a strident priority. The whole fabric of society had to be re-woven. At the human level, one-quarter of the homes were completely uninhabitable and most of the rest were rubble-strewn, windowless, waterless wrecks. Dispossessed and still disbelieving Germans, hundreds of thousands of refugees, former prisoners and deserters, scavenged the land in medieval misery. Every adult had to be screened for the stains of Nazi involvement – not for nothing was the coveted de-nazification certificate known as a 'Persil ticket' – sorted for interrogation and, if necessary, hauled before a court (or, in more cases than anyone now cares to admit, carefully safeguarded for later use on the side of the West in the already looming struggle of the Cold War). Out of the woodwork swarmed, as in France, untold numbers who proclaimed themselves long-time resisters *in pectore*, if not in deed. Black marketeers, many of them members of the Allied forces, minted minor fortunes out of misery.

The myth was one of a hard-fought victory by the yeomen and bowmen of little England for freedom, warm beer, pork pies and the little Princesses over the goose-stepping battalions of evil cruelty, pickled cabbage, beer bellies bulging over leather trousers and all that regimented rallying. The reality was that, once past the euphoria, the British had emerged, but only with the help of the United States, morally and physically on the winning side, but by most longer-term economic yardsticks the losers. One-third of the UK's overseas assets had been sold to help pay the cost of the war, and its overseas income had been halved. It had run up huge debts to the US and the Empire, and its manufacturing base was antiquated. Germany, though smashed psychologically, had lost only about one-quarter of its industrial equipment under the hail of Allied bombs; even though Russian theft on a massive scale had removed whole factories and assembly lines, the fixed assets of German industry in 1946 were greater than ten years previously. The country was at a standstill – reviled, shell-shocked, resentful and horrified – but all the conditions for a massive economic recovery, at least in what was to become West Germany, were in place.

Almost ninety per cent of its mines and steel plants were relatively unscathed, and when peace broke out German factories held higher levels of raw materials than those in Britain. Even in the short-term, Britain seems to have lost out on the Occupation; the costs of maintaining its huge presence in Germany far outweighed any recompense it obtained through reparations. In May 1946, Dr Hugh Dalton, as Chancellor, told his Cabinet colleagues that against a cost of £31 million to administer the loser's ruined country and feed its people, Britain had received less than £2 million in compensation.

However, Elliott was not one for Keynesian musings on the economic consequences of the peace. His job was to investigate the Deutsche Arbeitsfront, the DAF, or Labour Front, which, despite its original professed role as a godfather to labour, actually ended up owning a vast jigsaw of commercial enterprises inside and outside Germany. In an early object lesson in Nazi techniques of smash and grab, ignored as so often by the rest of the world, the DAF had thrust itself to the fore in 1933 through a miniature coup d'état, seizing the German Trades Union headquarters and confiscating its funds. In 1934, Hitler formally affiliated the DAF to the Nazi Party, whereupon it promptly proclaimed itself to be a compulsory state union of both workers and employers. All other unions were suppressed, and the once-powerful and independent employers' associations began inexorably to be tamed into puppets of the state. The DAF was the creature of the underrated, unprepossessing but wily Robert Ley, one of Hitler's earliest henchmen, an industrial chemist with I G Farben by day, and a porky beerhall Nazi rabble-rouser by night. Control of labour would ensure an efficient and subservient workforce for the Nazi war machine. But the ideological aspects of totalitarianism were not enough for Ley, who soon became energetically entrepreneurial in exploiting the funds that DAF had seized at its illegitimate birth. He plunged the DAF into a host of business ventures.

With a reach broader than any other business combine in Germany, he made it into one of the first of the European conglomerates. In the Control Commission's preliminary evaluation, the DAF's 300 subsidiaries had total assets, in 1990s' values, of a staggering £33 billion. It owned all the Co-operative Societies' property; 50 factories, breweries, 137 distribution centres and 12,000 retail outlets. It owned building societies, banks, insurance companies, publishers, factories in Holland, oil companies in Austria and shipyards in Bulgaria. One of its crown jewels was the original 'People's Car', or Volkswagen, factory, but I can find no direct connection between Elliott's work and the 1946 memorandum by a Colonel Boas of the Commission of Whitehall suggesting presciently that Volkswagen should be taken over by the British auto industry. After consulting the industry's myopic dinosaurs – where are they now, those Austins, Armstrong-Siddeleys, low Standards and hollow Triumphs of long ago? – the Board of Trade in London concluded that the idea was not worth pursuing, since the Beetle design had little future. SOE had no monopoly on short-term thinking.

Elliott was told, 'the extent of the properties owned by the DAF, the widespread and conflicting claims thereto, arising both inside and outside Germany, and the practical problems in connection with food distribution, housing and banking created by its dissolution, call for urgent action,' action made even more pressing by a real concern that, despite the surrender, the DAF's overseas assets and some of its key officials might form the nucleus of an attempt at a Nazi revival. The official files provide a less than clear picture of Elliott's role as this 'urgent action' unfolded. On the one hand, he is the peripatetic bureaucrat, jolting – as a victor rather than a prisoner, and no doubt with a perfectly justifiable touch of sardonic *Schadenfreude* – between Cologne, Hamburg, Berlin and other rubble scrapheaps of the Reich, sprawled in the back of one of the Commission's often malfunctioning Wolseleys, helping to assemble 287 crates of DAF records. The negotiator bickering with the Americans about who should have custody of them. The administrator worrying about keeping the DAF's Co-operative shops alive so that food could reach a starving population. But at the same time the professional intelligence man, interrogating DAF leaders and tracking one of them, hiding under a false name in a displaced persons camp, by intercepting a postcard foolishly sent to a DAF secretary. Later, the cool businessman immersed in the records themselves, writing the succinct memoranda of an effective executive who understands the complex accounting material well.

The general flavour of the files of the DAF Branch of the Commission is far more that of an administrative machine than of an intelligence outstation. But tacked without explanation on the back of one of the routine memoranda which flowed to and fro, is an organisation chart with a less routine, more curious flavour. Embroidered with names that might have been invented by Beatrix Potter or Ian Fleming – Captain Squirrel, Miss

Hunnybun – the chart shows that the Branch had three sections. The first dealt mainly with the overall task of dissolving the DAF and analysing its records. A second focused on denazification, 'Policy, Inspection, Interrogation'. A third is designated baldly as Intelligence, with all the trappings of the trade – an Information Room, a Librarian, a Map Section. Elliott is shown within it as responsible for Frankfurt and Berlin. What this seems to mean, though one cannot be certain, is that within the relatively straightforward work of the DAF Branch, Elliott and others were looking rather more closely, and perhaps with other, unseen, customers in mind in London, at anything and anyone of likely intelligence interest, especially Germans who in the post-war world might aspire, or be encouraged to aspire, to leadership in the new, purged labour and trade union movement. One of the DAF files suggests that even then a *soupçon* of Nazi Party involvement might not be an absolute bar to work in the movement if the man or woman was otherwise the right person for the job. Much work had to be done on the origin of the DAF's assets. Which were stolen by force from Jews or the conquered nations? Did some otherwise innocuous business deal provide interesting leads to trade between neutral countries and the Germans? Were there areas of industrial or scientific research that might be appropriated to Allied benefit? Whatever the job was, it changed after Elliott had been in Germany for about seven months. He stayed on, according to the War Office records, for another six months or so attached to a unit identified only as Special Operation 3, but of what he did, and where, there is no evidence.

There is, though, evidence of something else behind the files. Not a torrid love affair, no more than the close affection and respect, the *amitié amoureuse*, of two people from, on the face of it, very different backgrounds, but beneath that face both bright, iconoclastic and bold.

In an early browse through the Commission's staff list, I had noted with mild amusement that Elliott's nominal and perhaps real boss had been a woman, a Civil Service principal named only as 'Miss H. Makower' with the acting rank of colonel. Reporting to a woman, I speculated, hair in a bun, sensible shoes and a brisk way with line-shooting playboys, must have struck Elliott as on a par with saluting German officers. But I had no reason to think any more about it. Until, as the exhumation was almost at an end, the soil already thumping wetly on the coffin lid, and well after I had tracked down two subsequent mistresses and a second wife, serendipity decided to give me another nudge, putting into my hands three battered volumes: the *Oxford Books* of Russian, German and French verse. Elliott had kept them by him to the end of his life. Halfway round the world and back, shielded from bailiffs and the prying eyes of girlfriends, wives and children. On the flyleaf of the Russian volume I was jolted to see the ownership inscription 'H. Makower, 1931'. A quick check of my amateur card index made the Commission connection. Beneath, the same neat hand had written: 'Given to K. J. Elliott 1945 because it is one of the few things I have I really like.' Dated just a few days after his birthday, is it proof of love? Certainly not, but certainly an indication that the relationship was more than formal. And taken with the two other contemporaneous inscriptions, a suggestion of considerable affection, even hero-worship.

In the French volume, Elliott is hailed as 'Kavan, who for the sake of us that waited in safety risked and endured beyond understanding', to which Miss Makower has added Goethe's tag that '*Nur allein der Mensch, Vermag das Unmögliche*' ('only Man could achieve the impossible').

Inappropriately for a language so formal and structured, the inscription in the *Book of German Verse* suggests an admiring tease of her dashing demigod of a subordinate, a daring war behind him and a musky whiff, like expensive aftershave, of the world of agents, parachute drops by moonlight, nasty times with the Gestapo. 'To Kavan, who claims to be thirty-seven but who looks twenty-three', she wrote and, having used a German quote in the French volume, the inscription here seems to have been a very free translation of a Latin verse. 'I hate your vulgar epic', she penned, 'and have no taste for roads where crowds litter and I litter haste. Home the vagrant loves, and from the public springs . . . I drink not all common things.' The translation is actually so free that it is incomprehensible; the sort of effort for which thirty years ago one would deservedly fail Common Entrance, but which, outside Oxford, would today be thought good enough for an honours degree on the grounds that the candidate could at least do joined-up writing. I have no proof, but equally no doubt, that it was to Helen, his polyglot bluestocking boss, that Elliott dedicated that commanding studio photograph in December 1945. I also suspect that while she liked and admired him, intelligence and commonsense gave Helen Makower the X-ray vision and the sixth sense to see what lay beneath Elliott's barathea and the medal ribbons and pull up well short of any entanglement.

She had a remarkable life. Born in Chiswick, the daughter of a barrister, in a family which can trace its roots, via Switzerland, back to eighteenth-century Poland, she was a brilliant student, a senior civil servant, including a spell in Churchill's wartime office, a lecturer at the London School of Economics and, when she got tired of lecturing, an indefatigable and courageous smuggler of Bibles from Hong Kong into Communist China, a voluntary assignment for which she learned Chinese to match her Russian, French and German. When I met her, late in her life and in the life of this work, her memory had been eroded by the intervening years, and I could not fathom what Elliott really meant, if anything, to her. That he had kept her books suggests that she meant something to him, which given her grace and talent is not surprising.

At a more mundane level, back in England, my mother announced out of the blue that we were moving house. No more going away to school, no more Dr Morgan. *Auf Wiedersehen* to Appenrodt. Goodbye to Grodzinski. On with the English motley, to Purley we would go, to wallow in its suburban leafiness. My mother might just as well have said Pernambuco, and I had to look it up on a railway map. As she explained it to me and my round-eyed sisters, a friend of my father's had suggested a far better school for me – a public school (this said in tones of some awe, my sisters' eyes grew rounder), though lacking the real cachet of a boarding-school. This was in Croydon, about fifteen miles south of London; in a way it was also of Croydon, or even personified Croydon itself, since 400 years of shrewd land accumulation and investment by generations of clerics and local businessmen serving as governors had made the school the town's largest landowner. Our new Purley home was only two consecutive bus journeys away; its four bedrooms and larch-lined garden, with the tottering remnants of a chicken coop and a vegetable patch, made it seem like Chatsworth compared to the flat on the Hendon Way with its vista over the roof of the Blue Star garage.

After a minor hiccup, when Whitgift wrote to say that I had failed the entrance examination, but followed this with a note almost by the next post to say that they would take me anyway, I began, like John Betjeman's Uncle Dick, several years of journeys:

> Satchel on back
> To Whitgift
> Every weekday morn . . .

David and Maria Redstone: from Siberia ...

... to the Savoy

Colonel Hudson
(left, in Chetnik dress),
a Montenegrin veteran
and General Mihailovic,
1942

Elliott under Croat
interrogation,
February 1942

Spangenberg Castle: Oflag IX A/H – Elliott's 'home away from home', 1942–5

My mother, Sonia, 1940

Elliott and his mother,
Walburga, in about 1936

Kavan and Sonia Elliott

Elliott and an uncomfortable
author, 1940

Glamorous grandmother:
Walburga Rice in about 1900

Ethel and Kavan Elliott

Kavan, Ethel and Leo Elliott, 1916

The Romanovka House, Yakutsk, after the siege

The Romanovka Group and their lawyers, Irkutsk, 1904. David Redstone is second from the right in the first standing row

Sir Dick White, Director of MI5, later Chief of SIS

Antony Terry

Elliott at rest …

.. and at play, 1952

Away to the races: Elliott (second right) with Jamaican Premier Bustamente and friends, in about 1953

The last lap, Berkshire, 1970s

Unlike pedestrian Dick, I took the 234 bus followed by the 197 or 109, reversing the sequence each afternoon. Betjeman tells us that dear old Dick liked the school, and enjoyed his carefree after-hours life black-berrying and all that good healthy stuff in the nearby North Downs countryside, where nowadays hollow-eyed perverts roam in iridescent shell suits and the grassy knolls are studded with rusty waste and sexual detritus. Each to his own. I can't say I either enjoyed or positively dis-liked school. It was something one did from 9 a.m. until 3.30 p.m., and I just assumed that everyone else, staff included, felt as solitary and bored as I did. Whitgift was a well-meaning moderately efficient machine for educating with Christian moderation the moderate sons of the north Surrey bourgeoisie. Most boys drifted placidly enough from year to year; the school, probably rightly, reserved the full force of its support and encouragement for the handful of boys who were of exceptional academic distinction, or who displayed beefy prowess at the cold, wet team games by which the school set so much store, a prowess curiously closely correlated with confused adolescent sexuality. Something to do, perhaps, with showers and shorts. The rest of us, the pimply lumpen-proletariat, were left to muddle along in tranquil obscurity, piping at morning prayers from the unashamedly elitist *Public Schools Hymn Book*. 'Lead us Heavenly Father, lead us, Over Life's Tempestuous Sea,' we chanted, our parents dreaming that over the sea lay respectable, steady employment as bank managers, town clerks, oil executives or solicitors. We were not, by and large, destined to be rulers of Empire. But against the day we might have to defend it, we dressed up in thick khaki uni-forms to parade with the Cadet Force on Tuesday afternoons, learned how to handle an oily Lee-Enfield rifle and how to burnish a boot with the handle of a toothbrush and melted polish. We paddled towards puberty in a pool of mild smut, stimulated by the carefully airbrushed nudes in *Health and Efficiency* and *Lilliput*. How curious that as old age approaches, it is advertisements for large estates in *Country Life*, or *Demeures et Chateaux*, or for used corporate jets in *AC Flyer*, which tend to make the juices flow. The writer Kingsley Amis, who grew up on the other side of Croydon, noted regretfully that he 'nearly got into Whitgift', but had to settle for the City of London School. I have no doubt he and British literature are better off as a result.

Who was the friend of Elliott who recommended Whitgift? And was it the same friend who perhaps exerted influence to get me in after my distraught mother had been told of my abject failure in the entrance exam? (Dr Morgan's seaside academy had made no educative impression on me, maybe because I didn't care for it, and maybe also because in those balmy days before the healthcare system became properly organised, no one had bothered to test my eyesight. It was only at the medical examination for Whitgift that I was revealed to be grotesquely astigmatic and thus incapable of reading unaided anything smaller than block letters. A bottle-lens for my left eye did the trick for my vision, if less for my self-esteem, but a few years of textbooks had passed me by in a grey blur which had never struck me as abnormal.) No 'friend' ever actually appeared on the scene, nor do I remember him ever being talked about again. The death in 1993 of Sir Dick White, the professional intelligence executive who rose to head first the Security Service and then SIS, prevented me from prodding him any further to answer – why should he have? – a letter from me enquiring whether he in fact had been the missing link. Before the war, White had been a Master at Whitgift, and so knew the school and its authorities well. After the war, White's path crossed with Elliott's, as we shall see later. Is it plausible that Elliott, casting around for ways to educate and above all to anglicise his son, would have asked for the view of a man who was at the time giving him careful advice on a difficult and emotional issue, a man whom he respected, a man with direct teaching experience? And equally plausible that White would have recommended the school he knew well, and which was not, in any case, a bad choice given the realities? A nice, unprovable thought, on which the school archives are silent.

Nineteen forty-seven was one of the vilest British winters on record. Vile for hungry adults, vile for power-cut, supply-short businesses. Everything and everybody froze to a halt. 'Starve with Strachey, Shiver with Shinwell', the Conservatives, now out of power, taunted Labour's new Ministers of Food and Fuel. But not vile at all for children seeing for the first time the quiet magic of deep snow and silent streets, barred by drifts and the eerie absence of transport from even thinking about going to school.

Elliott was around then, briefly. Were they dreams, or were they real, those hazy memories of floating up momentarily, cold-nosed, out of sleep to hear muffled shouting from downstairs? One voice booming, the other shrill. Then, in the white light of morning, watching entranced, oblivious to the numb cold of the house, as Elliott painted huge and meticulously limned Disney caricatures on the playroom wall, conjuring comic-book magic out of a few small pots of paint, with the skill of the wartime 'nose artists' of the US air force, who used to paint Flying Fortresses with leggy images of Betty Grable or a shower of bombs falling on a skulking Hitler. Elliott showing me, God knows why, that it was much easier to overpower an enemy who stuck his pistol in the small of your back than if he stood back a pace or two. He got me to play the heavy. Nervously I jabbed a water-pistol in his spine. Elliott whirled like a cat, his hand simultaneously darting behind his back to grab the pistol. The trick, he carefully explained, was to play the gun, not the man, to jam your hand tightly over the top. 'That way, with a revolver you can stop the cylinder turning, and with an automatic you've got a good chance of stopping the slide. On a real gun, that's the part at the top here,' he pointed out helpfully. 'But it isn't the gun that's important,' he said seriously, 'it's whose finger's on the trigger.' A fine, if recherché, principle to leave in the doughy mind of an impressionable youngster. (The only time in my life I had a gun pointed at me in anger, it was a .375 Magnum held a careful three feet from my forehead at 2 a.m. When, in a fit of folly and fury and not remembering Elliott's lesson, I went for the throat of the balaclava-shrouded Italian who was holding it, he smacked me and then my wife very painfully over the head with it, before he and his three partners stole everything we had. The $1,000 a day we were paying to stay in the Hotel Villa San Michele in Fiesole had included continental breakfast, but this nocturnal irruption by the local *banditti* was by way of an à la carte extra; as our blood mingled on the flagstones rather like some rather extreme gypsy wedding, there seemed something appropriate in the fact that we were lodged in the Medici Suite.)

In a more normal family setting, I might have been given insights into music and literature, the finer points of cricket, even shrewd comments on business. But we take what we get and we get what we deserve. I thought nothing more of the advice, until I began to put down these memories of Elliott. Then, by chance, I saw for sale in an auction catalogue a bulky file in which Ian Fleming had recorded fragments of plot ideas, character sketches and coolhand quotes, many of which he later wove into his James Bond books. One of them was virtually word for word what I remembered Elliott telling me on the stairs all those years ago. I can only speculate that at some stage in their intelligence careers, both had heard this sort of maxim from a training instructor. It is just the sort of macho homily beloved of a pot-bellied but still stone-tough street-fighter rejoicing in the arcane rank of Corporal of Horse, who gave lessons in weaponcraft and unarmed combat, 'Go for the eyes, then kick 'em in the balls', is one I remember from my own rites of passage, along with other nuggets of sage, if not widely applicable, advice about how to use hot radiators, army steel wardrobes and radio static to good effect in extracting answers to questions without leaving marks.

Good moments and bad. Elliott dancing round with my younger sister singing, 'A she's Adorable, B she's so Beautiful, C she's a Cuty full of charms', or the nonsense patter of 'Mairsie Doats and Dosie Doats, and Little Lambs Itivy'. Fun and games with the water-taps. When the sun went in, the cold anger. One of my sister's favourite dolls thrown into the kitchen boiler: 'Give it here, it's an absolutely filthy thing, and besides, there's no such thing as a boy doll.' And Elliott one day brandishing what looked like one of my mother's crochet hooks, though made of flat blued steel with a wooden handle. Outside the front door, I watched puzzled as he pushed another straight piece of metal into the Yale lock, explaining that he was 'creating the tension', then thrust the hook carefully in and out of the keyhole, sometimes pushing up, sometimes rocking it energetically to and fro until suddenly the lock clicked and the door swung open. He was justifiably proud, but became quickly bored when my own fumbling efforts failed miserably to produce anything more than scratches on the lock's brass surface. How hard, if briefly, he was trying to reach out. How dumb I was not to be able to respond.

One day he was there, the next he was gone again. No goodbyes. No explanations. 'It's his job,' my mother said. I was never conscious of a moment at which I knew for sure that was it, that he wasn't coming back. Even into my late teens, when I knew about the divorce, his remarriage and all of that, there were moments when I could convince myself, either that I would soon be sent for, like a suddenly remembered suitcase to be retrieved from the dusty recesses of the left luggage office at Waterloo Station, or that he would come back. Purley, Whitgift, my sisters' own very English new schools too, were I suppose all part of an attempt on his part to wean us away from the introverted Slav world north of the Thames, which after so much closeness during the war and in the following years was, he must have felt, about to absorb us totally in its smoky foreignness. And who is to say he wasn't basically right to try? Although he was not around to see the result, it was largely successful, although it was an uncomfortably schizophrenic process.

South of the border, down Purley way, we played by conventional English rules. The school's annual performance of Gilbert and Sullivan operettas. Stereotyped radio comedies from which we culled and wore to death a litany of meaningless catchphrases. The hit parade of records crackling from far away Radio Luxembourg with its flavour of mild illegality. How hard to credit, in the days of rock groups named after every well-used part of the body and most sexual dysfunctions, that considerable popularity once attached to bands of elderly Jewish musicians led by fat middle-aged men named Cyril, Joe, Edmundo or Ambrose, with their roster of second-rate vocalists, shiny suits, shaky mid-Atlantic accents for the males, beehive hair and Doris Day smiles for the chunky girls. Wails of worship over the airwaves for Dicky, Lonnie, Alma, Lita and Helen. Collecting in a small ledger in an early and surrealistically pointless example of *das Ding an Sich* the numbers neatly printed in white on the red-painted bonnets of a bewildering range of different makes and styles of bus. A short-lived passion for following cricket scores in interminable detail (games as such I avoided like the plague, and once, in an unconscious emulation of my father's forgery of his record of music lessons, put a fine version of my mother's hand into a brief but compelling and not wholly implausible note about groin strain which took me out of gym classes for a whole blissful term). The tear-jerking theatricalities of the Coronation in 1953, seen in minuscule black and white on a friend's new TV. 'Who is that small fellow sitting next to the Queen of Tonga?' a commentator asked Noël Coward. 'Her lunch?' the Master drawled. Lonely as a cloud, I roamed my neighbourhood on a blue Hercules bicycle, making the first timorous contacts with girls from the local High School. Adolescent blood surged, hair threatened to sprout on sweaty palms, in pathetic response to those coy air-brushed nudes on the pages of *Lilliput*. How tame they were compared to the in-your-face obstetrics now available alongside *House and Garden* at every corner newsagent.

For my sisters, there was netball, Brownies, marching in to assembly two by pigtailed two to the ultra-English strains of Percy Grainger.

Our friends had fathers who went off in bowler hats and stiff collars on the morning trains. We had no father to parade, but that could be glossed over – first steps in deceit – by boasting about his unspecified but surely glamorous life abroad. In that prim and nosy community, it was more difficult to explain away the manifest lack of money and my mother's exuberant, un-English ways. We went to Church less out of fervour than a fervent desire to fit in, which over time we did, despite a secret fear that our essential phoniness would one day be exposed to a gloating world, by peremptory demands for proof of Englishness from the ticket collector at Purley Station.

The Thames was as real a frontier as the stretch of cracked roadway between Austria and Hungary. The journey from the orderly middle-class suburb of Purley to the accented, cosmopolitan streets of Golders Green was a couple of hours in time, but half a continent in its contrast. In the early post-war years, there were still trams, rattling and swaying from their terminus at Purley through south London to Blackfriars Bridge, and several choices of bus route. Or the train to Victoria, and a long run in the sooty warmth of the underground Northern Line, on whose platforms for years red, cast-iron vending-machines stood as empty, mute reminders of the forgotten time before sweet rationing.

After clattering in the dark past the ghostly non-station at Mornington Crescent, through Belsize Park and Hampstead, the train popped out in the light again at Golders Green, as though it had negotiated the Simplon tunnel. It wouldn't have been a shock to have been asked to show a passport. In so many ways I have better memories of my grandparents' little three-bedroomed house than I do of Purley, and David and Maria Redstone were kind, patient and loving far above the call of grand-parental duty. But children are without passion, except for their passionate interest in themselves, and I was certainly no exception. Racked by snobbery, self-doubt and even intermittent envy, since some collateral branches of the Redstone family lived in what seemed to me then considerable comfort, I saw myself, saw the Russian-ness of my mother's family, not as something exotic, interesting, a feature to be made much of, but as an embarrassing foreign stage play watched through the astonished, mocking eyes of all those English classmates down south. Who were these people, I could hear them scoff. My grand-father, though impeccably tailored, was the only bearded man I'd ever met. The English language had long since retired hurt from its vain, bruising struggle to make an impression upon my grandmother, who communicated in an excited torrent of Russian and fractured English, emphasised by waving arms and stabbing gestures, a process which reduced a succession of Irish housekeepers to gibbering incomprehension and covert appeals to my grandfather for interpretation. (A risky procedure, this, especially in my grandmother's later years, when she was given to misconstrue it as an attempt by whichever poor biddy it was to seduce my grandfather. A hissing barrage of Russian imprecations would rain upon the poor woman's head while a blameless David Redstone did his best to calm things down. Thank God the women didn't understand; when, years later, I learned the language and remembered phonetically some of her often used oaths, I was mildly surprised at the breadth, or perhaps depth, of her language, more the sort of thing to be expected from a stoker on the Trans-Siberian railway than an elderly granny.)

There was wholly different food. Breakfast meant sour rye bread and plump oily black olives, rather than Weetabix and fried bread. Tea was slurped with noisy gusto from a saucer instead of a cup, with dainty tastes of Morello cherry jam from a silver spoon. At dinner came fried fish, but astonishingly to anyone used to the hot, grease-heavy offerings of English fish and chip shops, served cold. Carp and venison, bizarre contrasts to the roast beef of old England. The cultural divide was accentuated at Easter and Christmas, always oddly unsynchronised with the high days and holy days appointed from Canterbury for conventional British worshippers. For days before the Orthodox Easter my grandmother would be dyeing hard-boiled eggs in cochineal, saffron and indigo ink, chopping cabbage and still more egg to make a deep, deeply satisfying but curiously appetising pie. She would drain curdled milk from a platoon of United Dairies glass bottles stored for a week or more in the larder. By endless straining through a muslin bag, and the addition of heavy cream, butter, eggs and raisins, this unappealing goo would be magically transformed into *Paskha*, an irresistible mega-cholesterol cream cheese pudding shaped into pyramids in a set of carved birch-wood moulds, which had travelled with her halfway around the world from Siberia. From high-sided metal dishes plopped the tall, rather dry, sponge cakes known as *Kulichi*. The meals themselves were watched over by an icon of the Mother of God Kazanskaya in a silver-gilt *oklad*, and a sepia picture of the Redstones' third child, Valentin, sad and huge-eyed, who had died of tuberculosis a few years after they reached London. In matters of religion my grandmother slightly hedged her bets in true primeval Russian tradition. God was God. No doubt of that. But there were other traduitions and superstitions to be observed and from time to time other deities whose aid could be invoked in matters of health, pregnancy and the general well-being of the household.

It would take a good, indeed very well-spent hour just to sample the starting snacks, the *Zakuski*, meat-filled pastries and pancakes, eggs, pickled cucumbers, chicken liver, salt herring, bread that was jarringly but tastily black, instead of fluffy, flavourless white, and yet more cold fish. Rivers of tea. And a permanent haze of cigarette smoke. But none of the lethal vodka toasts which traditionally fuel so much of Russian life. When there was talk of Russia, it was not of nostalgia for past Tsarist glories, or a yearning for a restoration. It was rather of a revolution which had been hijacked and betrayed by the Bolsheviks, but a revolution which had been a necessity, not an evil. In the background, scratchy gramophone recordings of Tchaikovsky, Chaliapin, or hollow reedy voices chanting Russian nursery rhymes: '*zhil byl u babushki serenki kozlik*' – 'the old granny had a little grey nanny goat'. We were diverted as children by an aluminium stereoptikon, in which yellowing daguerreotypes of Siberia, Moscow and Japan would acquire a vaguely three-dimensional aspect; my grandfather would explain patiently what we were looking at, but so foreign was it that little of his history and geography stuck in the mind. More solemnly, there were the basso profundo midnight mysteries of the Russian Orthodox Church. The one in Buckingham Palace Road for preference; the church near Hyde Park was roundly condemned by my grandmother and her kerchiefed cronies as being 'in Moscow's pocket'. We clutched candles in cardboard holders and gazed in incomprehension at the silver, gold and scarlet of the icon screen from which an unidentifiable heavenly host stared impassively down through a thicket of facial hair. At some signal unperceived by the uninitiated, my grandmother and the black ranks of dumpy, devout babushkas would prostrate themselves – foreheads touching the carpeted floor. We were left standing, like the losers in some children's party game whose rules no one had explained. As the unseen male-voice choir launched into its litanies, the Church Slavonic sentences sliding up and down the scales without a pause for breath, the spade-bearded thurifers swung their heavy silver censers and grey puffs of incense rolled over the cold floors in throat-grabbing, theatrical billows. The ladies crossed themselves with the syncopated rhythm of a battery of pious tic-tac men. I was a spectator only, a mute, nastily condescending witness of some foreign bloodsport.

The overnight switch back from this exotic and rather embarrassing ceremonial to the prosaic 1930s' cloisters of Whitgift, where classes for those about to be confirmed as members of the Church of England were conducted on behalf of a very different sort of god, by Canon Tonks, a gaitered frog with a fine line in earnest Anglican aphorisms, was as abrupt a culture shock as the three hours, twenty-seven minutes Concorde flight from New York to Paris. Confused by the two flags I flew, I was in the end never convinced I rightly belonged under either of them. In all of this, partly perhaps because of the snobbish feeling that I needed some distance between me and my roots, I never acquired a word of Russian as a child, understanding my grandmother by instinct more than linguistics. Much later, when, as a comfortable alternative to orthodox military service, I was launched into an organised, disciplined study of the language, becoming in the process fluent to a degree which surprised my teachers as much as me, I'm sure it helped that at least the sounds, the cadences, were somewhere in my head.

# 16

# Welcome to Hungary

> Love, oh love, oh careless love,
> You fly to my head like wine,
> You've ruined the life of many poor boy,
> And you almost broke this heart of mine.

There are genuine New Orleans versions of this sad old song, German versions, English suburban versions sung rather flatly by Ottilie Patterson with Chris Barber's band working valiantly at the harmonies, and for all I know versions groaned out in smoky Budapest cellars by well-meaning Bessie Smith imitators. This part of the story is about love, in part. And certainly 'careless love', verging on the reckless. It is about betrayal and disillusion. It comes, Ayckbourn-like, in a number of over-lapping versions. And even though we know a lot of the story, as I was warned when I embarked on the journey, 'Even when you have all the facts, you can't be sure you know the truth.' All the more so when the facts are those not of some world-scale drama but a minor Cold War incident. Agents blown, networks rolled up, show trials, long sentences, suspicion of betrayal. Happened all the time. 'Small cock-up in Hungary, not many dead,' Claud Cockburn might have written. And in any case those who plan secret operations, or clean up after them, take care to cover their tracks.

We are back, in fact, in Hungary, whose border we watched Elliott cross with nonchalance on that cold December morning in 1946.

Once the barrier had swung down behind it, the Studebaker rumbled comfortably into Hungary over the cobbles and clumsily patched pot-holes. The fog lifted reluctantly as though the landscape was somehow ashamed to be seen for what it really was, the junk-strewn aftermath of marauding armies. Budapest itself was less a city than a miniature alpine landscape of heaps of snow-covered bomb rubble. In between, vague shapes hinted at once substantial buildings now little more than scorched grey façades and shrapnel-pocked walls that creaked and whistled in the icy winds. Elliott was entering what its new rulers, moral swindlers on a massive scale, like all totalitarian regimes, told their people was to be the new Jerusalem. 'Enjoy the war. The peace will be terrible,' Hungarians had joked as the bombs fell and the fronts crumbled. The new terror of the peace was to last some forty years. Hungary was a proud nation, with little in its recent past to be proud about. The pain and shame of the post-Armistice amputations of land and peoples still flared along the psychic nerve-roots where its legs and arms had once been, and the Second World War caught it badly placed and morally confused. There were strong temperamental affinities between Hitler and the Hungarian leader Miklás Horthy (admiral in a land-locked country, regent of a kingdom without a royal family). Hungary was a German ally. Its industry, its mines, its farms were integrated into the Nazi war economy. Its troops fought and were slaughtered alongside the Wehrmacht in Russia, and its actual occupation, delayed until March 1944, was a peaceful affair. Asked how long it would take to occupy the country, a German general answered, 'Twenty-four hours.' 'And if they resist?' 'In that case, I would only need twelve hours, because there would be no speeches of welcome.'

While Hungary's toadying to Hitler, compounded by its endemic anti-Semitism, led to a raft of repressive and unpleasant legislation against its Jewish population, Horthy balked, initially, at the round-ups and con-centration camp convoys which the French and others embarked upon with such barely concealed glee. As the Hungarians began to have second thoughts about the war, Horthy's bombastic rallying cry, 'This war is our war', was less and less heard, and the country's emissaries began to put out peace feelers to the West, portraying themselves as an unwilling, blackmailed satellite who had gone along for the bloody ride because it had no choice.

After the occupation, deportation of the Jews began in bloody earnest, with some 500,000 of the 800,000-strong community shipped to their deaths under the management of Adolf Eichmann, until international pressure and Horthy's continued distaste for slaughter brought a halt to the killing machine in July 1944. But a few months later, Horthy was snatched into exile by Otto Skorzeny's paratroopers on Hitler's orders, and the unabashedly Fascist Arrow Cross regime was installed as a German puppet. The killings began again, notably in Budapest. As the Red Army began to sweep the Germans out of Hungary, thousands of Jews who had huddled praying in the ghetto, almost believing, as the guns of the liberators thumped ever louder on the approaches to the city, that they would be spared after all, were bundled off screaming in trucks to the Danube quayside near the Vasarcsarnok or Covered Market, there to be bludgeoned and machine-gunned by frenzied Arrow Cross hoodlums, many of them teenagers. As their blood slicked the cobbles, the bodies were flung like abattoir trash into the muddy waters at the point where today the sleek hydrofoils await the tourists and businessmen eager to begin the four-hour scenic run to Vienna. The Red Army swept brutally across Hungary. They were after all conquering an enemy. They were also taking control of a country which Stalin had long since determined, and had cynically agreed with Churchill in 1944, was to become an undisputed part of the Soviet empire. Stalin moved slowly, perhaps because he was keen to avoid a renewal of the Western outcry which had followed the Communist takeover in Poland. Perhaps too because his Hungarian henchmen had bitter direct memories of the failure of the short-lived Communist regime of Béla Kun, following the First World War, which had foundered on its haste and extremism. So, while being bled dry by Soviet expropriation of property and demands for reparations, post-war Hungary began with (it would be stretching a point to say 'enjoyed') a multi-party system of elected government. But the sharks were already circling.

Soviet foot-dragging delayed the signing of a formal peace treaty until September 1947, providing justification for the continuing menacing presence of the Red Army, while the Communists planned their takeover. For the majority of people, politics had little relevance to the grinding daily reality of trying to pull their lives back together. Men, women and children would do strange and awful things for a packet of cigarettes or a fistful of dollars. Petrol, penicillin, exit visas and ration cards replaced art and antiques as society's most sought-after possessions. Conscience about the past, the present or the future was a luxury few could afford. Love, trust, loyalty, were meaningless words. Fear and hunger, getting by and, increasingly, avoiding the bony finger and secret whisper of the regime's ubiquitous informers, these were what life and death were about. When, in a while, we meet Kati and try to follow her life with Elliott, remember that she especially, and he too, were victims of these mad times. The Communist leader Mátyás Rákosi, squat, bulletheaded son of a Jewish grocer who had spent fifteen tough years in jail under Horthy, returned with a cadre of colleagues from Moscow to plot the way forward from a minority position (only some 1,500 Party members had survived the war) to absolute power. In a felicitously Hungarian metaphor, he later described his strategy for taking control as 'slicing up the opposition like pieces of salami', a process better described by a Jacobean dramatist than a historian. Rákosi's much quoted notion may in fact be no more than an adaptation of a quip by Vittorio Amadeus about Italy after 1713, which he described as 'like an artichoke, to be eaten leaf by leaf'. But it is doubtful that anyone in Hungary actually stood up and told Rákosi he was borrowing other men's aphorisms. Democratic politicians were flayed for espionage and 'counter-revolutionary' activity. Elections were rigged, and although even all the effort produced only a twenty per cent Communist vote at the first attempt, unambiguous pressure gave the Communists the key to ultimate power through control of the Interior Ministry and its secret police resources.

Like the People's Courts, originally targeted at Fascists and wartime collaborators, the *Allam Vetelmy Osztaly* (AVO), or Political Police, was an essential weapon of Communist power. Omnipresent and omniscient, it was an intriguing blend of imperial tradition and new blood. It was headed by Gabor Peter, who, like nearly all of the Communist leaders returning from Moscow, was Jewish, formerly Anspitz, a physically uninspiring but sexually appealing individual with a Goebbels-like limp, a fondness for geraniums, and the distinction of having had an affair in prewar Vienna with the vivacious agitator Litzi Friedmann, who went on to become the first of Kim Philby's four wives. From the Hapsburg days, the AVO inherited the country's built-in culture of police informers and civilian sneaks. From the Fascist Arrow Cross, it took over its Italianate headquarters at 60 Andrassy Ut. The cellars had already seen years of torture and brutality; only the ideological underpinning changed. Across the wide street, one of the most handsome arteries in Budapest, stood the headquarters of the AVO's political masters, the Interior Ministry. No. 102 housed its real boss, the Soviet Embassy. In the other direction, going back into the city centre, on the corner of Nagy-Mezo Utca, were the bars and nightclubs – the Arizona, the Moulin Rouge – where the informers and bar girls in the AVO's pay usually outnumbered the customers. From the Arrow Cross too, Peter recruited the lower-level professionals essential to the smooth running of a secret police operation of any persuasion – the gaolers, drivers, torturers, telephone tappers and filing clerks. For them, it was a relatively easy passage back to some sort of respectability, in the same way as the thin ranks of the Communist Party itself were soon swelled by the arrival of thousands of former Arrow Cross and extremist supporters keen to demonstrate loyalty to what was obviously going to be the winning team. Many in the AVO's lower ranks were Jewish, provoking one commentator to write from the safety of exile of the 'Jews and Nazis idyllically reunited' in the AVO.

Peter also picked up from the Fascists a valuable cache of dollars, diamonds and gold, looted from Jewish victims of the old regime who had vanished into the Holocaust or the cold embrace of the Danube. It was turned over to the AVO, in exchange for his freedom, by a former Arrow Cross luminary, and provided a critical source of capital for the AVO's swelling operational budget; it had a staff of 4,000 in Budapest alone, allocated among seventeen divisions. Division 2 monitored diplomats and the foreign business community, and Division 3 had done a thorough job of penetrating the Catholic Church. Hungarians are a people of complex emotions. Before the war, Budapest had the highest suicide rate in Europe, fuelled by the streaks of melancholy, self-pity and rashness which flaw an outwardly cheerful, resilient if venal disposition. It is said, only partly in jest, that the standard Hungarian recipe for an omelette requires, 'First, steal six eggs.' As Communism tightened its hold, resilience was ever more important, the reason for melancholy ever more apparent. But no one could safely express their feelings. Even among friends, there might be an AVO informer, and it was best to stick to safe, non-political topics. Mothers and fathers guarded their tongues, keeping thoughts and beliefs to themselves in case, in the political hyperactivity of the classroom or the compulsory Young Pioneers' meetings, a child would repeat some fatally damaging parental comment.

No one dared ask what had happened to a neighbour, or what was happening to the country as a whole, let alone why. People vanished. It was safest not to ask questions, safer still to go along with the great lie, the mass schizophrenia, to join the marches, sing the hymns in favour of Rákosi, Stalin's 'wise Hungarian pupil'. And get your own denunciations in before someone denounced you. The AVO worked fist in sweat-stained glove with the Soviet NKVD, later the KGB, mirroring the ventriloquist and dummy relationship between Rákosi and Stalin. When in 1947 Stalin told him to stop the 'political pirouetting' and get on with the job of taking complete control, the AVO was ready, willing and able to assist, as were the People's Courts. Gulya Alapi, the Chief Public Prosecutor, frothed in one notable courtroom speech that the accused were 'no better than dogs, and the only way to get rid of mad dogs is to beat them to death'.

On New Year's Eve 1946, only a couple of weeks after Elliott's arrival, the left-wing press announced the 'smashing' of an ultra-right conspiracy to restore the Horthy regency, a plot which, though wildly inept, did actually have some substance to it, unlike many other such allegations, making it difficult for the Americans and British to protest too loudly when the Communists began to capitalise on the opportunity by impli-cating opponents. First to go was Béla Kovacs, Secretary of the Smallholders' Party. Snatched by the Russians themselves on the grounds that the plot was directed at the Red Army as much as Hungary, he vanished without trace, but not without first denouncing, at the behest of his interrogators, the Prime Minister Ferenc Nagy. Fortunately in Switzerland on holiday, Nagy was blackmailed into resigning, handing over his formal letter at the Austrian border in exchange for his five-year-old son, whom he had left in Budapest and who was brought to the checkpoint in confused terror by a posse of dour AVO and Russian officers. Stalin added fuel to the fire, balefully warning Rákosi: 'The more numerous our enemies, the more dangerous the sur-vivors of the crushed exploiting classes will become, and the sooner they will adopt ever more violent tactics in order to inflict as much damage as they can.'

By May 1947, as Hutter es Lever's plants creaked back into produc-tion, Rákosi was in the saddle as Prime Minister, pressing the buttons, signing the warrants, taking his Russian orders like a man and relaying them brusquely downwards through the hierarchy like the boor he was.

Prodded by Stalin, he proclaimed 1948 as 'the year of the turning-point'. Sound democracy, he belched, was dead. A bourgeois state had been conclusively transformed into a true people's democracy, one of whose first manifestations was a decree significantly lengthening the working day in factories, on the Orwellian grounds that since these now belonged to the people, the employees themselves would benefit from their longer hours. For reasons that had probably less to do with public morality than the new regime's realisation that with power, such things could be had for free, Budapest's rather comfortable Biedermeier brothels were closed down. The City's second-hand dealers snapped up their bevelled mirrors, china bidets with flower-painted rims and the engravings of partly clothed, enviably gymnastic Hapsburg ladies and gentlemen engaged in what in the discreet language of auctioneers' catalogues is nowadays referred to as 'amorous dalliance'. Once the regime of terror was in place and the levers of propaganda safely under control, the regime could move against its targets by using the brisk application of torture, intimidation and blackmail to produce a huge interlocking mosaic of confessions and denunciations. The target list was broad and refreshingly ecumenical. Real or alleged deviationist supporters of Tito. 'Wreckers and saboteurs' working for the West. Ex- and not so ex-Fascists. The Church, with its immense moral authority and worldwide reach. Even, yet again, the Jews. For a regime composed rather substantially of Jews, this might have involved at least a presentational difficulty, but this was neatly solved by attacking them as disloyal Zionists, under the control of the US, rather than as a matter of race.

In the first hectic months, Elliott had little thought for matters clandestine. His 'control' left him alone, though they had seen each other at Legation receptions. His business dealings with Hungarians were coloured by the prevailing fear, the chaos of war's aftermath and their natural tendency to dissemble, neatly characterised by the Blimpish sales representative of a British machine-tool maker at the Park Club: 'The trouble with these gypsy fiddlers is that they're bent as a box of frogs. Know the difference between the Swiss and the Hungarians? Both will offer to shop their grandmothers if the price is right, but the Hungarians will actually deliver.' Until he heard from SIS, it was the job that mattered. Disinterring the ledgers from beneath the heap of coal in the Hutter es Lever cellar, where a long-vanished bookkeeper had hidden them from German and Russian eyes. Grimly surveying the shattered and leaking factories, grimy icicles trailing from the pipework. Steering the protesting Studebaker down what seemed like half the rutted tracks in Hungary, negotiating with canny peasants, wide-eyed children cowering behind their mothers' skirts, to ship to Budapest the cattle and sheep carcasses without which there would be no yellow tallow bubbling evil in the company's huge copper vats and then no soap for the good burghers of Hungary to wash themselves. Not, he reflected, that soap was something they seemed to miss very much. Back down in the cellars below the Joszef Korut Boulevard, with a team of complaining clerks mixing up into washing powder gritty green and yellow granules laboriously shipped by train from Holland. 'Where there's a Vim, there's a Vay' was a bad joke he kept to himself, since it was, in any case, untranslatable into Hungarian. Interminable meetings with civil servants in draughty offices about permits, quotas and red tape, with the Hungarians managing to be defensive and offensive simultaneously.

His command of their agglutinative language he explained with the truth – the crushing boredom of those days, months and years behind the high walls of Spangenberg, the happy accident of a British medical officer with a Hungarian mother, taken prisoner at St Nazaire and eager to offer lessons as a way of passing the slow time. Compounded by the ease with which he had always managed to slip into a language as though it were a new suit. From the office of Hutter es Lever, the reports Elliott sent back to Unilever in London painted a grim picture of a business tied down like Pearl White on a railway track with the juggernaut of expropriation thundering towards her down the track. This time, though, there seemed little prospect of a miraculous escape in the third reel. Following straightforward principles of theft, thinly disguised as dogma about the evils of capital, the regime set about seizing all privately owned businesses. Those owned by Hungarians were easily dealt with. All the more since, following the European pattern, big industrial shareholdings were held by the banks. When the latter were swiftly taken into public ownership, effective control of much of Hungarian industry followed automatically. Expropriating the Hungarian operations of major international companies, which obviously had political clout at home, was a bit trickier, but still, in the Communist view, feasible. Nice pickings, those factories, buildings, warehouses and fleets of vehicles. In the end, after years of argument, some trifling compensation might have to be paid.

But so what? It was best to squeeze now, and squeeze hard. Hungarian managers of foreign-controlled companies were harassed and, at judiciously chosen opportunities, hauled away by the AVO to be interrogated about allegations of spying, or a conveniently broad catch-all accusation of 'economic sabotage' as a prelude to being blackmailed for information and false testimony about their employers. As one of Elliott's colleagues whispered to him over coffee one morning, 'Don't forget, Herr Direktor, there are just three classes of employee in our firm. Those who have been police informers in the past, those who are actively informing now, and those who are certain to be pressured into informing in the time to come. You don't know which class even I belong to, so please take care.'

Girls and boys on the AVO payroll swished their hips at foreign businessmen and diplomats at every opportunity. Phones were tapped, offices bugged and cine-cameras lay hidden in hotel rooms. The foreign companies were assailed in the press and, more dangerously, attacked through the financial system. Debts due from Hungarian customers, especially state-related enterprises, became impossible to collect; the cheque was not even in the mail. The Hungarian tax department, not an arm of the state normally distinguished for its assiduity, suddenly sprang to life, spewing out demands for immense sums in back taxes on 'illegal profits' said to have been made by the foreign companies from trade with the Nazis during the war. At the same time, credit facilities from local banks were withdrawn abruptly, leaving the foreign holding companies with the uncomfortable choice of shrinking their Hungarian businesses to unattractive levels or injecting more working capital from outside, in the certain knowledge that this too would soon be lost.

As early as February 1948, the Hungarian press had given banner headlines to 'explosions and oil theft' at Hutter es Lever, attributed to the black hand of 'Fascist sabotage'. One of the company's Hungarian managers was pilloried in another press attack as a 'ruthless military commander' under the Horthy regime; others were accused of black-marketeering. In Unilever House, that Lutyens lighthouse beaming out eternally on an empire of gurgling palm oil and frothing detergents, its Overseas Committee was coming to the inevitable conclusion that the issue was not how best, but how long, to carry on. How to negotiate for maximum compensation when, inevitably, the time came to leave.

In Hungary, the process of destruction of life, property and the national character rolled inexorably ahead, taking on a momentum of its own which needed less and less central stimulus from the Government, a hurricane growing in power from the water vapour and heat thrown off by its initial burst of energy. Ministries, universities and the professions were purged of political undesirables, all too often people denounced by others who wanted their jobs. Even the Party, like a moral cannibal, began to devour its own, rooting out under the guise of 'Nazis' anyone suspected of any hint of ideological wavering. Worried that Stalin might suspect him of being tainted with the liberal heresies of Tito, who was inclined to leave his farmers alone to get on with the job of providing Yugoslavs with food, Rákosi rushed headlong into the collectivisation of agriculture, dealing another serious blow to Hungary's economy, compounded fatally by his manic determination to create an iron and steel industry which could never pay its way, and to squander vast sums on a defence budget whose only beneficiary was Moscow, which could spend commensurately less of its own money.

# 17

# Layers of Truth

While dealing with Mammon with its right hand, the regime kept a powerful left fist free to deal with God, or at least his terrestrial representatives. To wrest control of Hungarian hearts and minds meant that the powerful voice and conscience of the Catholic Church had to be stilled and its leadership discredited, all the more given the spiritual revival which had followed the ending of the war. The Church's Prince Primate, forty-seven-year-old Cardinal Joszef Mindszenty, had been warned by the Pope at his Vatican ordination that he was bound to suffer for his faith, all the more since it came dangerously combined with courage and extreme obstinacy. In the elections of 1946, Mindszenty had challenged the Communists by urging his flock to vote 'for candidates who represent law, morality, order and justice', and he had strongly attacked moves to secularise Church schools and youth organisations and to shut down its newspapers. As a British Foreign Office official put it in the acid-drop prose style much favoured in King Charles Street, 'one cannot help feeling some sympathy with the Prince Primate, whose tactics [of opposition] are refreshing, if suicidal'.

Surrounded by his prelates, some of them loyal, not a few of them AVO informers, the Cardinal sat in his palace at Esztergom. Once the seat of the Kings of Hungary, it gazed stolidly out across the Danube into

Czechoslovakia about forty-five miles north of Budapest. Mindszenty was increasingly reviled in the press, spied on, his telephone tapped and his mail intercepted. Visitors, when not roughly discouraged by the police guards outside, were photographed and questioned.

So where does Elliott fit in? The basic, Mark One, version of the story, is a minor triumph of damage limitation from the delicate quill pen of an SIS draughtsman. It saw the light of day as a report in the now defunct *News Chronicle*, which appeared in London on 11 October 1948. 'Briton Tells of Andrassy Jail', the paper's liberal-leaning British public read over their morning Shredded Wheat and the first cigarette.

Last night I met Mr Kavan Elliott soon after he had rejoined his wife and three children at his home in Purley, Surrey. Mr Elliott was made general manager of Unilever in Budapest in December 1946. Last Wednesday the Hungarian police gave him twenty-four hours to leave the country after holding him in prison for twelve days. This is the story Mr Elliott told me.

'On the night of 24 September, I was stopped at a roadblock outside Budapest. On producing my identity card I was bundled into a waiting car, handcuffed and blindfolded and driven to a house where I was placed in a cell. Twelve hours later, still without explanation, I was removed to the notorious Andrassy Jail in Budapest. All personal belongings were taken from me, including my watch, tie and braces. I was put into an unfurnished cell like any prisoner. The light was kept permanently on and the grille in the door open. For twelve days I was not allowed to communicate with the Legation, my family or my firm. No reason was given for my detention except that I was suspected of espionage. I learned what this amounted to during repeated spells of interrogation. One lasted twelve hours. In fairness, I must say that unlike the Gestapo, into whose hands I fell after being parachuted into Yugoslavia in 1942, the Hungarians gave me breaks for food, and I was allowed all the cigarettes I wanted. My interrogators – plainclothes detectives – were especially anxious to know about all my friends and contacts in Hungary. They grilled me especially about a Ministry of Agriculture official. My car was waiting for me outside when I was released on Wednesday, still without any apology or explanation. I was told I had twenty-four hours to

leave the country. It was time enough to leave the matter in the
hands of the Legation. A Commissar was put in charge of my
firm – which employs 1,800 Hungarians – during my "absence"
and I imagine he is still there. I am reporting the whole affair to
Unilever.'

As intended, this neatly conveyed the impression of an innocent
British businessman caught up in the machinery of a police state, whose
minions were at least better behaved than the hated Germans, though a
very careful reader might have wondered what sort of treatment 'especially anxious' really implied. But a straight bat and a stiff upper lip had
seen him safely through. Time to turn to the review of Ivor Novello's
latest musical and those ever so charming new Cecil Beaton photographs of the royal family. And, still wheezing from the last one, to light
another cigarette. I looked for more in the Foreign Office files for
Hungary. While some items are withheld from public inspection, what is
left seems, on the face of it, to be no more than you would expect: the
bureaucratic infrastructure supporting the Mark One version. An
insight, fascinating for students of such things into the handling of a
minor, temporarily troubling, diplomatic incident. But one which was
not unexpected, given the tense political atmosphere in Hungary and the
AVO's arrest only a few days earlier of two American directors of the
Rockefeller Standard Oil subsidiary in Budapest.

There is virtually nothing in the flow of diplomatic traffic to and from
the Legation – all marked 'OTP', to show it had originally been carefully
encrypted in the virtually uncrackable one-time pad system – to suggest
that there was anything more to it. It certainly called for deft, expeditious
diplomacy. But not a *cause célèbre*. Not on the face of it a 'one of our men
is missing' crisis to ruffle the fictional quiet of the top floor of the Circus,
Rose Pouchong tea from Fortnum's cooling forgotten in Control's delicate Wedgwood cup while he and those privileged to have a seat at the
top table fret about what to do. Elliott's disappearance was reported to
the Foreign Office in the evening of 26 September by Hilary Young, the
Chargé d'Affaires in Budapest. His cable was marked 'Most Immediate',
but curiously, despite its immediacy, it took Young nearly twenty-four
hours to file the report – he had first learned of Elliott's disappearance
and a police search of his house on the evening of 25 September. He presumably spent the intervening day making enquiries about Elliott with

the Hungarian authorities; whether at the same time there were other people who needed to be alerted, fallback arrangements to be implemented, we can only guess. Young's cable asked Whitehall to inform Unilever; there was no suggestion that Elliott's family should be notified. 'All branches of the police it has been possible to reach, deny any knowledge of him,' Young added.

On 27 September, Young reported that he had been officially advised by the Hungarians that Elliott was 'under interrogation'. British officials had not been allowed to see him. Young suggested lodging a formal protest, to incorporate a heavy hint that Elliott's arrest could affect Britain's trade relationship with Hungary, but back in Whitehall, cautious men with polished shoes concluded, before taking the 5.10 p.m. train home to the Surrey hills, that there was little they could do. Initially.

The first documented reaction to Young's suggestion was a classic piece of Foreign Office handwringing and buck passing. 'The home departments', minuted a senior official with an illegible signature, 'will not countenance anything which will prejudice soft-currency sources of essential supplies (such as Hungary) except perhaps as a last resort against some particularly monstrous action which Elliott's case isn't yet. Therefore, the threat of a reduction in the volume of trade or even of less enthusiasm in negotiations will soon prove empty.' Developing his argument from Elliott's situation to the general plight of British companies with interests in the newly socialist countries of the East, the faceless commentator wrote, 'we have always advised firms within the [Communist] orbit that we consider they should not hope by any action on our part to retain their present precarious position in Communist-dominated territory. Hence any action to drag out the existence of interests behind the Iron Curtain must to that extent go against our own policy.' Fortunately for Elliott, that Munichois view did not last the night. The next day the tone of the papers on the file changes to one of action (one of the memoranda on the main file has a note that it had been 'temporarily attached' to another file, separately circulated and no longer identifiable). The trade card was suddenly played with vigour.

At a practical, non-political level, Hungary and Britain needed each other. For a famished and freezing post-war Britain, with little to eat beyond the bitter fruits, whalemeat and groundnut promises of a Labour Government, Hungary was a valuable source of badly needed poultry and bacon. For a Hungarian Government desperate for foreign currency, the income from its trade with Britain, though in sterling rather than the higher-prized dollar, was a significant balance of payments boost. All the more so since under their mutual trade agreement Britain was prepared to make sizeable advance payments. (Though the point was never explicitly made to the Hungarians, British officials reminded themselves that under the Exchange Control Regulations, sterling balances held by the Hungarians in London could be frozen in an instant by Bank of England fiat.) Though prepared to hint at serious repercussions for the trading relationship, the diplomats were still careful to avoid any specific commitments to retaliation. 'Our relations with Hungary are too valuable.'

A senior Board of Trade official was carefully scripted to express outrage over the telephone from Whitehall to the British trade representative in Budapest, talking with especial clarity, for the benefit of the AVO eavesdroppers in the basement of the Budapest telephone exchange, about the possibility of withdrawing him 'for consultation', thus cutting off any trade dialogue, and of the risk that 'technical problems' of an unspecified nature might just delay the next advance payment due to Hungary under the agreement. In case a little oil might be needed to get wheels to move, Unilever's solicitor sent the Foreign Office a cheque for £1,000 (perhaps £15,000 today) for 'legal and other expenses' in Elliott's case. On 2 October, Young was summoned to see Laszlo Rajk, newly transferred, many said demoted, from the key Interior Ministry to the Foreign Affairs portfolio. Rajk told Young that Elliott would 'probably be charged with espionage'. He went on to murmur that while the matter was currently with the police and thus out of his hands, provided Elliott's crimes did not turn out to have been 'flagrant', if the British were to ask for the matter to be dealt with by his expulsion, it would be proper for his Ministry to intervene. Too well trained to take a fly like this without instructions, Young hurried back to the Legation to recommend to Whitehall that 'subject to anything Mr Bell [a Director of the British thread manufacturers, Coats, who was the unofficial spokesman for British companies with Hungarian interests] and Unilever might say', the feeler put out by Rajk should be taken up. Unilever and the Foreign Office agreed, 'even though Hungarian propaganda will doubtless justify the arrest by allegations of espionage'. But the Foreign Office noted solemnly that accepting Elliott's expulsion should not imply acceptance of subsequent 'propaganda excuses'. Back at the Foreign Ministry, Young and Rajk agreed that it would be 'undesirable that the case should go to the courts if this could be avoided'. Young reported: 'I got the impression Rajk was relieved' that the British had accepted the expulsion solution. Relieved? We can speculate on that later. Meanwhile, the Hungarian Government had installed a 'Government Controller' to take charge of Hutter es Lever. A spokesman asserted with a straight face that since Elliott 'had been absent for a week without leave' and urgent business decisions had to be taken each day, this was the only way Elliott's Hungarian subordinates could avoid finding a charge of 'economic sabotage' flung in their direction.

On 5 October, John Hansard (the senior Unilever director in charge of Europe, and last surviving member of the family that had begun the eponymous daily record of British Parliamentary proceedings) sent the Foreign Office a cable from Prague which is difficult to construe, at least in the context of the official record. In view of the 'reasonably satisfactory' news of the Rajk conversation, he telegraphed, he would not 'press further through the Czechs for Elliott's presence in Prague', especially since the only minister who could make such a request, Evgen Loebl, was away in Moscow. Just why the Hungarians might have been prepared to yield Elliott up, or what commercial, diplomatic or other reasons there might be, we do not know. Nor is it clear what part Loebl, around that time giving up his post in the Ministry of Foreign Trade to become Foreign Minister, was intended to play. (Loebl was arrested in September 1954 and charged, first, with having treasonable connections with the ambiguous American Quaker Noel Field, but also with economic mismanagement, including advocating payment of excessive compensation for the nationalisation of foreign businesses, among them Unilever's Czech operations. He went to jail, but was released in 1963.) It is also difficult to judge whether the communication channels with Hansard were normal for that time. He was in Prague, on a business trip, but was in touch with developments in Budapest via the Foreign Office in London. Messages clattered to and fro over the teleprinter between Budapest, Whitehall and the British Embassy, hidden away behind its Disneyland fortress gates in Thunovska Street under the walls of Prague Castle. On 6 October, Elliott was released. The British Legation felt that it deserved the 'many congratulations' cabled by Whitehall for its successful efforts. Young told the Hungarian Foreign Ministry, in no doubt carefully chosen words, that in any case he 'had no reason to believe that a charge of espionage would be well-founded'. He reported to London an off-the-record comment of a senior Hungarian official that 'our authorities had hoped to make a scandal but failed to obtain enough material'.

The day after Elliott's release, it looked for a moment as though the concern about the propaganda play was justified. The Legation cabled urgently to London that the Budapest newspapers were all reporting under banner headlines, in our first glimpse of the public Hungarian version of events: 'The British manager of Hutter es Lever at the head of an espionage organisation – eight arrests'. The newspaper reported that,

> The Political Police authority of the Ministry of the Interior has unmasked an espionage organisation [whose] members have passed on industrial secrets to a foreign power. The authority, on the basis of concrete proofs, has taken into custody eight persons who had been using their offices for purposes of espionage. The contact between the foreign power and its Hungarian spies was maintained by Kavan Elliott, British citizen, the manager of the chemical firm Hutter es Lever.

For some reason, whether through the operation of a D-Notice, or lack of interest, the British press did not pick up the story until the sanitised version appeared in the *News Chronicle* on 11 October. So much for the official record.

However, we also have Elliott's own notes of what happened. His version of the story, as you would expect, is far more personalised and much more graphic. It is plausible; but what he does not tell us is far more interesting, far more painful, than what he chose to reveal, and we can see this as the Mark Two version.

Elliott begins by recalling that he had returned in September 1948 from a brief trip to London, equipped with a white flag, a mandate from Unilever to begin negotiations to sell Hutter es Lever for whatever the Hungarians were prepared to offer. Then he reveals the key fact omitted from the Public Record Office's account, and the reason why an initial, rather blasé, hands-off reaction in Whitehall turned overnight rather more positive. He was, he admits, working for SIS. But, even years later, what he was doing, and for whom, he could not bring himself to say. All he tells us is that he was 'running errands' for 'someone at the Legation. The trip back was the first time they let me through the passport checks and the customs without a hitch. The Hungarians were usually so bloody-minded. It should have been a warning. Everything was normal for two or three days. Then I went into town for a dinner with some of the Legation people. There was almost always a checkpoint on the road back to my house. I had a Unilever car with a Dutch registration plate that the police knew and I was usually waved through. When I drove back from Pest after dinner, I saw the usual red light swinging backwards and forwards at the checkpoint. I slowed down. I was sure they would wave me on as usual when they saw the car, especially since the weather was foul, cold and sleeting. They didn't. I opened the window and some johnny with bad breath jabbed a pistol in my face, bellowing at me to get out fast, with my hands up. I didn't argue. I opened the door. A goon loomed up out of the dark and grabbed me. I smashed at him, but they pulled me down and slapped a chloroform pad over my face. I was dragged across the road, thrown into another car. I was pretty woozy. I sensed we had driven up a hill and then slowed down. We stopped, someone outside yanked the door open, and I was hauled out by my hair. We were in some sort of garage. There was a floodlight in the ceiling. They pushed me down some steps in the corner. I tumbled down into a narrow alleyway. There were half-a-dozen guys down there, Jews and gypsies they looked like, pointing pistols, yelling and swearing at me to strip off – fast. I didn't have much choice. Then they pushed me into some sort of cellar. It was only about five feet high and a couple of feet deep, so I couldn't stand up or sit down. Just squat.'

Though Elliott was snatched on the street, the timing, the late evening, was a routine procedure. Like Dracula, the AVO worked best in the dead of night. Its victims were usually tired and ready for bed when they were snatched away by the black-hatted men in black cars to face the first of many nights of violence and disorientation. Their families, left horrorstruck in a ransacked apartment, had to wait until morning before they could call around to find out where their husband, wife, son or daughter might have been taken, or to try to enlist the help of a lawyer or friends with contacts. Elliott remembers the next forty-eight hours as a sleepless blur. Hauled upstairs out of his cellar box to face bright lights and questions, over and over. Who was he really working for? Who was his boss at the Legation? Back in the box, as his head dropped, they banged on the door to keep him awake. If that didn't work, he would be shocked out of sleep by a bucket of cold water. But he stuck to his story.

He was a Unilever man. Nothing more to it. A life of margarine and Vim. A boring business. He had no 'boss' at the Legation.

Elliott had no idea then, or later, where he was. By courtesy of an old AVO expert, I went to see the place a little while ago, a gloomy, substantial, three-storey house, shut in by trees and railings at the end of a quiet cul-de-sac called Mecsy Street in the Buda hills. Mecsy means 'fairytale'. The Brothers Grimm would have loved it.

Over the years, the leafy hills had sprouted hundreds of these solid villas for the merchants, lawyers and doctors of Pest. After the war, abandoned villas were two a forint and were a handy, secluded base for the AVO's more discreet operations. There were few neighbours and those that remained were too fearful to ask questions about the cars crunching up the drive day and night, or the scruffy men with beady eyes loafing by the gates picking their teeth. The Gestapo too had been quite fond of the Buda hills, taking over two hotels, the Majestic and the Golf, for interrogation, beatings and murder. The Mecsy Street house is said today to be back in private hands; by the look of it, the Addams family. From the street you can work out that Elliott was driven into the garage. Underneath it are the tiny windows of the cellar, whose coal-holes and wine cupboards served as the cramped 'boxes' in which the AVO's victims were housed in between their visits. Upstairs was the 'working area', with its Klieg lights, concealed microphones and the blinds permanently drawn. The bathrooms were useful for the messier work.

After being softened up in that fairytale world, Elliott was driven off, blindfolded, to Gabor Peter's flower-flecked lair on Andrassy Ut. As the AVO drove him into the courtyard through the Czengary Utca side entrance, and the blindfold was removed, Elliott found himself in a rather larger, grander establishment altogether, but one which served the same functions and employed the same basic set-up. The cells were underground, where almost total silence prevailed. The warders, the same underworld types as inhabited Mecsy Utca, wore felt slippers, or plimsolls, and the prisoners went barefoot. The quiet was broken only by the occasional clink of keys, the warders hissing from one to another the number of the next prisoner to be led upstairs for interrogation, and the twice-daily rumble of the food trolleys. In the cells, a bright ceiling light burned for eternity behind an unbreakable wire mesh cover. Every few minutes a bloodshot eye stared through the gaolers' spyhole in the steel door, like a Dada poached egg. Elliott did not describe the physical layout at length, but one's imagination suggests a scene from Piranesi's *Carceri*, all vaulted ceilings, torture racks and braziers. In reality, Andrassy Ut was and is a rather ordinary office building, with a rambling basement. The small, damp and horribly intimidatory cells have now been replaced by the prosaic impedimenta of filing, storage and central heating. Elliott spent eight or nine days there – he lost any precise sense of time – on the same mind-grinding treadmill of lights and questions, questions and lights, and above all no sleep. No sense of day or night. 'Why not', an older interrogator asked him solicitously, 'just write down for us what you are saying. That you are just a Unilever man, that your Legation contacts are only on Unilever business. We know the whole story. But you tell us in your own words.' So Elliott wrote, at a deal table in a room next door to the black-curtained interrogation office. 'You haven't given us enough detail. Write another one,' the interrogator chided. He wrote, and wrote again. Each time the sheets of yellowish paper were taken away by the guard only to be brought back by one of the interrogators either in sorrow or in anger, often torn to pieces. 'You haven't written about your journey to Romania in July. What was it for? And write it out in German, not English.'

Then he was pushed into a different room where an older man sat alone. Elliott hadn't seen him before. I found out years later that his name was Gyula Decsi. He offered the lung-racking relief of a cigarette. 'Mr Elliott. You have a lot to tell us. But you aren't co-operating. I'm telling you now. Tell us the real story. Or I'll send you out of here tomorrow and stick you in front of a People's Court. That will be that. Fifteen years at least. Possibly a death sentence. So do yourself a great favour and see sense. Go downstairs now, and we'll talk again later on.' Elliott was taken back to his cell, wondering in the darkness what to do next? Stick to the Unilever story? Start teasing out a few facts in the hope that this would satisfy the questioning men? But even with any halfway proficient interrogator – and these fellows were not bad at all – admitting one fact would inexorably lead to another less minor admission, and on it would go. It was better to try to tough it out. No rack, no thumb-screws, no electrodes, no truth serum . . . but unless you have been through it for real, how can you know what it is like? On your own in a black box, God knows where. Outside the steel door are men who care for nothing, and will stop at nothing, red-eyed night people with the power of pain and freedom, outside the law because they are the law. Does anyone else know or care where you are? You are bone-weary, dirty and scared. Tiredness, fear and confusion tug temptingly at the last vestiges of your resistance, your training and your self-confidence. And above all, in Elliott's case at least, you have real secrets to hide.

The opening of the door, the mute gaoler's beckoning finger, crystallised the fear into a flood of bile in his throat. Taken back upstairs, he found himself not in an interrogation room, but 'a damn great bathroom like Claridges. Tiles, towels, steam and mirrors. Before I had time to think what the hell they were going to try on me now, a guard came in, smiling now. Very unusual. He waved a pair of clippers at me and told me to sit on the stool. I was pretty shaggy, and he started to snip at my beard. Very jovial, but wouldn't say a word about what was going on. He told me to climb in the bath. I'm pretty edgy at this point in case he pulls some stunt, but no. Just left me to soak. This amazing long, hot soak. Then another fellow comes in with my clothes. All pressed and the shoes gleaming.' Elliott wondered if he was being spruced up to stand in the splintered pine dock of a People's Court. 'But then the senior fellow comes in and says straight out that they're letting me go. No explanation. Though he was quick to add that I was being expelled from Hungary.'

Decsi took Elliott along the quiet corridors, down the imposing main staircase and into the courtyard. 'He shook my hand, and said he hoped there were no hard feelings. Cheeky sod. I asked where my car was. He stared at me as if I was barmy, which at that point I probably was.

'"Aren't you satisfied with being free, with being allowed just to walk away from this building? That doesn't happen to many people."

'"No," I said, "it's an expensive Studebaker which belongs to Unilever and I want it back."

'"All right," he grinned. He put me in the sentry booth. I waited, dog-tired for about a quarter of an hour until he came out again and ushered me on to the side street like a hotel doorman. There was my car, washed and gleaming, the engine running. He repeated through the open window that I had just twenty-four hours to cross the frontier.'

The Canadian Military Attaché drove with Elliott into Austria, providing an element of friendly protection against some last-minute change of heart. 'When I got to Vienna, Antony Terry hid me up.'

\*

Like a Chinese meal, half an hour after Elliott's version, you find yourself salivating for more. What was he actually doing? Who was his control? What went wrong?

Despite the ferretings of journalists, authors, academics and trouble-makers, SIS keeps most of its secrets, and even today keeps the identity of most of its overseas officers well camouflaged from those who make a hobby of trying to spot the spies from the heavily coded career histories and the bland biographies of the British Diplomatic List. Unless an officer stumbles into brief notoriety by being irrevocably 'blown' in some *cause célèbre*, or chooses in retirement to write an elegant little memoir lifting an insignificant veil or two, SIS people live and die without much fanfare. Among friends in the snug bar of the Bull and Bladder in Cheam, the sun lounge of the Hotel Eiger or in the marbled halls of the Reform Club, they may permit themselves the occasional coy reference to the inwardnesses of life in the service of the Firm, but by and large they do not name names. (Thus, whenever out-of-date SIS orders-of-battle or budgets are apparently divulged without hesitation, it is usually as well to wonder why.)

What follows – compiled from a range of sources – represents, if you will, the Mark Three version.

Many in post-war Budapest, not least the US State Department's deep-cover intelligence representative, Jim McCargar, thought the SIS man on the spot was friendly Freddy Redward, with the local rank of First Secretary at the British Legation then often used as a substitute for the discredited Passport Control Officer cover to give SIS officers a measure of camouflage and diplomatic immunity. Redward, in his fifties, had an appropriately E. Phillips Oppenheim background. Service with the fledgling Royal Naval Air Service in the First World War, then a spell with the Allied 'Danube Flotilla', part of the rather futile Armistice arrangements. He had gone native, settled in Budapest and married a Hungarian girl. From 1935, he was the Legation's Press Attaché. With the approach of the Second World War, he had made himself useful to Section D; a later attachment to SOE's Hungarian section ended in dissatisfaction and unspecified mutual recrimination with a monetary flavour. Any ill-feeling can only have been temporary, since after serving with the post-war British Military Mission, Redward settled smoothly back to a diplomatic role – or perhaps quasi-diplomatic, since by temperament and force of circumstance he continued to be a useful intelligence odd-job man. As with Grinovich in the SIS Station in pre-war Bulgaria, it was convenient all round to have a man with local flavour generally perceived to be the wearer of the black hat. It would have done Redward's ego good for the old Magyar hand to be the object of 'nudge nudge, wink wink' identification with SIS in the chancelleries and cocktail-parties of Budapest. It certainly suited the actual SIS Head of Station, Harry Morris, lodged unobtrusively towards the bottom of the Diplomatic List as a Second Secretary (local).

Elliott had first been introduced to Harry Morris before he left London, over a cup of Camp coffee extract in an anonymous room in an anonymous building in Northumberland Avenue, down from Trafalgar Square. Like Elliott himself, Morris had survived what the fellows in the mess called with gruff mock modesty 'a good war', meaning just the opposite. Though their paths had not crossed, Morris had also served in SOE, where he had come to the Firm's notice after some especially malevolent double and triple dealing in Lisbon (pleasantly unexpected in a City solicitor, who had been plucked from the wood-panelled parlours of the National Provincial Bank) had neatly unhinged several key Abwehr operations.

Back in London, the well-worn cover of Elliott's SOE personnel file, now like all the remaining SOE records under the control of SIS, was carefully annotated with a 'C' reference to indicate to any future researcher that its subject now had a formal connection with the Secret Service. At first, Elliott seems to have done no more than any of SIS's 'UAs', or 'Unofficial Assets' around the world might be asked: Budapest business gossip; character sketches of civil servants; chitchat on indiscretion and infidelity. Whatever the real value of the scraps he brought in, he would have been lavishly praised, as the agent-running courses prescribe, asked a few debriefing questions and in his own, as well as his control's, interests told almost nothing about what his information might mean, or where his work fitted in the overall scheme of things.

Then as East and West beat their chests and postured, and as Rákosi tightened the screws on the Hungarian people, Elliott was asked to play for higher stakes. First came the Hungarian businessman, call him Laszlo. He had an important job in international trade, and was authorised to travel abroad provided his wife and family stayed in Hungary as hostages. Pervasive at home, the AVO could not be everywhere abroad, and missed the evening when the old Adam triumphed over caution.

Laszlo slipped the leash, slid like a randy tomcat out of the service entrance of his hotel, and let down what was left of his greasy hair, carefully combed over the growing bald spot, in that contradiction in terms, a Swiss nightclub: a night of merry widows, padded bar stools, padded bills and squeaky sexual calisthenics. An SIS 'occasional' passed the word, and on Laszlo's next trip, a pass was made at him involving the straightforward offer of money and the rather less than firm promise of eventual safety in the West. He rose to the bait; whether he was told what the harsh alternatives might be if he failed to co-operate, we do not know. When Laszlo was in Hungary, he needed 'servicing'; a job that was obviously difficult for Morris, while Elliott had at least superficially convincing reasons for meeting Laszlo at his office or at business receptions. Elliott took on the task of passing on requests for information, picking up in casual contact or from dead-letter boxes Laszlo's hard-won nuggets of information, and acting as counsellor, confessor and, all the time, like a suspicious spouse, checking for the hint of an unfamiliar perfume, the nervousness of betrayal or blackmail. Morris then brought Elliott into a far more complex and infinitely more risky operation.

For the Vatican, the Second World War had been little more than an interlude, painful, ambivalent, at times less than glorious, in what it saw as the far more important long-term struggle against the forces of the ungodly, the militant atheists of Bolshevism. Even before the German surrender, the Vatican worked hard, with covert support from the US Office of Strategic Services and SIS, to organise the infamous 'Ratlines' down which German, Croat and Romanian war criminals, whose staunch Catholicism and anti-Communism far outweighed, in Rome's eyes, any unfortunate ambiguities about their record, vanished through Bolzano and Trieste into the humid neutrality of South America. A process described rather one-sidedly by one of its Nazi beneficiaries as 'saving the best of our race from the demented victors' mad craving for revenge and retribution'. From there, it was planned that they would re-emerge after a discreet interval with bland new personalities and passports to act as standard-bearers in the next round of the Church's war fortified in the case of the Croats by the plundered gold coins and bullion which an ever helpful Vatican laundered for them through its ever so discreet bank. For this next round, the Vatican would continue to need badly the help of the US and the UK spymasters. Equally, the latter's rather more practical plans for rolling back the Communist menace – just then taking shape in

New York in the quiet rooms of the Council on Foreign Relations, by quiet firesides in panelled Federal homes in Washington and in the Spartan offices of the newly formed CIA – would benefit from the warm glow of Vatican support, from the grassroots intelligence the Church across Eastern Europe could provide, and from the Church's power over the hearts and minds of its flock.

In his palace at Esztergom, Cardinal Mindszenty was the Church Defiant and Militant wanting not just to resist but to fight to bring about the Vatican's dream of creating a new pastoral confederation of Catholic states at the heart of Eastern Europe, centred on Croatia and Hungary (800 years or so previously briefly one country), as a buffer against the forces of the ungodly just a few kilometres further east. The dream, rather reminiscent of that earlier Mihailovic–Dimitrov fantasy of linking Serbia and Bulgaria, might come to nothing, Western intelligence analysts reasoned, but at least the plans and the plotting for it would add useful momentum to the overall attempt to destabilise and confuse the new enemy. Behind Mindszenty in the shadows stood Intermarium, an ambiguous alliance of militantly anti-Communist Catholic lay organisations established in the 1930s and very soon courted and used by every Western intelligence service, beginning with the German Abwehr, followed in short order by SIS, the French and the Poles. It had played an important role in the Ratlines scheme. In a neat parallel with the way in which the AVO garnered Jewish plunder to fund itself for the post-war struggle, including the struggle against the Church, Intermarium too seems to have got its hands on a valuable trove of Budapest art treasures originally seized by the Arrow Cross, providing the clerics with a handy nest egg for their divine anti-Communist crusade. If Intermarium was the Church Militant, the Cardinal had also to contend with the Church Flexible, in the shape of the Jesuits, who susurrated seductively about the risks of making things more difficult by pushing obviously radical concepts, via the Vatican and the Church overseas, which provoked the wrath of the regime and even more intense attacks. Why didn't the Church simply make its powerful voice felt through the Hungarian political process? There was, after all, a Liberal Catholic Party. Surely it was better to reach a solid modus vivendi with the new secular power, rather than fight and lose, a line not out of harmony with the accommodating equivocation which had marked the Vatican's relationships with Nazi Germany. The Church was further weakened, and the independence of its priests compromised, by the agricultural 'reforms', which snatched away the Church's income-producing land holdings and forced priests to live instead on state subsidies, which could so easily be withdrawn at the AVO's behest if they made trouble.

In the spring of 1947, Elliott moved out of Budapest to Tahi, a wattle and thatch village, basically still a farming community, but with a small resident colony of artists and writers adding a touch of intellectual paprika to the otherwise tranquil setting on the banks of the Danube, about twenty miles north of the capital. Even though the traffic on the rutted highway to Budapest was light, it was an unusually long commute in those days. It made more sense, as an observant friend in Budapest pointed out, when you realised that twenty miles to the north of Tahi up Route 11, Cardinal Mindszenty waited for destiny to catch up with him. Even today, the spiders' web of country roads and wooded hills between Tahi and Esztergom offers countless opportunities for a rendezvous in leafy obscurity. Five miles south of Tahi is the little town of Szentendre, today a charming jumble of cobbled streets, tiny squares, cafés, flowery riverside promenades, antique shops, art galleries and onion-domed churches. In Elliott's time, the commercial attractions were fewer, but the churches were very much there, as they had been since the end of the seventeenth century, when Orthodox and Roman Catholic communities from Bosnia, Croatia and Serbia had fled to the tranquillity of Szentendre out of the path of the Christian armies savaging the Ottoman Empire. Esztergom and its brooding primate, the clerics of Szentendre, Harry Morris and his SIS colleagues in Vienna, Rome and London, were the compass points in Elliott's daunting task of orchestrating the lines of communication between Mindszenty and the Vatican. How it was done, who was involved, we cannot know for certain, since after nearly fifty years memories fade at the edge of the detail. There were carriers, post-boxes, codewords and high risk. What passed along the network, hand to hand, dead-letter box to the basket of a rusty bicycle to a rolled-up newspaper handed over on a railway station, is equally shrouded, though some sense of it comes out in the record of Mindszenty's own show trial.

This I read in the tranquil Georgian building, once, slightly improbably, a school for the Welsh community in Clerkenwell, which now houses the Marx Memorial Library. Beneath a mural painted by the 'Red' Earl of Huntingdon in 1935, showing cheery workers at toil under the benign gaze of non-working intellectual giants of the labour movement, I revisited the madness of it all. The Mindszenty trial was a vicious classic of its kind, one of those infinitely humiliating, infinitely rehearsed productions by the demented Busby Berkeleys of the Hungarian Prosecutor's Office. Like most of the regime's victims, Mindszenty and his co-defendants recited their lines by rote, dully admitting at the prompting of the Court President their involvement in an encyclopedia of 'crimes' aimed at bringing down the Communist state. And yet like so much of the background to Elliott's story, one is left wondering. Those whose political reflexes were conditioned by growing up in the Cold War are trained to the belief that all such show trials were entirely evil manifestations of evil regimes, trumped-up displays of totalitarian power, innocent men and women shovelled down the courthouse steps to death or prison. The trials were a brutal ritual aimed more at discouraging others than establishing any sort of legal or objective truth. But looking back over forty years later, might there not have been aspects of the Mindszenty and other *causes célèbres* where the myth of the persecution of the innocent and the reality of the deep undercurrents of the time once again find themselves strangely intermingled?

Communist regimes, built on the quicksands of falsehood and murder, told lies on such a staggering scale that it is easy to overlook the grains of truth. The Rákosi regime made much in its internal and external propaganda of the plotting of Western agents, exaggerating the threat to increase the sense of a nation beleaguered, a nation in which vigilance and arbitrary justice were a necessary price to ensure the triumph of the socialist dream. At the same time in Hungary as elsewhere in Eastern Europe, the increasing terror also suited the West, whose strategists reasoned that as the paranoia bloomed the resulting repression would stoke popular discontent and encourage eventual destabilisation. Mindszenty's co-defendants were a stereotyped cross-section of the regime's targets – Jesuit priests, a former landowner, a Jewish banker. They also included Miklos Boresztoczky, the Budapest head of Actio Catholica, like Intermarium one of the many Church organisations whose names appeared and disappeared during the Cold War years in the mostly unmapped marshlands which lay between the Vatican and the intelligence services of the West. In the prosecution's allegations about how the lines of communication worked, and what passed along them, the principal 'correspondent' at the Vatican end was said to have been Canon

Zsigmond Mikalovics, Actio Catholica's Director, who had escaped from Hungary via Austria early in the Communist clampdown. Messages from Esztergom to Rome and back again passed through what the prosecutor called 'an official trusted agent of the British power' who was 'well-versed in secret matters'.

From Mikalovics in the Vatican, the line brought to Esztergom news, encouragement and, allegedly, reports on contacts with US and British intelligence: half-baked schemes to restore the Hungarian crown to the Hapsburgs; and a fanciful plan, said to have been taken seriously in Washington DC for a brief and lunatic moment, in which the US would pay the Russians many millions of dollars for their assets and installations in Hungary, and their reparations claims, whereupon the Red Army would immediately leave the country. From Esztergom to the Vatican, the traffic was valuable grist to the intelligence mill. Reports from the Catholic clergy about everyday life in Hungary, on peasant attitudes, on labour relations and the behaviour of the Red Army; comments on politics, on personalities and on the regime's increasingly tough attitude towards the Church. After sifting by SIS and the OSS, some of Mindszenty's news was enthusiastically used by Actio Catholica as propaganda material to stir up anti-Communist sentiment in the West and to stimulate fundraising among the Hungarian community in the US.

This Mark Three version of that first tale told to the *News Chronicle*, full of sound and fury but signifying nothing, is still incomplete, since it ends in Elliott's arrest. What it does not tell us is what went wrong. Why was Elliott arrested? More to the point, perhaps, why was he released, instead of starring in a show trial of his own? What happened to the 'eight persons' taken into custody with him?

There is no official source available to give answers to questions as sensitive as this. Not even a semi-official one. Indeed, it would not be realistic to expect any official source in London or Budapest to admit that the questions in themselves made sense. I still felt Budapest might be easier. Despite, or perhaps because of, its massive Brezhnev-era leatherette furniture, Suite 315 is one of the nicest that the slightly shabby but still comfortable Gellert Hotel has to offer. It has two balconies, one with a sweeping view of the Danube, the lines of Russian and Bulgarian barges labouring heavily upstream against the brown tide, and the passenger hydrofoils turning into the quay like shiny dragonflies after their highspeed run from Vienna. The other looks across to a little

Catholic shrine in the cliff face, reopened after the passing of the secular
state. In the street below, pensioners shuffled into the foetid thermal
baths, where, over the centuries, Romans, Turks, Hapsburg hussars,
Gestapo officers, KGB thugs and now Western tourists have eased their
joints. It was in the Gellert that, thanks to the courtesy and efficiency of
the 'new look' Interior Ministry, I first read a photocopy of what remains
of the Budapest Prosecutor's file on Elliott's case. It was chilling to see
Elliott's name on the front of the file, in precise Gothic copperplate, as
though it were to serve as the lettering on a tombstone. The file itself is
No. 547 of 1948, which gives some indication of the scale of operation of
the Rákosi salami slicer. Let us think of it, thin thought it is, as the Mark
Four version.

The charge on which Elliott was held translates as 'Disloyalty', and
the first paper on the file orders him detained for thirty days as 'there is
reasonable cause to believe he would [otherwise] flee the country'. The
details of the charge, the evidence and what is alleged to have been
Elliott's 'confession' have all disappeared, and other than bureaucratic
minutiae, we are left with a memorandum signed by the Chief Public
Prosecutor, an interpreter, Madame Laszlo, and by Elliott himself, in
which he professes to

> fully maintain my confession which has just been read to me
> from the transcript drawn up by the AVO, and hereby request
> that this should be considered as a confession made also to the
> Public Prosecutor. Its contents represent the truth in every
> respect. In addition, I would like to state that I have no com-
> plaints regarding the behaviour of the police.

That does not tell us much, and in his own notes Elliott says that all he
'confessed' to, since it was demonstrably false, was that he had visited
the Romanian border on a certain date of interest to the AVO. One minor
feature of the document is that Elliott's signature is spidery and unfamiliar. Over the years, he would win small bar-room bets, by
demonstrating that he was ambidextrous. When he prepared the notes
on his AVO experience, he recorded that he wrote the last of the many
versions of his confession with his left hand, hoping to argue later that it
was different from his normal script, and thus written under coercion.

Possibly his memory was slightly deceiving him, and what he used his left hand for was the signature on the file copy. After Elliott had signed, the Prosecutor read out to him the expulsion order and passed on to the AVO a formal order of release, telling them in language reminiscent of the Red Queen that 'this detention is to be terminated because the legal reasons for ordering it have ceased to exist'. For some time, deflected by gossip and surmise in Budapest, and the 1950 rantings of James Klugmann, I wondered whether Elliott and Laszlo Rajk had something in common, which might well explain why the AVO arrested Elliott in the first place, why they released him and why Rajk was thought by the British to have been 'relieved' at the news that Elliott's expulsion was an acceptable outcome. Could this be yet another version? When, like the solid citizens of Salem crusading against witchcraft, the psychotics in Moscow scoured the reddening skies for enemies, they could hardly have failed to light upon the jerky, East European orbit of the ambiguous, ubiquitous American Quaker Noel Field.

The well-born Field, described by one who knew him as an 'unctuous hypocrite', had been recruited by the NKVD while working in the US State Department in 1934. But he turned out to be weak-kneed, backing off in a hurry when asked for the certainties of hard intelligence rather than gossip and platitudes. Calling up the buff files from the Lubyanka's basement annexe in 1947 as the witchhunts gathered momentum, the Russians carefully tabulated all of Field's high-minded bustling across wartime Europe resettling refugees as Director of the Unitarian Services Commission. The analysts noted that in the process Field had got to know suspiciously well all the leading Hungarians, Germans, Yugoslavs and other Central European exiles, most of them Communists, many imprisoned after fighting in the Spanish Civil War, many who had simply fled from their homes in the late 1930s a brief jump ahead of one Fascist police force or another. Field's contacts were very much the same people who, as the Second World War ended, had stepped back naturally into the senior echelons of the emerging Communist regimes of their native countries. Wasn't Field, the Russians asked themselves grimly, an old acquaintance of the American spymaster Allan Dulles? Wasn't it Field who in 1943 had convinced Dulles of the need for US support of the archdemon Tito? The case of this all being part of some grotesque Western plot was building nicely. With the halogen-bulb clarity of vision characteristic of true madness, the Kremlin noted that among those whom Field had helped and befriended was none other than Rajk, whose release from a French internment camp had been arranged by Field. Rajk who had then been smuggled back into wartime Hungary by none other than the Yugoslav Communists (that he then fell unpleasantly into Gestapo hands was thought irrelevant). The same Rajk who was still friendly with Tito's Interior Minister Aleksandr Rankovic. Rajk who saw Communism in an ideological framework heretically close to that of the apostate Tito. Rajk who was so friendly with the sizeable Yugoslav military mission established in Budapest when all had been sweetness and light in the Communist camp. Rajk the persuasive, crowd-pulling politician who might dare to see himself as a rival to the puppet Rákosi as a candidate for the leadership of Hungary. It all fitted. Certainly Klugmann's polemic drew a direct and superficially plausible line between Rajk, Tito and the 'plotters' of Anglo-American imperialism, all working together to bring down the rancid Hungarian regime. So neatly did it fit that some have even argued that the whole affair was designed and helped along surreptitiously by Dulles himself, who disliked and mistrusted Field, and who could see benefit for the West in a heightening Soviet angst to provoke even sharper repression and purges if only to help convince the soft-dough Third World about the real face of Communism. On a visit to the Kremlin in August 1948, cap twisted in his hands like the foreman of a near bankrupt Victorian foundry visiting the high-collared mandarins of Head Office to hear his fate, Rákosi was told that Rajk was guilty of plotting with Tito and the West. Incidentals such as evidence and the orchestration of a set-piece trial, at which Rajk would confess, would be left to the AVO to fix, though not without the guidance and professional skills of a team of some forty Russian military and secret police advisers.

Back in Budapest, Rákosi broke the news to his trembling inner cabal (had a cartoonist dared to draw the scene, the collective bubble of thought above their heads might have read, '*Hala Istennek, hogy nem en vagyok*' – 'There but for the Grace of God go I'), and glibly negotiated Rajk's change of Ministry on the grounds that he would benefit by broadening his experience. For all his Saxon charm, Rajk had the feral instincts of a man who had lived his life on the edge, often on the run, and he must have had chill night thoughts about just what the endgame might be. All the more, had he had any idea that Gabor Peter had put his two closest AVO henchmen, Colonels Erno Szucs and Gyula Decsi, on the job of building the Rajk case. As September crisped the leaves along the Danube valley, they set grimly to work. This was a priority, full-time task requiring a delicate blend of creativity, brutality, patience, low cunning and the ability to guess what the Russians expected the case to look like. All the more curious then that at the end of September, in the middle of it all, it was Decsi who personally took charge of the snatching and questioning of Elliott. It could be argued, and was, seductively, to me in the Gellert, that when Elliott was arrested – a step which, in the case of a foreign businessman, could only be taken with express Russian permission – the AVO had no idea what he was really doing for SIS. Rather, as part of Decsi's far more important brief of nailing Rajk's hide to the wall, Elliott was pulled in because of his Yugoslav background, perhaps because he had been spotted around the Serb clerics in Szentendre, or because he was suspected of having ties with the Yugoslav military mission. The AVO would thus have hoped to exhaust, beat or blackmail him into saying something which could be used in the scenario Decsi and his Russian puppeteers were crouched over their typewriters trying to compose for Rajk. In the first ten days or so, Elliott says that he could not be brought to admit to anything beyond a drive to the Romanian border, which he had never actually made and which he felt he could safely deny later on. The AVO did not have the luxury of time. The diplomatic clamour about trade sounded serious, and the timing was too awkward to risk calling the British bluff. Hungary's peak season for food exports to Britain was less than a month away, and the country could ill afford to miss out on the advance payment now due, and the cash due to flow in before Christmas. So, the thesis goes, the Russians decided it wasn't worth it. In any case, if Elliott was expelled, the Hungarians could take control of Hutter es Lever even sooner than they anticipated, and Rajk was a dead man anyway. It was just that no one had yet bothered to tell him, so Decsi ordered Elliott's release and expulsion. And two weeks later, Rajk had another secret and terminally compromising meeting on the Yugoslav border with Aleksandr Rankovic. Szucs and Decsi ploughed inexorably ahead, breaking minds and bones in the holy cause of filling the files with statements about Rajk's perfidy. The trap was sprung on Field at the beginning of May 1949; arrested in Prague on a ruse, he was rushed to Budapest by the Russians, but was not directly used in the trial when Rajk's time came two nerve-racking weeks later. Rajk was arrested the day after. In a fine Borgia touch, he and his wife had lunched *en famille* with the Rákosis in an attempt to convince him that, despite Field's arrest, nothing was really amiss.

The AVO's senior inquisitor of the period is Vladimir Farkas, who lives comfortably in retirement in Budapest, a grizzled Walter Matthau lookalike, helping Western researchers in their quest for records and memories of the period in return for bottles of Johnny Walker, the Black label, not the Red. Since my Hungarian is too weak, and unusually for a Hungarian Farkas speaks little German, we communicated, ironically enough, in Russian, his father's native language. He did not recall Elliott's case, probably because, whatever Irish luck Elliott could lay claim to, he was expelled before Farkas and his men, backed up by the sinister Russian doctors with their hypodermics of scopolamine, could get to work on him. Rajk had withstood Horthy's police and the Gestapo, and even Farkas and the doctors failed to crack him physically, but in the end what broke him were threats to his family, and a last-minute promise by János Kádár, totally convincing to a desperate man, that if he confessed for the Party's sake any sentence would merely be part of a script, and in fact he would be released quietly a short time later. The promise was worth exactly the same as every other promise made by or about a Communist regime, and in September 1949 an AVO hangman snapped Rajk's spine as he choked on the prison noose. His last words, heard by among others the Russian 'advisers' who had come to watch the final act of their own version of *Titus Andronicus*, were 'long live Communism'.

However, at the end of it all, the thesis is just that: conjecture. Apart from Decsi and the Yugoslav connection, there is no known link between Rajk, his 'relief' and Elliott, so I was left to look elsewhere.

# 18

# The Final Veil

I have made much of the coincidence of curiosity and chance. Here they are again without apology, the curiosity a random question from me to Antony Terry and the chance which led him to lay his hands on a copy of a letter Elliott had written from London, dated 6 January 1949, to him and his then wife Rachel, deservedly better known as the author Sarah Gainham.

> Salud! If only, by God, you would stop sousing yourselves on Pernod and send me a couple of bottles instead, maybe you would answer your bleeding correspondence a bit quicker. Anyway, happy New Year, dearies. Having said that would you kindly stop wishing me a happy New Year, when you both know full bloody well that it is NOT going to be happy at all for anyone outside the Kremlin. Why don't you ask me how I am – because you don't damned well care, I suppose. Well, I am lousy, low-spirited, irritable and full of dread at going to firkin Hamburg and get hopping mad when anyone tells me how lucky I am to be going there, so careful. Maybe if I had a long heart-to-heart with Victor Gollancz [the left-wing publisher] before I go, I might soften my attitude, because I have really felt for years now that

we really are too, too beastly to the nice little Germans. We must
co-operate with them of course and I cannot see why you wouldn't
get this into your thick hide when you were told this ages and
ages ago at Spangers. Think what fun we should be having by
now. Talking of Victor and Spangers makes me send you the
enclosed cutting [about General Victor Fortune] and I hope it
makes you as sick as it made me. Jesus Christ . . . I cannot tell
you the whole long story of the plot, counter-plot and bloody
intrigue that has gone on in regard to Kati. And most of it British,
my pets. I hate the whole God-damned lot of them and you know
who I mean. Lily-livered lot. Anyway, I am still hoping to get her
here shortly – by which time I shall be in Hamburg of course.
Seriously, the whole affair has really been an intense worry and I
am quite ill as a result. Of course Margit doesn't write to you.
Why the hell should she, since it takes you bloody weeks to
answer. Poor girl, she sits brooding on top of her mountain, waiting for uncle to send some green-backs, which he doesn't. I have
met Mama and step-Papa here, they are quite nice. Once I go to
Hamburg, I am supposed to come back here for one week in
every eight, which will be something. And I don't go to Purley
either, which is more still. That place has driven me even nuttier
than I was before.

    In re bally Leica, for Christ's sake make up your mind. I'm not
taking it to Hamburg, just in case I don't get it back. In any case, I
should probably be accused of pinching it off some sodding
Goon.

    Life here is bloody expensive and I hate it. And I still love you
both very much and I miss you. I'll write you shortly from
Hamburg, if I can resist cutting my bloody throat. Ever yours
ever, Joe


When Terry sent this to me, he said he had no recollection who Kati
had been, or what the problem was. 'I cannot remember, even if I ever
knew,' he told me, lying in his teeth over the Transpacific telephone,
though at the time I did not realise this.

Curiosity again. If Terry did not know, perhaps someone else did. So
many blanks, so many dead ends. And again, chance. Someone put a ten-
tative name to the initial, a second added a surname, and in a final spin

of the roulette wheel, perhaps the twentieth person in the chain said, very matter of fact, 'Oh, I know who you mean.'

All of a sudden there we were in a small North American town, the railway's mournful whistle echoing behind the WalMart parking lot, hearing the Mark Five version of the story, rolling away, so it seemed, many of the mossy stones beneath which the memories had been so long buried. And, in the process, adding some dimensions of truth, sadness and continuity to Elliott's self-censored account. Whether her story was the whole truth and nothing but the truth, in a courtroom sense, I doubt if even she knows after all this time.

If he saw today's Kati Lechner, in her seventies, cropped hair and a mist of pain behind the eyes, would Elliott recognise the girl he met in Budapest's Park Club one rowdy evening soon after he arrived in November 1946? Then she had been a vivacious, petite Ingrid Bergman lookalike, with wavy auburn hair, and as smart as endlessly re-hemmed, laundered and re-stitched pre-war dresses would allow.

Before the war, the Park Club had been a snobby rendezvous for rich businessmen and landed gentry up from the country to visit their bankers or their mistresses. Now a down-at-heel oasis amid the post-war rubble, missing a few windows and the hundreds of bottles of Tokay once the pride of its cellars, it had become a louche watering-hole for the staffs of the British and US Legations and the hangers-on who fluttered around them, some simply craving the glamour and warmth, others fawning for favours of one kind in exchange for favours of another. It even figured in a minor honeytrap subplot at the Rajk trial. Not the sort of place that Kati's parents cared for her to be, though at twenty-six she had an impulsive will of her own, and an instant fascination with Elliott. She came from a *haut-bourgeois* Catholic family, which, until the war scythed through, had lived in comfort on the Buda hillside below the Citadel. Her father was a musician, and their circle was one of intellectuals, lawyers, doctors and senior civil servants. Béla Bartók had been one of her godfathers.

She was no ingénue, it must be said. In 1942, a few days after her twenty-first birthday had put her out of legal reach of her protesting father, and as the forked lightning of war flashed, she had married a Hungarian with an ambiguous blend of entrepreneurial Schindlerish qualities. 'By 1944 we had eleven apartments around the city in which we had hidden away Jews. We took them food – it was very difficult with the rationing – and did our best to get them to keep out of sight, which was also very difficult as they hated being cooped up. The apartments originally belonged to Jewish families and straight after the war we gave them back to their owners or, if they had disappeared, to the City.'

Kati divorced her husband in 1945. 'My father was right, it had all been a big mistake.' A brief reconciliation in 1946, by which time he had become a captain in the Budapest Police, ended unhappily when his new colleagues arrested him for unspecified monetary offences. Her mother, not content with seeing it as her dangerous duty to incommode the German occupiers by puncturing tyres and dropping sand into their petrol tanks, had done her best to provide cover for Jewish girls, giving them false papers and temporary jobs in a legal typing bureau she ran. (By what has to be coincidence cubed, one was a girl who after the war worked briefly at Hutter es Lever as Elliott's secretary before taking advantage of a design scholarship to go to London to study and never return. She became a successful lawyer and many years later as a civil servant handled the compensation claim lodged by Unilever for the appropriation of their Hungarian business.) Kati's father had reached New York just after the end of the war, and her mother was due to follow. Kati could have gone too, but in the face of parental pleading, 'I told them I wanted to stay with Kavan. I was always obstinate, a bit of a spoiled child. Unluckily for me I grew up to reality just a few months too late.' At first, she was just one of a platoon of girlfriends. 'All the women threw themselves at him, and he didn't want to settle down in a relationship. But in the end we did. Forget what happened later. It was the happiest time for me, and I think I made him happy too.' It was a madcap, frenetic happiness, rather than mahjong and slippers by the fire at Tahi. Parties, dinners, nightclubs, any excuse for a good time to ward off the black shadows that hung heavily in the streets. 'How sad and bad and mad it was — But then, how it was sweet!' Helen Makower would likely have recognised the Browning quote; Elliott probably thought Browning was no more than a manufacturer of useful small arms.

There were curious constraints though, and, with hindsight, a lot of holding back on Elliott's part. Though he spoke of his family in England, especially my younger sister Jennifer, and once enlisted Kati's aid to buy embroidered dresses as a birthday present, 'he lived with a tension he would never discuss'. At night he would scream and shout in his sleep, but simply pass it off as nightmares.

'He told me he was Irish by birth, and often blustered about how much he disliked the English. He never told me about the war, and I had no idea he spoke Hungarian. We talked in German until he taught me English. One day I did hear him asking the housekeeper to prepare some food, using a lot of Hungarian idiom, but when I teased him, he just said he had picked up a couple of phrases at the office.

'He drank more than anyone I've ever known before or since, but it usually had absolutely no effect. He stayed buttoned-up. The worst thing was that he often had people at the house in Tahi, but I was never allowed to show my face. If they came unannounced, I had to stay upstairs. Otherwise, he'd tell me to go to my aunt's for supper and not come back until 10 p.m. It drove me wild, because I was convinced he was seeing other women, one of them he even had smuggled out, someone told me. Once I got so cross I left him, but when he came to my aunt's to say sorry, I couldn't go back fast enough. I had no idea, not a thought in my head, that he was doing anything in the spy business. It wouldn't have crossed my mind, and I wouldn't have known the signs of whatever it was anyway.'

That Elliott's notes do not even hint at the relationship is perhaps understandable. That in describing the arrest and what followed as something in which he alone was involved, suggests the confusions of a guilty conscience as much as it does a discipline about secrets.

Because the night the mirror cracked, Kati was with Elliott in the car. They had spent the evening at a party given ('thrown' is actually a better verb for the diplomatic revels of those days) by Knox Helm, the British Chargé d'Affaires. Kati and an unobtrusive Hungarian were the only foreigners present. As the Famous Grouse flew and the jokes flowed, Helm decided that everyone had to do a party trick. A Scotsman stumbled through a few incomprehensible verses of Burns. Someone balanced – too clumsily for the good of Mrs Helm's carpet – a half-empty bottle on a tip-tilted nose. Coins were made to appear by magic from the heavily powdered décolleté of someone's sturdy wife from the shires. Then Kati was appalled to hear someone suggest, to British bays of approval, that she and the Hungarian guest should dance a czardas. Turning to Elliott in embarrassment, she got a tumblerful of fiery *Baracs* instead of sympathy. The half-drunken peasant dance ended in a laughing clumsy sprawl, from which she was plucked by Elliott's unfriendly hands and propelled out to his Studebaker. As usual, Elliott angry was an Elliott silent and cold, rather than yelling. They sat stubbornly mute as the Studebaker squealed on the slimy cobbles, headlights flashing across the stage-set silhouettes of burned-out buildings. Once or twice at the drizzly edge of the beam a squirrel's scurry betrayed a furtive night-walker shrinking out of sight.

The repairer's rickety wooden scaffolding and flapping tarpaulins still closed off the bomb-smashed portals of the Chain Bridge ('British designed and British built, don't forget,' Kati was now used to being reminded by the occasional visiting British businessmen who cornered her at parties under Elliott's disapproving eye). So Elliott crossed the Danube by the rather more prosaic Liberation Bridge, swearing to himself as the Studebaker skidded on the wet tramlines when he swung right on to the Embankment. To their left, the mock Turkish cupolas of the Gellert loomed out of the night. As he settled the Studebaker for the run north along the Danube, Elliott began to let loose. 'Stupid drunken cow,' he snapped. 'You made a damn fool of yourself and of me. If you can't control yourself, you'd better stay at home.'

'I wasn't drunk,' Kati sniffed, slipping under pressure from English back into German. 'I just felt such a fool prancing about like that in front of people I didn't know. And anyway, you were the one who gave me the last drink.'

'Stupid cow,' Elliott repeated unimaginatively as he glared ahead through the half-circle cleared by the wipers. Balanced on the slippery slope between warm drunkenness and cold nausea, sweat already chilling on the nape of her neck, Kati shut her mouth, breathed deeply through her nose, and clamped her hands ahead of her on the dashboard to try to keep steady. The car rolled them homewards in awkward silence. Like Elliott, Kati saw nothing unusual in the red light swinging in the road ahead. Like Elliott, she was instantly sobered by the shock of the next few seconds, which seemed to last for hours, each noise, touch and gesture hugely magnified in time and effect. For Kati, the nightmare would be a long one. The AVO's snatch squad worked with a synchronised precision which might have been rehearsed at a surreal school for doormen. The Studebaker's two front doors clicked open simultaneously. Hands which seemed starkly white against the dark reached dexterously in, and Kati and Elliott were pulled out on either side, sprawling shocked and winded, her knees grazed, on the wet cobbles. Torch beams fixed them like rabbits. Behind the glare, a hoarse voice shouted in Hungarian, 'You are under arrest. Get up slowly, and put your hands on your heads.' Kati half heard the scuffle from Elliott's side of the car. As she turned her head, her arms still outflung, a rough canvas hood was slipped over her head, with a hangman's practised skill, and iron fingers crushed the fabric into her mouth. The AVO's polished orchestration provided separate cars, and separate routes, so that Elliott had been safely locked away in the Mecsy Street cellar before Kati arrived, ran the same jeering gauntlet and, half-stripped, was bundled into a cubicle on the other side of the cellar. Neither had any idea of the other's presence, either there or later, when Kati was herself shipped down the hill and across the river to Andrassy Ut.

In Kati's version, for the next week or so her days and nights followed the same routine as Elliott, though in her own terror and confusion it never occurred to her that he might be in the same building, let alone perhaps in the next room.

'Kavan was a foreigner, and I just felt that even the AVO were pretty careful how they dealt with them. Since I never suspected anything, I assumed they were getting not at him but at me for some reason. But in all the sessions with the lights and the not sleeping, the man who was talking to me never seemed to actually ask any questions. He knew something about every subject. Music, which was our family's big love, art, life, people, and just talking.' The interrogator, unidentified, has marked similarities with the AVO officer who, about eighteen months later, worked on the Hungarian Paul von Gorka, who described him as 'a well-educated Jew in his late twenties who was very familiar with literature and classical music, one of the Jews who never used or even threatened violence'.

Like Elliott, like so many others before and after Elliott, Kati lost her bearings. As she recalls, 'One night – and I know it was night by the time of my evening meal – I was taken up. The light in my eyes was so bright it hurt, and I asked, as I so often did, if they would turn it off, or away. But all of a sudden, the AVO man said, "What light, that's the sun. Look." I looked again and it was bright daylight, the blind was up, and the sunshine streamed in. But it seemed just minutes since I'd come in. On the table in front of me was a stack of paper. He pointed to the top sheet and said, "Look, you've been a good girl. You did what we asked in the end. You signed for us."'

Kati told me that she had no idea what she had signed, or when. Equally, while she remembers vividly her feelings about what happened about two hours later, she cannot recall what was actually said when, escorted into a different room, the intellectual Jew at her elbow, she found Elliott there, flanked by two AVO guards, an officer and an unobtrusive woman who was probably the interpreter recorded on the prosecutor's file. Elliott makes no mention at all of this brief and painful encounter. Nor can Kati recall much except a memory of being told that this was her chance to say goodbye, as Elliott was being expelled, and she was very definitely staying behind. Also left behind, in a shallow grave in their garden at Tahi, was the Alsatian, grey with a black stripe, she and Elliott had loved and spoiled and which the AVO search party had shot before venturing into the house. After Elliott's expulsion, Kati was detained for several weeks, then released, though kept under surveillance and required to report weekly to the AVO. Any contact with Elliott was to be reported immediately.

Elliott's first debriefing by SIS in Terry's Vienna apartment ended by Terry's recollection, on a reasonably comforting note, 'Yes, he had had a tough time, but he had held up well, and had not told the AVO anything compromising. In fact, the debriefers concluded that his recollections of the questions he had been asked were useful for the counter-intelligence task of figuring out just what the AVO did and didn't know.'

Reading in the comparative sanity of the post Cold War 1990s a recently declassified CIA memorandum on Communist interrogation techniques, I was struck by the parallels with Elliott's own experience. The memorandum had been circulated in the CIA in the 1960s, with a 'health warning' to officers that care should be taken in briefing potential agents about its contents in case they took fright at what might happen to them if they fell into hostile hands. By the 1960s, the CIA and SIS had at their disposal reports from large numbers of agents, assets and hapless victims who had been through Communist interrogators' hands. In 1948, when Elliott got into trouble, little such experience can have been available, but his responses suggest that he too had been briefed quite accurately by someone on what to expect and what to do. Since *au fond* there was little difference between the totalitarian rough justice of the Gestapo and that of its socialist successors (the Nazi and Communist systems at the lowest levels often used the same people, as we have seen), Elliott's SOE training probably gave him the basic grounding in what to expect and how to react.

The CIA memorandum begins by differentiating the two types of arrest. 'Overt indicates the interest of the authorities to liquidate the operation and formally charge and sentence the persons apprehended.' When the AVO pulled Elliott's car over in the dead of night on a lonely road and bundled him and Kati off to the house in Mecsy Street, they were following to the letter CIA's blueprint for a 'secret' arrest, which 'as a rule means that the arresting service has plans which require that the fact of the suspect's arrest be concealed as long as possible'. These plans could, the CIA memorandum suggested, be simply to avoid scaring others before further arrests were made. They could mean that the hostile service planned to 'turn' its victim if it possibly could. But 'occasionally', as perhaps in Elliott's case, 'a person is arrested on trumped-up charges in the hope of getting him to provide evidence against himself by surprise and under high pressure'. Hence the first bout of intense questioning in Mecsy Street. The CIA also counselled, as rather cold comfort, that an arrest might have been carried out in secret 'in order to avoid embarrassment if the prisoner has to be released for lack of evidence later – that is to say, the arrest is a bluff'. But the cool, rather detached author also notes that, 'in a good percentage of the cases there is a substantial prospect that the person detained [in secret] may be let loose to function as a double agent'.

In another dose of ambivalent reassurance, the CIA noted that 'harsh or violent treatment and hasty interrogation are indications that the arresting authorities are on a "fishing expedition" and do not really have sufficient information and evidence in hand'.

In the back of his mind, we can surmise, Elliott must have heard some earlier instructor's echo of the advice recycled twenty years later by the CIA: 'Never give up hope.' Remember that 'in espionage matters so much is clouded and confused, even in the clearest cases, that prisoners who know the game can frustrate their opponents – if they persist'. Like Elliott's wartime mentors, the CIA warned of the cramped cell, the bright lights, sleep deprivation and the deliberate attempt to distort the prisoner's sense of time. Even Elliott's wartime standby of the distorted signature on a statement or supposed confession becomes part of the CIA's agent lexicon, which goes on to guide its protégés through what they are likely to encounter at a trial, in prison, in any (not recommended) escape attempt, and even on release. Here too one can see Elliott's own drinking and sleeplessness in Vienna in the CIA's depiction of the 'first wild elation of release', and catch echoes of that first carefully anodyne *News Chronicle* statement in the CIA's other bureaucratic admonition that any publicity or 'spontaneous disclosures' must wait until 'co-ordination with the original sponsor has been effected'.

There it might have ended. Elliott, rested, could have gone on to other SIS tasks elsewhere, maybe joined the permanent staff as an Established Intelligence Officer, after training at Fort Monckton, case-studies and field exercises by day, and the evening sessions in the mess, enthralled by some ascetic Alpinist veteran of the Service reminiscing cryptically about past operations in 'Neutralia', or 'Southland'. Or he might simply have continued under his grey-flannelled cover as a Unilever executive in some other troubled part of the world. 'Might', 'Maybe'. It didn't happen. Since Morris must have known about Elliott's ménage with Kati and, even if he had warned him of the risks, still allowed the operation to continue, Elliott should not have been open to too much criticism about his personal security. But when the network was rolled up, and the post-mortem started to raise legitimate questions about Kati's role in the imbroglio, Elliott (obstinate, lovelorn, guilty?) refused to listen and instead began to create an unBritish and very unSISlike fuss about getting Kati out to the West, with a frenzy and lack of judgment that had the cool watchers in the shadows wondering whether in fact he had blown more fuses in the AVO's hands than they had first thought. 'Elliott appears to have gone off his head,' I can imagine someone minuting coolly. The story then moved into the 'plot, counterplot and bloody intrigue' of Balkan Joe's letter to Terry (quoted above), Héloïse and Abelard separated not by the Seine but by razor wire and searchlight-swept minefields. SIS were bound to be suspicious. The organisation is suspicious by nature and, given the particular circumstances, their suspicions could alight only on Kati. And perhaps Elliott. There was no reason to doubt Morris, who was one of their own, though they might with hindsight have been critical of his professional handling of an important asset in a high-risk situation.

Quite how and when, why and where it was decided that the botched operation ought to be looked at by the counter-intelligence specialists of MI5 rather than kept inside the Firm, one can only speculate. Perhaps the case was seen rather more clearly than we can today as an attempt either to compromise the Legation or to recruit a British national, both legitimate fields of MI5 interest? Was it conceivably because about this time MI5 was beginning to try to piece together the trail of the moles inside the Foreign Office, a trail that would lead to Burgess, Maclean and Philby, and therefore wanted to take a harder look at failed SIS operations than SIS itself might have done? From one small scrap of the valuable evidence unearthed by the indefatigable Nigel West from the KGB's archives, we know that in 1946 Philby betrayed at least one SIS asset in Budapest to the Russians. Privy in his counter-intelligence duties to almost all SIS cable traffic, he fielded an enquiry from the Budapest Station seeking guidance on what to say to a Hungarian civil servant and valuable SIS source whom the Russians, unaware that he was already a British asset, were seeking to recruit and infiltrate into the UK. The Hungarian turned to his case officer for guidance, the case officer turned to London, and Philby with his habitual alacrity turned to Moscow, with predictable results for the hapless civil servant. Perhaps even then the antennae of the counter-intelligence experts in London were beginning to twitch. Whatever the reason, the files of cables and internal memoranda went by green Commer van to MI5's offices, then in Leconfield House in Curzon Street. The delicate quest for intelligence, the intricate cardhouse of secret operations and Vatican plots were swept aside by the sensible brogues and gaberdine macs of counter-intelligence, subtle tradecraft replaced by the less flamboyant, prosaic police methods of the Security Service. On to the stage, and perhaps into the planning of my education as well, came Dick White, then plain Mister, but later, following his apotheosis as head of SIS itself, Sir. A Vienna veteran with fragmentary memories of what went on told me that White inserted himself directly into the SIS dialogue with Elliott, without bothering to add to the confusion by declaring himself to be from the sister service, and it was White and MI5 who began to sift the embers. Looking back, the concerns are understandable, though the unanswered questions and inconsistencies are legion. Though Elliott was convinced that Kati had no hand in the network failure, Curzon Street common sense led briskly to the conclusion that they should *cherchez la femme*. All the more when three more Hungarians connected to the network were hauled in by the AVO in December 1948.

If indeed Kati was working for the Hungarians, had she been a plant from the beginning? Or had she been turned by the AVO along the way? Neither would be surprising, though since the risks of Elliott being caught in a honeytrap were so clear, one wonders why Morris and London allowed him to carry on as he was. Unless of course they had a different version of the script, one they had not shown him, which had him tethered out in the clearing, the goat in the tiger hunt, to lure the Hungarians and their Russian bosses into false moves. Against this rich backdrop of actual and potential deceit, what are we to make of the letters Kati wrote Elliott in the eighteen months after the operation blew up? Letters which must have been analysed by SIS and MI5 as carefully as though they were the Dead Sea Scrolls. Letters, the possession of which is a debt I owe, at one remove, to that old fox Antony Terry.

I assume that the letters are genuine, in the sense that Kati wrote them, and somehow got them via an intermediary to the Legation. And genuine too in that after a long journey in the familiar canvas diplomatic bag chained to the rheumatic wrist of a retired Colonel of the Blues now pensioned off as a King's Messenger, and careful scrutiny by the counter-intelligence analysts, Elliott duly received them. But were they genuine cries from the heart, complete with their misspellings and fractured English, or were they instead the careful craftsmanship of some MVD counter-intelligence psychologist seeking to undermine Elliott's morale, to blackmail him, or to compromise the Legation through a botched attempt to use diplomatic cover to arrange her escape?

One or two of Kati's letters are clearly missing from the sequence. Likewise, we know Elliott sent at least one reply. I read them first in executive comfort drifting at 38,000 feet between Emporia, Kansas, and Lamar, Colorado, where the wheatlands are laid out in vast squares, some ploughed in circles, giving the endless landscape the look of a giant's chequerboard. I did not have the stomach to send them to Kati; they had come my way only after I had had my long talk with her and I felt disinclined to scratch any more at the scabs of her, or indeed my, past.

I have left the spelling and grammar untouched. Just to illuminate the more obscure references, we know who Harry is (and can thus wonder whether the AVO did too). Fred is presumably Freddy Redward, the spyworld groupie. The girl Elliott met 'that last day' may be the mysterious Madame Laszlo, the interpreter at his interrogation. 'The 60' refers to the AVO headquarters. The kindly Mrs Markos is unknown. Quite how easy it was for a Hungarian to make an overseas call, as Kati clearly had done just before she wrote, I do not know, but she would have to have assumed her call was tapped.

Budapest, 17 April, 1949. Dearest Kavan! It was dreadful the telephone this morning, I could not hear nor understand much, I
hope today or tomorrow to talk again, and hear you! Well Darling,
this is the long letter I promised – and I am afraid that it will cause
you lots of trouble and worry. I am fearfully sorry about this – I
really tried very many things to get out from here without asking
for your help (I knew you have enough troubles yourself), but
now I am at the point that I cannot go much further by myself. I
start from the beginning. Last time I wrote you what the black-
going possibilities are. Since then I heard that even with the
Russians it is very difficult and round sixty per cent of them get
caught. The way I know is perhaps better than the other ones –
now somebody just tried it – but there is no news yet if he arrived
or not. Anyway what we know about him is that his wife was
pulled into the 60 [Andrassy Ut] and she is still there. With
Hungarian smugglers all the ways are dead, because all of this
people were caught once already, and they were let free under
the consideration that they will bring their next passengers strait
to the police. Of course they do so, as they have not got to sit for
five years or more in jail – and they even are allowed to keep the
money. . . . I would never trust a Hungarian, but perhaps a
Russian. With this I have to wait now for some time. But now I
have to tell you about another very unpleasant and horrid thing.
Last time I wrote you, how I could not get in touch with the
people in No. 60 about my passport, and how I could not see the
gentleman you wrote me about to see him. Since then I kept on
trying and trying, and all I could do was to get hold of that girl,
who speaks some English too. You saw her last day, remember? I
asked her if I could meet her, and we had a date one morning. I
told her everything, how they promised me the pass, how they
asked me to ring up etc., etc. I asked her to find the gentleman
who was telling me these promises and ask him if I could speak
to him or find out what the position is. She promised to do so,
and afterwards talking to me again. I must say that she was the
first who kept her promise, she did what I asked her to do – and
the result was absolutely shocking and dreadful. Now I see what
they are after, and I see what they were after, and I see what they
were after during this six months. They simply want to blackmail

YOU! They asked me to tell you to get a job in Switzerland or Austria, and if you are there already for good – I get the Pass. This means that they want to get in close touch with you. I ought to persuade you to do so, and they needed this six months time to make you worried and weak, that you should do what they want you to do. During this six month they were blackmailing me – to make me stay here until it gets nearly impossible to go away black. Now the frontier is closed – and they came out with their proposition. They have forbidden me to go near to anybody from the Legation, because they knew, that if I go there, they will tell me what and how to do – and they would never be able to get in touch with you. Of course they watched me, and I was told that if I see anybody, particularly Harry or anybody I knew before – I am not only not getting the Pass, but also I go to concentration camp. Like this nothing was left for connection with you than letters, which they were reading and calls to which they were listening. They reached what they wanted, and I am still here – you are blackmailed – people's life is not important to them at all. And now, I know what will be the next, if you even did go to Vienna or Switzerland which I do not want you to do! (I have to talk to you about it on the phone, I have to write you about it, I have to ask you to try to go to one of these places because they must think that I believe them, otherwise I am lost.) Well, next thing if you were in Vienna would be, that they would get in direct touch with you and ask you to do something – and when you did it – I get the Pass. After the first would come the second offer – until God knows when I would never get the Passport. So this is finished – I play my game towards them as if I would still trust them (thank God they think that I am naïve and stupid) and in the meantime I have to try to disappear. Please do not even think of going to Vienna or Switzerland – I definitely refuse in your name to try to do anything with those people and as anyway they are not keeping their promises it has no sense at all. Apart from this, I most certainly would never ask you to do something against your own people – and what they want you to do is exactly this. I want, that you should stay yourself, a BRITISHER, and nothing else. This is how I love you, and I want you to stay like this! I don't care about myself if only I know that you are all right with yourself and I never would be happy with or without you knowing that you gave up your conscience for me! The thing is a million times more important than two people's life and I am sure that your opinion is the same! Darling, promise me that you do not go to Switzerland or Austria for a job! I am going to write you often about this, I shall beg you to go there – but I do not want you to do it! You have to write me about it too, that you try, that you do your best, etc., etc. I shall know it is only kamuflage. . . . I understand there is a possibility to get some false British papers. The Legation here cannot give it and won't give it, if such papers are. But there is a way from London I think. What I ask you: try to do it from your end. If they give instructions to the Legation here – I may get out somehow. In this case only by car with an English or American car, as the airport and stations are watched, and very many people know my face. Even on the frontier there is a chance, that somebody remembers my face – but this risk I have to take. Of course if I could go with a CD car, the possibility gets less of looking at me too closely. In this case I ought to go from Vienna direct to the British zone, where you or one of your friends (Fred perhaps?) could meat me. I think it goes without saying, that the papers I give back immediately to whom I am told to give them. As I have a visa to England, this is no problem anymore if I am out of here . . . Kavan Darling, try to arrange this. I am sure they helped other people [?leave], persuade them to help me out too! I know it is possible! I don't know, if you understand why I need false papers! I cannot travel with my own name – it is a too much obvious one. I don't know if it wouldn't be best to travel as somebody's wife or so, this you know the best. Anyway I do what you tell me to do! And there is a third thing too, which I am thinking of. I don't know if it would help a lot, I don't believe it would give me a Passport, but it is worth to think about it. What do you think, how would those people lose interest in me? I thought, that perhaps, if they would think that you left me, they would give up blackmailing you and me! Once they asked me, that what do I think, what would you do if things would go wrong, would you leave me or not. I said then, that I am sure you would never let me down. They said it is good then, because if you would let me down, they would know how to

deal with you and how to brake you down. Well, I am not afraid
from them until you are not reachable for them! This is why I
want you to not go anywhere, but stay in England! And what I
thought is following: What would happen, if you would let me
down on paper? But you cannot do it from Hamburg! I know they
can get at you there! For instance if you would get annoyed with
me slowly, letter by letter, and then make an end to correspondence. Or if you would write, that you tried everything, but you
cannot get a job in Austria and Switzerland, and like this you see,
that I got stuck here, you can't see any possibility for a mutual
future, and you think it is better to say goodby as friends. Well I
leave it to you how to do it if you think it would do good. The only
trouble is, that I don't quite see how this would help me. I don't
believe in getting a Pass though this way, as Passports only can
be bought for about 150–200.00 Forints, and even this is not
always. Anyway think it over, and let me know through the
Legation in a letter, what your decision is. Of course we can keep
on writing letters later too, only not so often, as the Legation
would not do it every day. In case you think this idea of mine
right, you ought to make arrangements, that we would write, let
us say once a week. Oh Darling, I hate this idea so much! It
means again losing touch with you daily and this is just too
horrid! Must we do it? Try to get my papers, this would make us
to meet so much sooner, and it is nearly sure to get away with
it! . . . Well Darling, that is about all I can tell you. I know this
letter won't make you happy, believe me it makes me terribly
unhappy too – but this is the truth. Kavan I tell you very sincerely
now: if I could not know during these six months that you love
and you are with me, if you wouldn't tell me all the time about
your faith in me and your love for me I would have committed
suicide. Very often I was close to it and once only Mrs Markos
talking to me till the morning brought me to sense (she saw what
I wanted to do). But now I am over this silly period since I see
clearly what these people want and why they did behave like they
did. I only want to fight and I am going to fight. They won't get
me any more and I am not frightened from them any more. I am
strong now and I shall get to you. I love you Kavan, more than
ever before, and I believe in our happyness! Please write me very

soon the same way, I am counting the days till your answer! All
my love, Kati.

In a postscript, which suggests that when she spoke to Elliott on the
telephone, someone from MI5 or a GCHQ (Government Communications
Headquarters) monitor had actually picked up his phone, she added:
'PS Who was the Hungarian-speaking gentleman in your place this
morning?' Dick White and his analysts must have been tempted by the
possibilities for bluff and counterbluff this letter opened up. Was it worth
persuading Elliott to seem to take the Hungarian bait, so that he could
penetrate their intelligence operations? Given Elliott's fragile state of
mind and the possibility that the Hungarians and Russians could somehow turn Elliott and the script around, they decided like cunning old
trout to ignore the tempting grey feathers floating on the water. And
White told a distraught Elliott that they viewed the whole thing as a put-
up job, and that he was to ignore Kati's appeals. Love was personal. This
was business.

On 11 June 1949, Kati told me that she took things into her own
hands, forgot her own advice and entrusted herself to the questionable
care of a Hungarian smuggler. As she had predicted, she was apparently turned over to the police at Szombathely and spent four months in
an internment camp. Her next letter, written after her release, is equally
straightforward, but was read in London with equally straightforward
cynicism. Her mother was at that time in England. The reference to
Elliott travelling to Italy is another strand we will follow later. 'Ted' too.
We can assume meanwhile that the 'L' he was heading to was in fact
London.

Budapest, 17 October, 1949. Dearest Darling Kavan mine, Now,
here I am again in Leanyfalu, writing to you, with a very very
heavy heart. What can I tell you about those last months? I think
you know it better, than I do how I felt – specially after that I
didn't know anything about you. Yes, Kavan, I . . . often thought
of putting an end to everything. I grew tired from everything and
everybody – and all I was longing for was to die and make an
end! But as you see, I didn't do it – and now here I am with more
worries that I ever had before. Why did you stop writing? What
happened? There was one letter from my mother, I got it the day

I came out, where she says that you cannot write to me. But why Kavan? It does not do any harm to me, this is sure – but of course I don't now if it does any harm to you. If yes, well try to explain it to me, I shall try to understand it. Anyway people were horrid to me. I was told that you have been in Italy with somebody, I was told to give you up, because you forgot me already since a long time, etc., etc. I think you can imagine, how I felt. There was only one thing to help me: your last letters, which said that 'anything happens you have to trust me'. Well, I do trust you, and I keep on trusting you until you don't tell me to stop it. Kavan listen, I am deadly serious: I belong to you just as I did before, only my long-ing for you grows more and more every day. But when Kavan? When shall I see you again? When shall I feel safe in your arms again? Oh, dearest, life is just too hard to me. Do you think, that I shall ever get back to my ownself again? I got old and bitter – and I hardly can believe in something nice. There is only one wish in me: to get to you. But shall I? and how? Until now what hap-pened? I've spend a dreadful lot of money first on going, then on sitting, and what is the result? I am being on the same spot where I was before – now it is worse, much worse. Don't think, Darling, that I am weak – actually I am stronger than before – but how to start again, this is the question? If I get caught once more – 12 months prison first and internment camp after. And I am watched again like I was till March. I have a shadow, and God only knows when I shall get rid of him. I hope that they soon stop it – but unfortunately things like this nowadays get only worse and never better. It can happen any day to me, that they simply put me to camp, as you know, they don't need any reason for doing it. But I really hope that they won't do it. Now listen, this is what hap-pened to me during the seven month. I was taken away for a whole month to a place, which is worse, than the last-year place. They want me to keep connection with you – they want to send me to some school (I think I can guess what school) – and they want (or at least they say so) to put me over the frontier black! Ted is going to L. tomorrow or the day after tomorrow, I ask you Kavan, to go and see him. He will know everything that interests you – and I am waiting for your answer. Until I don't get any answer – I don't know where I am, because I am nearly sure that you are blackmailed. And please Kavan, don't tell these things to my mother. I want that she at least should stay as quiet as possible. And now, Kavan, I want to be very serious, and I think you can see from my letter that I am not exactly in a joking mood. Kavan, I swear you, that I love you still as much as I ever did – no, more than this. Really more Kavan, because I am ready to do anything for you whatever you want me to do. Kavan, listen Darling, I offer you freedom. I know that you did everything for me, what you could. You do not owe me anything, I have to offer you the possibility of leaving me, because I know, that you would not do this by yourself. It is now more than a year that you are waiting for me – a whole year with troubles and worries, you are blackmailed and you are unhappy. I love you Kavan, and my only wish is to make you happy. Don't laugh Kavan! I know you are at least smiling now – but I am speaking seriously. My own happyness is you – but I cannot be as selfish as this – I have to let you go – if you want to go. I understand many things – and I had a hard lesson just now. Darling, I even offer you one thing more: if you feel bad because of my parents – I am willing to take all the blame on myself. I think you understand, that I cannot offer you more than this – and I hope you know that this all I would do, because I love you, and I love you more than I love myself. (You always said that I am selfish, well, I don't want to be selfish – only want to give.) And Kavan, yes, I love you – I think I shall always love you – even if you leave me. You cannot spoil any more the beautiful past I had with you. Those times will always be the most beautiful times of my life – and I am grateful to you for this. There are not many people in the world, who can say that they had 21 happy months – and I had it. I love you Kavan, my longing for you is here just as much as before, if not more – but I must not be selfish. I think it is needless to say that if your answer is that you still wait for me – I shall only be too happy – but I cannot really believe in this answer. Are you not tired yet? I, from my part feel 80 years old, and tired from everything. Oh Kavan, if we only could get together – and die! – how beautiful this would be. Sweetheart, I love you so much – and you are so terribly far away! If I think that you are reachable for other people – and only for me not, I simply want to cry and scream – sometimes I feel

hysterical about this. But it is madening Kavan! Why just I cannot
go to you? And I need you so much! what about my dreams, of
having a home? What about my great wish of children? Oh
Kavan, this is all too bad! And I do not want anything from my
wishes if it is not from you. Only you exist for me, and no other
man could ever take your place. Kavan, I am getting mad one day
really, I am crying now, and I was crying through so many nights
already – where are you? Are you still mine or are you gone?
Dearest Darling, Darling little Pet, who do you belong to? I
cannot write any more, it is much too trying – I would like to beg
you on my knees to not leave me – and I must not do this!
Sweetheart, answer me please quickly. I am not really living until
I don't have your handwriting. And tell me the truth Kavan, I
must know everything, because I shall have to use my brains in
the next future about 'these things', which T. knows about! Trust
Kavan please, and some advice I need! Once more: I love you,
only you and for ever. You must be sure about this! And Kavan,
Darling I am yours like I was when you still were here – and this
is going to stay like this! What is your answer? Yes, or no? Yours
ever, Kati. You must answer me through Ted! This is possible in
any case!

If indeed Kati was writing under control, whoever was drafting the letters, some Barbara Cartland of the KGB, was doing a pretty convincing
job, since this letter in particular struck me, and continues to strike me,
as a real *cri de coeur*. But then I am not in MI5, in the middle of a hot
Cold War. The art and the curse of counter-intelligence lies in the fact
that every supposed fact or alleged truth can be turned completely on its
head. Suspicion is always the better part of valour. For instance, Kati's
original prison sentence, London knew from the British Legation, had
been six months. Why was she released after four? Had she done some
deal? How do we know, a cynic asked, that she had even been inside at
all? When mistakes cost lives, and even more important reputations and
promotions, it was surely better to be safe than sorry. There may well
have been collateral evidence in any case. This remains unknown. Nor
do we know by whom Elliott was being 'blackmailed' and how Kati knew.

At some point in the sad and finally pointless sequence Kati remembers that Elliott did write but to her mother, rather than through the

British channels. What was it he wanted to say, but very much did not want Dick White's cold eyes to see? We don't know. Nor does Kati. When her mother told her she had received the letter, Kati told her to destroy it unopened, leaving her prey for years, even today, to the thought that if only she had read it, things might have turned out otherwise.

# 19

# Sanders down the River

Kati was an outcast. Most of the British community avoided her like dogs circling a piece of poisoned meat. The Hungarian mistress of someone expelled for spying was not high on the dinner-party invitation list. Her Hungarian friends smelled AVO, and smelled trouble. As part of the process of stringing along, watching and waiting, Kati had received small amounts of cash, ostensibly from Elliott, to keep her going. These had been channelled via the Legation through Ted Sanders. What happened next is both an extension of Elliott's and Kati's story and a new story in itself. Its hero and victim is the Ted mentioned in Kati's letters; fall-guy might be a better phrase. If Elliott was myopic about risk, bamboozled by the bottle and Kati, Sanders must have verged on the certifiable. But yet again you are left wondering why, with the concerns felt by London counter-intelligence after the Elliott débâcle, Sanders was not warned what might happen if his role as amateur postman and occasional cash delivery boy escalated into something more torrid.

Perhaps he was indeed warned, but ignored the warning and decided to run the risk. Perhaps again there was a script, to the rehearsal of which they had forgotten to invite him, in which London simply sat back and watched to see what would happen. Born in St Petersburg to English parents in 1906, and reportedly related to the actor George,

Sanders was a natural candidate for wartime service in the Intelligence
Corps and, by some accounts, MI5 as well. He was later attached with
the rank of captain to the British Military Mission in Budapest. When the
Mission was dissolved, Sanders took a job with the Hungarian subsidiary
of the US International Telephone & Telegraph communications empire,
then and in later years much targeted as having US intelligence and
political connections of considerable scope and effectiveness. Though
Kati says she saw Sanders as just an amiable bear of a businessman
'interested only in girls, beer and having a good time', it is difficult to
imagine anyone more likely to be seen by SIS (and the American secret
services) as a useful resource, and equally viewed by the AVO as a prime
candidate for suspicion. Sanders actually looked more serious than Kati's
word picture suggested – a later photograph suggests a beefier version
of Stafford Cripps – and he had a serious job. He also, inevitably, got into
serious trouble. Kati refused, as she recounted to me all those years
later, to let go of her fixation with escape, the Holy Grail of the infinitely
desirable, always elusive papers. Sanders offered to help, at one stage
even suggesting that they might get her a British passport by a handy
*mariage blanche*; something, perhaps the reminder of an existing wife,
held him back. In October 1949, about the time of her second letter, a
carefully planned rendezvous with Kati in a coffee house, when she
expected to be given a forged exit visa, came disappointingly to nothing.
In November, Sanders said that he had found another source. On 21
November 1949, Kati pushed through the smoke and chatter at the
Gerbeaud coffee house on the north side of the bustling Vorosmarty
Square. Sanders sat glumly, stirring his coffee and sipping from the
glass of water, which, as in Austrian coffee houses, always comes with it.
'No papers. I'm so sorry, but the man didn't come last night. If you
haven't heard, the AVO have hauled in Bob Vogeler, my boss, and I think
I'm on their list too. Let's not hang around here,' he muttered, glancing
around at the self-absorbed crowd. As he and Kati crossed to the dividing strip in the centre of the street, by the tramstop, he turned to say
something. She didn't hear it, melting instead in deaf apprehension as a
black saloon swung around the square behind Sanders and pulled its
nearside wheels over the pavement. Before it had stopped, the doors
were swinging open. Men in raincoats padded towards them. All around,
Hungarians with a nose for danger scuttled back across the street, eyes
averted.

Kati remembers a square-shouldered plainclothes man snapping, 'Tell the man we are the AVO. He is to get in the car and come with us. If he makes no fuss, it will help him later on.' Sanders stood still, hands held a little away from his body, his eyes darting from the car to the men, to Kati, and briefly to the corner of the square: 150 yards away, but it might as well have been 150 miles, stood the diplomatic safety of the British Legation in Hormincad Street, its Union Jack limp on its pole in the cold, still air.

Taking the chance that the AVO men did not speak English, Kati turned towards Sanders and said quickly, 'It's police. Run into the crowd. Get away.' Sanders blinked, looked at her, back up the street, shrugged and walked quietly to the car. Kati stepped back, saying to the AVO man in Hungarian, 'I have to go to the office. That guy just picked me up in the café. I don't know who he is.' He didn't bother to reply, simply taking her hand and pulling her to a second car, which had moved smoothly in behind the first.

Against the sadly familiar background of bright lights, sleep deprivation, threats and false promises, Sanders, Bob Vogeler and two Hungarian civil servants were trained like battery chickens in the routine they followed with dull exactitude in the People's Court the following February. Yes, they had conspired to cut back production at the Standard plant, to keep telephone equipment out of Russian hands. Of course, their interest in rebuilding the Hungarian telephone system was simply because of the unrivalled opportunity the new network would provide for Western interception. Certainly they had passed Hungarian economic and business information to SIS and Washington. Yes, sir, no sir, three bags of secrets full, sir, if that's what you want. (The AVO were too discreet to bring out at the trial that they had some benefit from the ITT plant themselves. Unknown to its management, a group of engineers worked on after closing time three evenings a week making the bugging devices the AVO spread so liberally around Budapest.)

This time threats of retaliation from Washington and London made no impact at all. Perhaps because the script was better written than in Elliott's case, the Hungarians were unyielding. The two civil servants were sentenced to death; Vogeler and Sanders heard their thirteen-year sentences without flinching. They were, after all, only the well-signalled curtain lines of a very well-rehearsed play. Each sat out four long years, and was then released without fuss or publicity on either side. Kati spent the months in another basement cell. Years later, she told me, she learned from a friend that one of the pages of the script, deleted as superfluous at the last minute by the Hungarian or Soviet producers, had called for her to denounce Sanders, and then be denounced in her turn by her friend as a long-time British agent. But the cancellation of this minor walk-on role did not help her. She too went to prison, without any trial, and served four grey and hapless years, before being released without warning or explanation.

Another letter survives. The date is difficult to make out, but by inference it is October 1949, less than a month before Sanders's arrest. Once again Kati's jealousy about Italy is raised. If the 'certain gentleman' is Sanders, it is almost as though she is warning Elliott in advance of the arrest that something untoward is on the cards. But one can only guess. She wrote:

> Kavan Dearest, I had a letter from my mother this morning when she said that you are still waiting there for me and she said that you were not in Italy. I am glad that I didn't believe the stories! I wrote a letter to her today and I hope you will understand everything what happens here concerning a certain gentleman and you must be sure that there is no need to worry about it. I know very many things – actually I knew them before too, but you'll see. My only wish is to be with you again and I hope you have the same wish! My mother writes to be patient. I try to be patient as much as possible but it is not easy. Do you love me, Kavan? Do you believe I shall get to you in the end? Do you really want it? Sweetheart I must go now to Ted, can't write any more but I think of you always and I hope that I shall be able to find a connection with you somehow. I am still yours forever, Kati. Dearest one problem more. I had 4500 forints from Ted. I suppose this will not be quite enough for the rent. Please do some arrangements how much I can draw monthly. I think if I am sitting quietly I can manage with 600 a month. Would this do? Then I can pay the left sum to the rent too.

As Lady Bracknell might have said, to lose one British lover to the AVO was unfortunate, but to lose two was carelessness, at best and at worst suggestive of something much more unpleasant. London should have gone, and for all I know did go, into shock. Certainly there were more and more questions. Had Elliott really told SIS everything? Had the last encounter with Kati at Andrassy Ut just been a sad goodbye, or had harder things been said? Things like, 'The woman has confessed and betrayed you, so you may as well sign your own confession' (the confession which curiously vanished from the Budapest file). Or, 'Unless you do what we want, the woman will be shot. And what we want you to do, once you get back to the West, is to be ready to help us with information. Nothing very difficult, and if it works for say six months or a year, you have our word that the woman will be allowed to join you in the West.' In the pressure of the moment had Elliott promised to work for the AVO if they let him go?

As time passed there were many more important things for SIS and MI5 to worry about, and Elliott's file, with its red warning label, sank lower down the pile of priorities. In Budapest, Sanders too sank into the thankfully numbing prison routine, soon oblivious of the bad food, body odour and boredom – forlorn but, as it turns out, not entirely forgotten either in London or in Moscow.

Although only a walk-on part in our story, Sanders managed to leave an enigmatic later trace in the British records of the 1950s. Deep in the steamy, leech-laden jungles of Malaya, Chinese Communist terrorists were intensifying the campaign which drove the British colonial authorities and their supporting army to distraction and eventual defeat. In the inevitable cycle of those post-war retreats from Empire, violence begat repression, followed in turn by still more violence. When the British captured Lee Meng, an attractive woman who was a key terrorist courier, they swiftly had her sentenced to death and locked her in a white-washed cell to await the hangman's dawn call on his next scheduled visit to sunny Malaya from the gloom of his pub on the Yorkshire Moors. Suddenly, from a grimy Hapsburg building more than half a world away, the Hungarian Government offered the British Sanders's freedom in exchange for hers.

From Kuala Lumpur to Whitehall teletype bells rang, hands were wrung, memoranda were drafted, and consensus took shape, a process likened by some to the setting of a blancmange. The Cabinet, including Churchill, agonised and ministers puffed about the consequences of being seen to give in to terrorist blackmail. In the event, according to the files, despite the pleading of Sanders's wife, the exchange offer was robustly refused. Lee Meng must face the ministrations of Mr Albert Pierpont and Sanders would have to serve his time and eat his goulash. No deal could be done.

And yet . . . after the official decision had been recorded for posterity and for the benefit of future policymakers, Lee Meng's sentence was quietly commuted by the Sultan of Perak, who had legal jurisdiction over her, and a few months later Sanders was home. No deal was done. How could it have been, if the record showed otherwise?

Whether the arm of SIS had proved to be as long and as deft in support of one of its people as that of the Communists, and what surreptitious contacts may have taken place between cool professionals in Vienna and Budapest to achieve this result, we shall never know.

When Sanders got back to Britain, he avoided the press, but after a decent interval to allow him to glue mind and body back together, he found himself reliving the painful past step by step under the patient prompting of a team of MI6 debriefers, who had his and Elliott's files stacked on the table in front of them. Sanders told a strange tale. But not one entirely unexpected by those congenitally conditioned always to fear the worst. Not long after his arrest, Kati had been proudly ushered in to his cell. With a smirking plainclothes AVO officer hovering, she had told him that it was she who had reported him to the AVO. And she claimed that she had shopped Elliott too. What was more, Elliott had agreed to provide information to the AVO if he were released; perhaps Sanders would like to consider a similar bargain with the same devil. Even if these second-hand accounts of what Sanders said are correct, and they come from informed sources, not from any documented record, they are not necessarily condemnatory: Kati could so easily have been forced by the AVO into performing for them in front of Sanders. But they were received gloomily in London, where the files had stayed open; and some years later, even Kati's uncle was questioned about her on a trip through London 'in a very unfriendly and suspicious way' by unidentified 'men from the Home Office'. What had Kati known? What had she done? Had she ever really been in prison? This latter question became another small and unresolvable puzzle since, in the 1960s, unable to get work in Hungary without revealing her prison record, which, in a neat Catch 22, would have made her *ipso facto* unemployable, Kati was able, as she told me, to pull strings to have the files doctored so that no note of her jail spell remained.

In 1956, when in the aftermath of the Hungarian revolution one of Elliott's network broke out of jail and reached England, he told another pair of quietly anonymous men again claiming to be officials of the Home Office that he too was suspicious of Kati's role in the débâcle. The Hungarians in the network first and foremost, then Elliott, were the ones who took the real risks. As far as I can ascertain, no one in Elliott's group was actually sentenced to death, though most served at least eight years, and would have spent longer inside had the 1956 revolution not intervened. Ringmaster Morris had diplomatic immunity. Elliott was legally unprotected, but at least had a government prepared to rattle the cage for his release. The Hungarians had only belief and commitment, for which they paid a very full price.

Kati too took risks, whichever view you take of her allegiance. If, as she avers, she was not a plant, to become romantically involved with the mysterious Elliott was to put herself, naïvely, at real risk vis-à-vis the AVO. If (which must remain an 'if') somewhere in the sad saga they did force her into an ambivalent or even hostile role, with Elliott and later Sanders, she was running a risk of a different sort, since SIS has an elephantine folk memory and a longish arm. Despite what the rotund and orotund Canon Tonks claimed in my Confirmation class many years ago, there is no absolute truth. Especially in the piranha-infested waters of spydom. Truth is in the eyes and the typewriter and the scissors of whoever has charge of the files. Files may lie by perpetuating on cheap paper with official stamps and smudged signatures the false testimony beaten and bullied out of hapless witnesses. They may mislead by error, selectivity, falsification or subsequent pruning, a prime example being the archives of SOE, which, in a successful effort to expunge all references to SIS and its wartime secrets, have been weeded more thoroughly than the gardens of the Royal Horticultural Society, the edited pages ironed flat to conceal the emendations.

There is no reason to think that the Hungarian archives are better or worse than others in recording the real facts, nor to believe that what they hold is necessarily the truth about Kati, Elliott, Sanders or anything at all. Assembled in their dusty volumes and microscopic personal detail for the trial of Sanders and Vogeler, and unearthed for me by the diligent Dr Laszlo Varga of the Budapest City Archives, they put a different gloss on key parts of Kati's story, a gloss closer to the cool and cynical view of her taken by SIS and MI6. They suggest that far from not knowing that Elliott was a spy, she realised what he was up to early on in their time at Tahi when she overheard him talking on the telephone to a man named Darwill. The files even suggest that she became part of Elliott's network before being turned against him by the police, who had captured her on an early attempt to escape to the West. They may be right. They may be wrong. It doesn't matter any more. I am not sure I have the right to try to judge events of which I know so little, but which meant so much to those involved, but on dry human interpretation of what happened, Kati was much more a victim of her times than a villain.

When I originally cross-checked my views on Kati with him, Antony Terry wrote to me, with a politician's adroitness: 'I still have no recollection of hearing about her from Kavan . . . though his reference to her in his letter indicates he must have assumed I had some prior knowledge. I did not know for instance (or do not recall) that he had been picked up with her by the Hungarians.' Summing up, based on all his experience of that twisted, forgotten post-war Europe, he told me:

> I would not necessarily assume the worst. . . . Life in a
> Communist country and in that line of business meant that things
> are not always as straightforward as they are in other walks of
> life. The lady may even have been anxious to help Kavan, but got
> caught with him and only talked her way out of it by undertaking
> to work for the other side. Or, of course, she could have been
> working for them all the time. Kavan was no fool, however, and
> had been in that game for a long time; if he was anxious to get
> her out to the West, he must have thought she was genuine, at
> least at one stage. In these matters, I hesitate to draw easy con-
> clusions because one hardly ever knows the full story. For
> Kavan's employers at SIS, things as seen from London are more
> cut and dried. They trust nobody and despise nearly everybody

in Terry's lapidary summing-up, which might well serve as a super-scription over the doorway of SIS's grotesque and grotesquely visible new headquarters at Vauxhall Cross. Terry never volunteered to me what had turned him against SIS, beyond vague references to a 'friend' of his who, after many years of risk as a legman and errand-runner for SIS, discovered that they were reneging on what he had understood were his long-agreed pension arrangements and, on complaining, had found himself dropped penniless from the charmed circle with the chilly alacrity that might attend the discovery that the Chairman of the Racing Committee of the Turf Club worked in Stamford Hill on Saturdays as a Hassidic rabbi. We have neither space enough nor time to record here Terry's many other off-the-cuff comments to me on SIS and its people. Both he and Elliott had known in Vienna George Young, who rose to be the Service's Deputy Chief before his embrace of his wife's extreme right-wing political views and the knowledge that the top job would never be his led to a mutually agreeable parting of the ways and a new life in the City, which must have tested what Terry termed Young's 'Presbyterian conscience . . . sometimes a bit too much of it'.

Echoing Malcolm Muggeridge's remark after a period of service with SIS that he had 'never met an intelligence man whom one felt one could trust', Terry wrote that Young 'was basically straight, not devious like the rest of the gang . . . I always felt that come what may one could rely on George to back one up to the hilt and even though he stood up for his principles and had no illusions about the frailty of human nature, there was never that slipperiness one felt in the others . . . .' Of another, unusually sociable, SIS figure of that era, who had better remain anonymous, Terry, misquoting Dr Johnson, said acerbically that he had 'the morals of a whore and the manners of a dancing master'.

Antony Terry died in 1992. Though we had spoken many times, and he proved an energetic correspondent, I never got around to organising the long trip to the ovine obscurity of New Zealand to talk face to face. A pity, since on some points, such as Kati and his own career, he was adept at evasive frankness, and a meeting might have flushed out more. But perhaps not; his first wife, Rachel Ames, who has sculpted several word images of Terry in her Sarah Gainham novels, found him incorrigibly devious, congenitally unfaithful and capable of icy cruelty. Like Elliott, Antony Frederic Aime Imbert Terry was born in North London, to parents who were not married. He spent much of his early life in Berlin, where his father was attached to the British Embassy. When he sheltered Elliott in his book-stuffed apartment in Vienna's Fleischmarkt, Terry was working for Ian Fleming as a correspondent for the Mercury News Service, a network of journalists established by Fleming in 1945 when he left Naval Intelligence, and which claimed to be principally serving Kemsley newspapers in London, including the *Sunday Times*. The network was also used to collect reports of a more political, strategic or sometimes downright eclectic interest, which, many of his orthodox correspondents noted with interest, never seemed to find their way into print despite Fleming's compulsive interest in gathering the material. A network, in short, that often seemed to have as much to do with interesting intelligence as it did with publishable news.

Terry was a war hero and an investigative journalist of resource and tenacity, skills well honed in his post-war work tracking down and interrogating Nazi criminals. He was not an easy man to live with; his obituary, which one suspects was his most polished piece of composition, records two wives, though there were in fact four, brief moments of stability in a life of compulsive promiscuity. Terry always exhibited a considerable familiarity with SIS, matched by a cordial distaste for its people. When I asked him whether he had in fact worked for SIS, his smooth reply was on the line of, 'Oh, I used to come into contact with them a lot. Couldn't avoid it in my work.' I did not press the point, and it was only after his death, and talking with two of his ex-wives, that I learned that one at least had no doubt at all that he had been formally engaged by the Firm, and recalls detailed talks about pensions and insurance. When and in what capacity is obscure; one SIS source seemed convinced that while Terry was 'sort of in the family', he was never a 'card-carrying member' of the Firm. The relationship probably began before the war, a period about which he would only say that the proprietor of the small news agency which employed him 'had intelligence connections'. Whenever he started, and whatever the formal ties, he was certainly working closely with SIS in Vienna in 1948. Rachel Ames recalls that they had actually been required to marry as a condition of his posting there, as SIS felt it unwise to expose a bachelor to the blackmail and pressure risks inherent in the gourmet menu of temptations of the flesh then (and now) readily on offer in Eastern Europe (a pity those Arnold of Rugby attitudes were so singularly absent in briefing Elliott for Hungary). It was only after he had died that I found Terry's own version of his relationship with that enigmatic body of men and women who cheerfully deny the truth in order to serve it. He had settled in New Zealand late in life with his fourth and last wife. In 1989, stung by allegations in a Wellington gossip sheet that he was the SIS New Zealand Station Officer, masquerading as correspondent of the *Sunday Times*,

Terry instructed his lawyers to write a rebuttal. The hand might have
been that of the august firm who represented him, but as with the obituary the voice was pure Terry. The letter recounts his career in some
detail, though it omits any reference to his pre-war work for the little
Westminster agency. Nor does it mention the 'intelligence backdoor' by
which he claimed he and Elliott had joined the army. Terry says of himself: 'He was posted to Vienna in 1947 on a part-time correspondent
basis (for Mercury) and for a limited period also continued his part-
time intelligence work.' He goes on: 'In 1949, Mr Terry was taken on as
a full-time staff member for the *Sunday Times* of London and was posted
to Berlin. From then on he ceased all intelligence work and for forty
years has never worked for any intelligence organisation . . . .' Much
depends on the real meaning of 'worked for'. Over the years Terry was
associated even from remote New Zealand with *Sunday Times* scoops
and claimed scoops of an intelligence nature. And I was amused on
rereading one of his letters to me recently to recall his pride that 'I did
have some input . . . in ditching Arthur Scargill by being involved in the
disclosure of his Libyan connections . . . . On the wall of my home here
is the *Sunday Times* picture of me with Arthur S. surrounded by tough
Scottish miner bodyguards. . . .'

Now that the allegations that the Mineworkers Union received
'Gaddafi gold' have been convincingly demonstrated to be at a mini-
mum without substantiation, and most likely a smear operation
contrived by MI5, Terry's further comment that: 'As I happened to be in
London from the South of France at the time I volunteered for the job'
can be cast in an ambiguous light, and may suggest that, while not
strictly 'working for' SIS itself in later years, he had a close relationship
with the inner sanctum of the Information Research Department at the
Foreign Office, whose supposed lack of connection with SIS was a distinction without a difference but which a Talmudic scholar could argue
was not 'an intelligence organisation'. But at all events Terry was a loyal
friend of Elliott's, and an invaluable help to me.

Hungary itself, though not free from economic pain and the alluring
old-time melodies of anti-Semitism and irredentism, has made progress
towards the broad sunlit uplands of democracy and capitalism, becoming
among other cultural achievements a major European centre for the production of pornographic films and proud owner of a booming stock

market. However, as in Bulgaria, the shadowy cadres of ex-Communists repackaged in Armani, lipgloss and Mercedes 600 SEL roadsters gives pause for thought. When, as part of this process of transformation, its Government announced proudly in the spring of 1992 that Unilever and an Italian partner had paid over £100 million to buy Hungary's 'largest manufacturer of margarine, soaps and detergents', of which Hutter es Lever had once been the cornerstone, few eyebrows were raised. Another deal, another dollar. But Geoffrey Heyworth, John Hansard and Elliott must have done a rattling, syncopated turn in their graves at the thought. A little like paying a mugger to give you back your wallet, though, to be fair, Unilever did in the end receive compensation of seventeen pence in the pound for the assets the Communists expropriated. The 'new' Unilever is now one of the twenty largest companies in Hungary; 'it's an ill wind . . .'

In January 1993, Gabor Peter's nasty little life drew peacefully to a close in a quiet Budapest apartment looking out over what else but a flower-filled garden. Caught up himself, the biter bit, when Stalin's paranoia fixed feverishly on Jews holding key positions in the Soviet Union and the satellites. Peter was bounced out of office and faced trial in 1954. Those who claim Stalin had no sense of humour are surely in error; in one of the era's supreme ironies, which must have had the old bastard rolling on the dacha carpet in stitches while Beria giggled in sycophantic glee, General Fyodor Belkin, the Soviet secret police chief who had masterminded most of the investigations and trials in Hungary and Czechoslovakia in the 1940s, was himself arrested in 1952 and promptly (hardly surprising considering he knew the script so well) confessed to being a 'Zionist' agent and to having recruited Peter as an agent for the unlikely duo of SIS and Mossad. Peter avoided both the rope and reprisals by the countless victims among his fellow prisoners, and served some ten years in jail before being released without fanfare. Fifty would not have been enough. He then made his living from his old skill, bespoke tailoring, a calling involving some of the same skills in fitting and stitching up as running a secret police force but, happily for him and his neighbours, without any of the concomitant screaming.

Colonel Szucs, one of the two inquisitors put on the Rajk case, went to Moscow after Peter's arrest because he felt that the purges were getting out of hand and that Stalin, the Great Father, was probably being misled by his henchmen. After stammering out his report in the Kremlin to The

Leader of all His People, Szucs was led away for a soothing glass of tea and an unsentimentally brisk session with the Lubyanka hangman, while in the Executive Suite the laughter swelled again.

Rajk's rehabilitation and reburial, for whatever good it did him, on 6 October 1956 was one of the powerful currents of national emotion which culminated two weeks later with the short-lived revolution, soon snuffed out by Russian tanks. The swollen-headed Horthy also went through the ritual of repotting in 1993, though many of his fellow countrymen felt that he might have best been left to moulder. Pale, trembling, but with his honour intact, Cardinal Mindszenty was freed from prison in 1956, but was unable to leave Hungary before the Red Army closed its borders. He was given asylum in the US Embassy, where he was immured for fifteen claustrophobic years, before eventually being permitted to leave for Rome and a peaceful death after a martyr's life.

Though SIS veterans maintain that he was never officially 'on the books', Freddy Redward saw his twenty-year career in Hungary draw to a no doubt completely coincidental close about three weeks after Elliott's little spot of difficulty. Combining a sense of loyalty with a sense of humour, the Foreign Office posted him to Iskenderun in Turkey as British Consul. His opportunities to put his fluent Hungarian to good use might have been limited, but he was no doubt good company for the locals.

The AVO offices at No. 60 Andrassy Ut are now a corporate headquarters, but will be very readily convertible back to their more unpleasant function when, inevitably, the tide of history turns again. Even now, the currents along the Danube bear careful watching. Jim McCargar, the American agent who lay low in Budapest during Elliott's time, summed up very well the stew of contradictory feelings in the mind of an operator facing that implacably hostile environment. 'Outrage, anger, worry, fear, suspicion, curiosity, pride, sympathy, hope, frustration, satisfaction, brief triumph, occasional humour and final sadness.' A cocktail powerful enough to drive most people a couple of degrees off true North. If you were a little adrift to begin with, it could do a lot of damage. Elliott showed every sign of going to pieces, in a way that might have been perfectly explicable in the light of his bad time with the AVO and the fact that Hungarian 'Joes' for whom he had been responsible had paid a high price for their loyalty and his carelessness. He drank. He screamed in his sleep at Antony Terry's apartment. He once drove, senselessly drunk, headlong in the direction of the Soviet zone and

Hungary, before coming to his senses in a ditch. All of this would have been carefully reported back to SIS. But he was well looked after, not only by Antony Terry and his wife, but also – another name I plucked from his letters – by the lady named Margit. Unlike Kati, of whom he professed stonewall ignorance, Terry seemed ready and able to sketch Margit for me, though he would not tell me where she was now living. 'She had nothing to do with the espionage stuff,' he asserted with the same convincing ring as his denial of any memory of Kati. Terry told me, 'Margit Novotnova was vivacious. Red hair. Red fingernails. Great fun. She and my then wife were good friends and I had introduced her to Kavan on one of the weekends he came to Vienna from Budapest well before he got into trouble. She was Czech. Happily married to a man with a good job in the Czech hierarchy. She came from a good Jewish family, she was essentially Central European, upper-middle class, and she simply did not fit into the rigid Communist society that she and her husband had returned to from Britain during the war. Her husband's *nomenklatura* friends tended to disapprove of her because she liked dressing well, and she longed loudly for the harmless luxuries of the old "*Kaiserlich und Koniglich*" world before Marienbad became Marianska Lazne, when one's parents took one to Bad Gastein for the *Kur* every year.'

It wasn't easy for a Czech to spend time in the West, but Margit had the right attributes: a medical problem, a husband with some influence, and a family that could stay behind in Czechoslovakia as some reassurance to the grudging authorities of her eventual return. And, above all, money. An uncle had emigrated to the United States, made a fortune, and was now back in Eastern Europe building textile factories with United Nations' funding. He had shipped to Vienna from New York a huge eight-cylinder Lincoln, which Margit drove around Austria with carefree flamboyance and an apparently inexhaustible stock of petrol coupons. (Did no one, I wondered, have small cars in Europe in those days?) The medical problem was polyps on her throat, for which the best surgeon in Europe – a frock-coated giant who had treated Tauber, Caruso and David Redstone's customer Chaliapin – happened to be in Vienna. Of Margit's husband Jan, Terry told me, 'He too came of a wealthy factory-owning family. His mother, despite that, was very left-wing which may be why Jan returned to Czechoslovakia and stayed there under the Communists. He was certainly a Party member while in Britain during the war but is cured of it now.'

Terry said the Novotnys were still together. 'He is well-established in the academic world, when I last heard of them some years ago . . . and altogether they have, like so many middle-class Jewish refugees, merged perfectly into the Western world . . . .'

At that point Terry drew the curtain, saying that he would not give me the Novotnys' address: 'I am not keen on the spotlight being turned on her.' There, for the moment, I left Margit, though tantalised by the thought of this bright light flitting like a cheerful will-o'-the-wisp through the grey streets of Vienna, hot nights under the goosedown duvet with Elliott on his weekends away from Budapest and from the idyll with Kati. The duplicity, indeed the energy, is breathtaking.

Terry told me that after Elliott had spent some time trying to decompress in Vienna and London, he went to Bolzano, in northern Italy. Where, he added, Margit just happened to be staying too. Terry claimed that (almost certainly through Terry himself, though he did not say so) SIS was informed about this new liaison, and was sufficiently concerned to advise Elliott while he was in London against making the trip. Advice which he professed to accept, only to throw to the winds when he returned to Vienna, rumbling off in the Studebaker in what seemed to be a rush of reckless lust. A nice enough place, Italy's northernmost city, but not exactly convenient, even today, for Vienna, Budapest, Prague or London, and in Elliott's time a long and difficult drive. That in 1945 and 1946 it had been the main staging-post for the war criminals running down the Vatican's Ratlines to Trieste and, prior to that, the 'last redoubt' HQ and art treasure cache of the Wehrmacht Commander in Italy, General Karl Wolff, is, as far as I can see, irrelevant for Elliott's story, although, as always, one can never be quite sure.

Bolzano sits in the lee of the Dolomites, German-speaking, appropriately for land that was once part of Austria – one of the ruins that the US air force knocked about a bit in the closing days of the war, but by 1948, tranquil under clear winter skies, its baroque charm well on the way to restoration. I am sure that in the SIS side of his heart Terry will forgive me for behaving like a journalist and ignoring his wishes about tracking Margit down. But as with Kati, the fascination of meeting someone else who had known, and been fond of, my father was irresistible. As indeed was the challenge of trying to unravel more of this tangled skein.

I dug in Prague, in New York, in London. Clues here and there. An old address. Out-of-date telephone numbers in central Vienna and suburban

London. Blind alleys and frustration. Then another telephone number in the American midwest, though eventually we met not among the wheat-fields but in the balmy 80-degree wintertime air of Naples, Florida (whose civic motto seems to be 'See Naples and Spend'). Effortlessly, indefinably European in a sea of bulging polyester and tanktops, Margit was petite, not much over five feet with reddish hair, slim and elegant; a slightly throaty voice overlain with the touch of an accent. Terry was right about Jan. A nice man, he told me he had been recruited to the Communist cause whilst serving in the Czech forces in England during the Second World War, convinced that, based on the record of the pre-war years, the Russians were the only people with a real commitment to help Central Europe against the Nazis. Jan himself stuck loyally and suc-cessfully to the one true path for twenty years, rising steadily in the hierarchy. As the promised land sank ever more deeply in grime and repression, Jan became a supporter of Dubček and democracy, and, when that brave effort failed, went into exile with Margit in 1968.

Margit's views on Elliott were a mix of the spontaneous and the con-sidered. Terry was unquestionably right in saying that she could have had little to do directly with the SIS side of Elliott's life. She is too straightforward, too nice, too unquestioning. But cynics might wonder today whether, despite the concerns voiced by SIS, Terry or one of his friends in the shadows of the Vienna Station might not have thought it worth taking a shot, seizing via the motive power of the mattress on the opportunity to compromise the wife of a man with a worthwhile position in the Czech *nomenklatura*.

Not that Margit was unaware of Elliott's other world. He was, she said, a man of great charm and kindness. But a drinker. And when a drinker, indiscreet, given to jovial nudge and wink banter with Terry, that the girls were not thought smart enough to understand. Those infuriat-ingly coy conversations between intimates, excluding the outsider, all boys together. Arch references to 'chummy up the road', or 'our big friend in Graz'.

'Not', Margit told me reflectively, 'a man you would marry. Too unre-liable.' (Not wishing to be cast in, indeed not being cut out for, the role of a homebreaker, she had asked Elliott early on if he was married. Economical as always with the truth, he said he was, but that he and his wife lived apart; he omitted to mention his ménage with Kati south of the border.) Searching for a portmanteau description, she called him a 'windbag', a term which puzzled me for a while, since I never saw him as a pompous waffler. Then it dawned on me that she was actually translating literally from the German, *Windbeutel*, bag of wind, an éclair-like pastry with an appetising exterior but nothing inside except a heart of cream.

Terry introduced her to Elliott at a time when, despite the gaiety and the Lincoln, her health was fragile and her marriage temporarily fragile. She recalls: 'The short time I did know him was one of the high spots in my life . . . he came into my life at one of its darkest moments and he helped me to come to terms with several problems. The time we spent together in Vienna and later in Italy was nothing but a succession of wonderful, happy and carefree days which I shall never forget . . . in my mind's eye I can still see him. One of the most charming, attractive and lovable men I have ever met.' What a strange unconscious echo of Kati's words when she told Elliott that their twenty-one months together 'will always be the most beautiful times of my life, and I am grateful to you for this . . . .'

If Elliott was pining for Kati and agitating to get her out of Hungary, why go off to Bolzano to be with another woman, who, despite more than her fair share of intuition, had no idea that Elliott had anything on his mind but her? She was there because, after her surgery, her doctors urged her to take 'a climatic cure' in Sopra Bolzano, nestling about 3,000 feet above the town at the end of a rack and pinion railway, which did yeoman years of service until the 1960s. So off she went across Austria in the Lincoln. Terry called her in her pensione: 'Kavan's on his way to see you. Meet him down in Bolzano tomorrow. At the Hotel Griffone' ('*Greif*' to the many German-speaking locals). The next day, hovering expectantly on her balcony over the Plaza Walter, she saw a dusty American car – always the touch of the flash in his vehicles and his women – bounce across the Plaza. Grey with fatigue, but as always briskly military, Elliott stalked into the hotel, his poise momentarily ruffled when, looking up at a waving Margit, he tripped over the deceptively pitched marble steps leading to the foyer. 'Shit,' was his unromantic greeting. (Nowadays, there's a garage underneath the piazza, with an elevator direct to the hotel lobby. Today's spies and star-crossed lovers will pay about $250 a night for their room, and $60 for dinner for two.)

Europe was a strange place in those days. The wires ran in all directions. In the best traditions of the hotel trade, which conveniently blurs hospitality with venality, the head porter was fawningly ready to exchange information for dollars, from anyone who had dollars to offer; in the world of high-class hotels, money has no smell. Reports on Elliott duly flowed back to SIS in London, to Prague, where Margit's presence was carefully noted in her police file, and a little later to Budapest, where a distraught Kati heard about the new relationship first from her mother and then from the AVO, who told her spitefully to 'forget your Englishman. He left you and went straight off to Italy with someone else.'

Probably Margit was no more than a distracting idyll, of little or no real intelligence significance. She is fortunate that she emerged unscathed and uncompromised, with happy memories.

Harry Morris slid discreetly back into the shadows, reappearing in Rome in 1951 as First Secretary (Visa). Whether he was still working those curious Curial connections we do not know, but in due course he collected his CMG, retired and died a few years ago. Judging from the published Honours Lists, SIS seems to get on average an allocation of one OBE a year, for a serving officer, and one or two CMGs for those shuffling unwillingly into retirement, sometimes with the consolation prize of the occasional night spent as a duty officer, watching the messages flow on the electronic screens and the lights glimmer along the Thames, hoping an old colleague or two will be bored or kind enough to drop by for a trip down memory lane.

# 20

# Island in the Sun

Post-Hungary, Elliott's trail recalls Lytton Strachey's view of Queen Victoria's life after the death of Albert: 'a veil descends. Only occasionally, at fitful and disconnected intervals, does it lift for a moment or two. A few main outlines, a few remarkable details may be discerned; the rest is all conjecture and ambiguity.'

A spell in sales with Unilever in London. A 1950 photograph shows him with a group of his colleagues at an office lunch, all of them dark-suited, sporting carnations, stiff collars, more like a bank board about to launch into a sombre review of foreclosure statistics than an 'up and at 'em' sales force. Elliott, who had the nebulous title of General Field Sales Manager is, as so often, seen with a smile that is more muscle movement than a mark of pleasure. A colleague, Derek Price, remembers him as 'clever, slim, always well-turned out . . . a man to work for, but it was clear there was a lot in his past that he wouldn't talk about. He gave you the impression of having gone through a very bad experience of some kind.'

My sisters and I can separately date incidents from 1951, simply because they centred around the hype of the Festival of Britain – marking, so the public relations myth went, Britain's Elizabethan renaissance in the post-war world, but in reality little more than a well-meaning attempt to relieve the drabness of the pyrrhic victory and economic defeat of 1945. Burbling down river from the Festival site by Waterloo Bridge to Kew on a lurching rusty boat that must have done yeoman service at Dunkirk, my mother waved her hand sadly at a stretch of red-brick, white-painted houses on the north bank and said, 'That's Cheyne Walk, where your father's living.' In those days, Cheyne Walk was more Bohemian, raffish and less cursed by traffic than today, but even so still a pricey place to hang your hat.

Around the same time, my two sisters, then ten and eleven, were summoned via my mother to spend a half-day with Elliott at the Battersea Fun Fair, by coincidence almost directly opposite Cheyne Walk. Its rather forced mix of roistering gaiety, candyfloss, dodgems and bad teeth was in keeping with the stagey bread and circus aura of the Festival. Elliott met them at Victoria Station in a Sunbeam Talbot 90 Coupé, star of that year's Motor Show, priced (I looked it up) at a cool $50,000 in today's money. With Elliott, of whom they noted sniffily that he was wearing too much hair oil, was a woman whose name they did not catch, and of whom they remember only that 'she seemed to be wearing a dead rat round her neck'. At one point in a stilted afternoon, Elliott asked them if they would like her 'to be your new Mummy'.

'No,' they said in firm unison.

The afternoon dwindled to an early close. Elliott's expensive living habits would in themselves have made it difficult for him to support my mother. But as the months went by, it was clear that he had no intention of doing anything anyway. The legal heat was turned up; that much I remember from family conversations I was not supposed to overhear.

In June 1952, word came that Elliott had a new job in Jamaica, running a Unilever associate. The old firm (which one?) was looking after its own. (That some at least of Elliott's Unilever colleagues had an idea that there had been another side to his life is hinted at in the menu card for a farewell dinner they gave him before he left for the Caribbean. At the bottom, peeping out from behind the 'Coffee and Liqueurs', is a little caricature of Josef Stalin.) The duties were light, the twilight of Empire atmosphere agreeable for a white man with military pretensions, the climate infinitely better than the UK. Above all, Elliott was out of reach even of the ingenious and persistent Lord Goodman, the redoubtable London lawyer.

I found several photographs in the archives of Jamaica's *Daily Gleaner*. Elliott, every inch the linen-suited colonial businessman, fondling a couple of Alsatian puppies he was given by the Jamaican police kennels, the commandant looking on respectfully. Elliott at the races with the Premier. At business gatherings. And at a Government House dinner for the Queen and the Duke of Edinburgh. Less formal photographs of the time show a Jekyll and Hyde divide. One shows the sober businessman quietly reading at home (I had the slide enlarged; he was immersed in, of all things, Nancy Mitford's *Noblesse Oblige*, that pointed send up of U and non-U English manners; perhaps he was still trying to learn), while in another, he is a berserkly drunk partygoer cheerleading a bevy of tottering revellers, managing in drink to look twenty years younger, the ghosts of so many Christmases past exorcised by an aspergillum of single malt.

In a 1956 interview with an evidently awestruck, if not actually drooling, lady reporter from a magazine that seems to have been the Jamaican equivalent of *Hello!*, Elliott rolled out what he must have seen as the definitive Revised Version of his life and personality, carefully plaited from twists of myth and sprigs of reality. Mill Hill became the childhood home, the upbringing Irish, his parents having 'emigrated to England before Ireland became the Republic of Eire'. He had left school at eighteen, not fifteen, and in a flight of fancy evocative of that peddler of myths Maundy Gregory, he even lays claim to membership of 'The High Order of Benedictines'. The wartime record has been invisibly mended, steamed and pressed. The spell in Cairo waiting for the DISCLAIM mission to take off acquires by implication a Desert Rat flavour of suede chukka boots and cord trousers, 'a period centred on Egypt. Rommel and his menacing Afrika Korps were still in the desert. After Montgomery finally knocked out Rommel, a more daring assignment (Yugoslavia) was given to the dashing young Irishman . . . .'

To be fair, much of this, and the odd note that his time in Yugoslavia between parachuting in and capture is stretched from days to two months, can probably be laid at the door of the journalist, who (who knows?) may well have been laid herself, if Elliott was on his usual form. The story makes much of Elliott's intelligence background, but curiously, like the dog that did not bark, the one episode which is not given any clandestine flavour is Hungary, being presented as little more than an unpleasant mix-up. But Kati was still in Hungary, and the warning of SIS about secrecy still rang in his ears. The oddest risk that Elliott took – and it could not have been a misunderstanding with the reporter – was that, in rhapsodising about his recent Jamaican marriage, Elliott allows himself to be portrayed as a handsome bachelor 'venturing successfully on the unexplored seas of matrimony'. Quite when he made it known to his wife, or more broadly, that there had in fact been a previous voyage which had ended in shipwreck, with several penurious adolescent castaways, is not clear.

Crossing a Purley road a year later, my mother was knocked down and killed by a drunken bookmaker in a silver saloon. The resulting flurry of telegrams and calls must have brought reality home to Jamaica, though Elliott's sister Ethel remembers his second wife, Pamela, on a visit to England six months or so later, being dumbfounded to hear that there were three children; she had been told of only two daughters.

Photographs of my mother tell less about her than all those disturbing shots of Elliott. In a sense there was less to tell, though she had her share of adventures. She did her best to play out the piss-poor hand of cards Elliott had dealt her. Three children, a Mauser pistol and a couple of suitcases aren't much of a start for the last lap of your life.

My sister's verbal snapshots are better than I can express: 'permed and loudly foreign . . . her laugh would have sufficed for a whole live studio audience. She played the piano beautifully, loved opera, music and ballet, dressed dolls to perfection and cooked terrible things to make the most delicate meals (we wouldn't touch the horsemeat or the bright yellow toadstools but the brains were delicious), spent forever choosing or making presents that were just perfect for Christmas and birthdays.'

She adapted less easily than her children to the leafy suburbs. 'These English people don't know how to cook. They don't know how to dress. They can't make coffee. They don't know about wine. Brown Windsor soup they give you everywhere you go . . . soda in the cabbage.' When Elliott decamped, she found it difficult to manage socially and financially. Single-parenting was not yet an acceptable mode of life. My sisters – I was above such things – grew used to the sighs of Purley shopkeepers, the frowning glance at the ledger, when they came winsomely in to get groceries 'on the account'. My mother took in lodgers (insisting, my sister recalls, on calling them 'paying guests' as somehow more genteel), worked in a teashop and spent hours, helped by my sisters, twisting paper flowers together at some derisory price per dozen. I know

David Redstone helped; I suspect my uncle did too. Somehow she managed, her gaiety undimmed. Until the lights went out.

After her death, life spun rather out of control for a while, a sensation I have since been at pains never to allow to be repeated. While I don't recommend it, the razor slash which cut off my adolescence at one Bobbit-like stroke and propelled me overnight into a state of being unnervingly grown up and self-reliant did at least curtail the tedium of those adolescent years. Her death left Elliott unmoved. The undertaker's men delivered a small wreath at the church with a card declaring 'Love, Kavan', but he made no effort, by cable, letter, telephone or visit, to see what he might be able to do for his children. Years later, talking to Ethel, I discovered that he had called her from Jamaica to ask her to arrange for the wreath to be delivered. Nothing if not consistent, despite a couple of polite reminders, he never paid her back the few pounds she had laid out.

The house was sold with disconcerting abruptness and we were dispersed among friends and relatives. In the process, the attic was cleared, all those memory-stuffed artefacts scattered, probably sold to some passing totter; whether his family now have the Mauser hidden under a floorboard, whether it passed swiftly into less respectable hands, who knows? I left Whitgift clutching a handful of examination certificates and the encomium of one of the masters, a bitter little pederast, rolling in my memory: 'We always found you, I have to say, rather sly, but if you'd gone on, we might have done something with you. . . .' I bounced around. Arnold Goodman, eternally kind, gave me a book to read called *Anson on Contract*. Though a far cry from Leslie Charteris and Hank Janson, it was as interesting as it was bewildering, and I must have spoken about it with enough glib charm, shades of my father, to justify being given a desk in his room as an articled clerk for a while.

Had Trollope invented Lord Goodman, he would have been criticised for overdoing it. Goodman was counsellor to princes, politicians, publishers, business potentates, playboys and performers; a brilliant jurist, a trusted negotiator for governments in a tight spot, an unstinting public servant, notably in the cause of the arts, a respected Master of an Oxford college and even, once or twice, a film writer. Throughout it all he was a non-orthodox but sturdy pillar of the Jewish community and, as in my case, infinitely kind to the offspring of very ungrand old clients and friends. His Oxford colleagues remembered him for his 'reassurance, toleration and good humour', to which my own memories would add boundless commonsense and, concealed until too late for the unsuspecting behind the vast, jovial exterior of a Yeti, a wellspring of acute cunning.

I learned a little about the law and much about human behaviour from the follies and sad antics of his eclectic range of clients. One, an impresario of distinction, had to sign an important document and I was sent around to attend to it. 'You will observe', his Lordship, then no more than Mr Goodman, instructed me, 'that he has a very pretty secretary. You will also observe, unless life in his office has changed radically since I was last there, that he has traces of lipstick around his fly.' He was, as so often, correct.

Some clients, not retained for long once a decent fee had been billed, were scoundrels; one at least a Mayfair murderer. Some were barking mad, material for Rumpole or the padded cell. In surprisingly many instances the problems, though the clients might describe them as something else, were *au fond* a combination of the domestic and the sexual, often colourfully so, turning Goodman's white-panelled file-strewn chambers, in the corner of which I tried to blend with the furniture, into a discreet British version of Dr Ruth's consulting rooms or a Joe Orton set. For someone who had become London's solicitor of choice, quite a high proportion of clients were throwbacks to the more prosaic beginnings of his career, kept on like my mother out of genuine generosity of spirit. He had been Balkan Sobranie's solicitor when it was little more than a couple of aromatic East End lofts piled with tobacco and bright ideas. Another, a lady being hounded by her insane husband, an idiot savant who conducted his own litigation, gave me an opportunity, slightly unusual at seventeen and a half, to attend nervously a hearing of the Law Lords and take a note of the demented husband's argument. Only the other day, a photograph of a justly distinguished member of the Court of Appeal brought back to me from nearly thirty years ago the wisdom he imparted to me as a youthful barrister when I trotted in his wake, clutching the files of evidence for the hearing of some messy divorce. 'Remember,' he said, 'two-thirds of husbands bugger their wives in the first eighteen months of marriage.'

A few months later, word, wrapped in the majesty of the law, reached me from my father's long-suffering and almost certainly unpaid solicitors, via Arnold Goodman, that Elliott would be in London soon. A date and time were set for me to meet him in the lobby of the Waldorf Hotel, a slightly déclassé but solid pile in the Aldwych favoured by middle-managers on business trips and county visitors unwilling to cope with the tweedy gentility of Brown's or the overbearing Americanised pseudo-suavity of Claridge's. Came the hour, and came the man. Or at least I came. Apprehensive, curious, self-conscious. And never without the twinge of fantasy. Was he going to suggest I came out to Jamaica?

Hair cut, shoes shined, I reported at 4 p.m. as instructed, to be told politely enough by the desk clerk that Elliott hadn't returned. Getting the same answer with slightly decreasing civility at 5 p.m., 6 p.m. and 7 p.m., and having by then read every brochure, every newspaper and telephone directory within range, and stopped just short of accosting in excitement a tall man with a vague resemblance to my memory of Elliott, I sidled out, losing myself in confusion among the theatregoers. The next morning, an explanation of sorts: he had been 'unavoidably detained', a phrase that might have been his epitaph, now I think of it. He was off to New York, but would see me next time. Meanwhile, the solicitor added, I could expect to get soon in the mail a present he was sending, a watch, no less. The postman never even knocked once. And I forgot about the watch for the next forty years.

Compulsory National Service was drawing peacefully to a close, but still on the statute books, and while I might have avoided the call, being both inept and grossly astigmatic, some residual insecurity or lack of judgment led me to be intrigued by the embrace of serge and the gritty artistry of blanco and I mistakenly abandoned the fascinations of Goodman, Derrick's Dickensian offices for the Lewis Carroll world of the army. My sisters were boarded with kind friends, whom Elliott had promised a regular cash allowance. Inevitably, as the weeks went by, discreet enquiries were made: 'Er, have you heard from your father lately? We'd been rather expecting him to send us something.' You and many others. From Jamaica, silence. From my grandfather, yet another shake of the head and another cheque.

Back in Jamaica, Elliott's Big White Bwana attitude to his largely black workforce caused increasing friction with local unions then beginning to feel their muscle on the road to independence. His marriage had in the end, and despite the high profile, not helped. His wife was twenty-one, and her father, understandably, was very suspicious of a relationship, beginning inauspiciously with an unwanted pregnancy, with this enigmatic hard-drinking ex-major, with an uncheckable and dubious pedigree from the netherworld of secrets, and no money. When he found out about the family abandoned back in England, his cup must have run over with fury and concern.

Now describing himself for the record as simply 'Christian', Elliott must have had a hard time just keeping up with, let alone paying the subscription for, the imposing, whiter-than-white clubs of which he was a member – the Liguanea, The Jamaican Jockey, Royal Jamaica Yacht and the Garrison Officers. But between the lines, the *Gleaner*'s social column of the time cast the first shadows of a professional life that was becoming unprofessional. A succession of one-month holidays, or 'combined business and pleasure' trips, to the US. In June 1957, a four months' holiday, hefty even by old colonial standards. No surprise then that a bland corporate announcement in 1959 recorded that he was giving up his Managing Director's job to concentrate on sales. Less than a year later, Geoffrey Heyworth had retired, and Elliott was out altogether within the month.

After the Hungarian débâcle, I find it hard to believe that he was up to any of his old tricks at the same time, although one Jamaica photograph gave me a moment's pause. It is curiously reminiscent of the opening scenes of Ian Fleming's *Dr No*, when the SIS Resident in Jamaica leaves his daily bridge game at the club to check in with 'M' on the short-wave radio concealed in the bookcase in his spacious home (Elliott's address was an evocative 'Allsides, Stony Hill, Jamaica'). Sadly, Commander Strangeways is gunned down by three pseudo-blind gunmen before he can pick up the microphone. In 1959, the *Daily Gleaner* photographed Elliott in front of a sizeable radio transceiver, all dials and matt metal (an Eddystone, if I am not mistaken). He is described in the caption as President of the Jamaica Amateur Radio Club. Even though as a colony Jamaica would have been more in MI5's sphere of influence in those days, one can see the value of having someone experienced with a plausible excuse for scanning the tropical airwaves from Jamaica night after night.

It is more amusing to speculate whether Fleming, a good friend of Terry's, ever met Elliott when he was at his Goldeneye retreat in Jamaica. If so, did some trace of Elliott, his style and his radio, lodge in Fleming's fertile mind for later use?

In the years after Elliott's return from Jamaica, he and Terry kept in intermittent touch. Terry was a staunch friend, always ready with counsel, but one can detect in their letters the slight flavour of Elliott as a friend best dealt with by correspondence. The frenetic pace of Terry's journalistic and clandestine life – Prague today, Warsaw tomorrow – made him a hard man to visit, but suggestions by Elliott of possible trips to Bonn tended to get a guarded reply on the lines of, 'We'd love to see you, but do send a postcard first, as I am so often away.' Despite the superficial cheerfulness of Elliott's letters, this was the period in which the financial pressures were mounting, when jobs came and went, and when he was borrowing money from anyone daft or loyal enough to lend it. So Terry, who had sensitive antennae, was probably only sensible to try to preserve the friendship by keeping Elliott at a slight distance. Perhaps, too, he was conscious professionally that Elliott had been red-carded by SIS.

But he was always ready with advice, if sometimes equivocal. In 1968, Elliott was after an intelligence job at the British army's German head-quarters in Moenchen Gladbach. What did Terry know about the set-up, he asked after the first interview. 'Mark you, I may not get the job; the Committee who interviewed me looked askance at my cloak-and-dagger upbringing as I gather we are all now highly respectable and play a nice little game called "overt intelligence".' Terry wrote:

> I would have thought, knowing the place, that what with barbed wire and the people it would have just about driven you nuts (or you will have driven them nuts) inside a month, but it does have certain concrete advantages. Maybe you are prepared in return for a comfortable villa, cheap NAAFI stores and the reassuring trappings of the Last Cornerstone of Empire (outside Gibraltar) to live in, far from wops, wogs and hippies. It all depends what you want. I know you were engaged in a spot of empire building yourself for a while so maybe this is what you would like. I would certainly have a look at it before you decide.
>
> The job would probably be elementary and I have no doubt you could do it on your head if you like working that way though some of the characters I used to know there would not be my choice of company on a desert island, if you see what I mean. I fear part of the Moenchen Gladbach set-up may be moving to that rather grim place in Belgium called Casteau. I should let your wife decide! Then you can always say 'I told you so' after-wards . . . .

In the end, the point was moot. Elliott was turned down. Another letter, in 1972, showed Terry at his subtle best as a friend. On the face of it, straightforward, saying that he had recently 'been at the Special Forces Club (what a ghastly name), where everyone was talking about you because what they call the Yugoslav Section had or were planning to have some dinner . . . . I gathered that they all miss you and hope you will call in and have a bitter there sometime.'

Inconsequential, except that I happened to find out that the letter followed a disagreeable episode in which a cheque Elliott gave the Club had bounced, with the Dunlop Rubber quality characteristic of most of his gestures at payment around that time. I have a strong feeling that in fact Terry himself settled the debt, and that his letter was a nicely phrased way of telling Elliott that he could show his face again behind the Club's anonymous red-brick façade.

# 21

# Hail and Farewell

My military service had been quite agreeable; in fact, not really that military at all. Basic military training in the Intelligence Corps was, shall we say, rudimentary, little more than a few limp-wristed passes with the bayonet at a straw dummy and an hour or two waving Sten guns by the seaside. It was felt that we were destined for a calling higher than mere soldiering and the full force of military discipline and stupidity rarely supervened. Once, though, I was detailed to spend a morning scraping several years' accumulation of bright green verdigris from the urinals in the commanding officer's hut with a used razor-blade; Gillette, as I recall. It did at least give me the opportunity to see and indeed look up to the great man, in reputation at least, as he stood at the next stall while I was crouched on my janitorial crusade. Wishing me a distant 'Good morning', he unleashed a gentlemanly jet over my newly brightened handiwork. There followed a short spell of so-called Field Security training, involving among other things brief exposure to interrogation techniques of startling unsubtlety and equally startling effectiveness, some involving standard-issue army metal wardrobes and the mega-decibel application of 'white' radio noise, others making liberal use either of cold water or hot radiators. This particular little sideline was tucked away in a unit designated the Joint Services School of Psychological

Warfare, under the direction of a red-faced cove whose uniform bore no shoulder flashes to identify his corps or regiment and who seemed rather badly in need of psychological attention himself. We learned where best to place microphones in interrogation cells, and how to follow each other around Lewes and other major enemy centres.

The Gods then smiled, as only army Gods can. I applied to learn Arabic and was promptly given a coveted place on what turned out to be the last of the courses for interpreters in Russian, dividing two happy, uniform-free years between Cambridge and London with a small group of gangling youths with intellectual pretensions from whom there later emerged, *inter alios*, two distinguished ambassadors, the Professor of Chinese at Oxford, the Governor of the Bank of England and a Discalced Carmelite friar. At the time, the story was that the courses had been closed because National Service was ending and, between them, the army, navy and air force now had enough Russian speakers to cope with whatever the Cold War might bring. Only when I read *Spycatcher* did I find out that, at least according to Peter Wright, they were terminated because the MI5 zealots of Gower Street were convinced that the training scheme had been thoroughly penetrated by the KGB. I have no idea whether this was true. I rather doubt it. Certainly and perhaps mildly disappointing, no raddled blonde swayed up out of the steam in the ABC off Russell Square to honeytrap me. No dead-letter boxes under the third seat in from the left in the back row of the Classic Cinema in Notting Hill Gate. Not for me the clandestine delights of supposedly chance encounters on that well-worn Regent's Park bench with some charismatic unfrocked Hungarian priest coyly sounding me out for membership of the Whitgift Twelve. No envelopes of cash 'for those little expenses'.

As far as I know all most of us did was learn, endlessly, word lists, rules of grammar, more word lists, more grammar and still more lists. Forty years on, so effective was the training, so firm the imprint of useful words such as the Russian for 'annointing balm' or 'capercailzie', that I can still dash off the crossword in the émigré newspaper *Novoe Russkoe Slovo*. And, reading a Russian version of John Le Carré's *Night Manager*, I can become professionally irritated by the translator's rendition of a self-deprecating quip by the effete Major Corcoran about his 'Wanker's colic . . . must be my limp wrist' as a flattened, meaningless 'Writer's cramp . . . must have sprained my wrist'. But so what?

Looking back, there was one little moment when Wright's colleagues did show their faces and suspicions. We had been told that we could expect to be trailed around London at times, but believed, rather naïvely I suppose one would say today, the official line that this was to provide practical field training for the plainclothes section of the Military Police. One summer afternoon, the course was summoned to a London University lecture room; a stern man in a blazer took the podium, the atmosphere edgy, rather like school when expulsion for over-indulgence in one of the alluvial vices is in the offing. Members of the course, he pronounced, had been seen going in to Collett's Chinese Bookshop in the Charing Cross Road. The place – like other haunts of the leftie intelligentsia – was a security risk. We would be in serious trouble if any of us were seen near there again. We were urged to report to our lecturers any approach to us to talk either about the course or those on it.

For a while we made jokes about suspicious-looking old ladies trotting past the vast Victorian pile in South Kensington, known for some arcane naval reason as HMS *President*, where the language students and a flotilla of tribadic Wren officers were housed. But it all died away, and I certainly never noticed any sign of Wright's later claim that a careful study was made of secret tape recordings of our classes, to see whether any of us was carelessly using modern Russian idioms absorbed from secret chats with our KGB controller.

I had forgotten too about the landlocked, barnacle-free HMS *President*, until I recently noticed it being offered for sale as surplus to Ministry of Defence requirements.

By coincidence, the same batch of mail brought me a photograph of that cerebral American spymaster James Jesus Angleton, on his 1944 visit to London with a group of OSS officers to learn the secrets of spying at the feet of the supposed grand masters at SIS; Angleton himself was specially tutored in counter-espionage during his stay by the stuttering turncoat Kim Philby. Angleton is standing, intriguingly, outside the same building, then rather more prosaically known as the South Kensington Hotel. Whether even then it hid clandestine links behind its Patrick Hamilton aspidistras, I have no idea. Nor whether the upmarket brothel which flourished in a hum of Daimlers and a twirling of moustaches in the mews behind the good ship *President* in the 1950s and 1960s had been there all along, patriotically ready to service the red-blooded Yale alumni of OSS as the bombs fell and the sirens wailed. Perhaps the brothel itself, run by a lady whose aristocratic name fought a losing battle with her Essex Girl origins as the level of the Booth's gin bottle descended, was an SIS or MI5 operation all along!

In 1958, Elliott was in and out of Hamburg, working for or with an unidentified 'Leroy', who seems to have been unconnected with Unilever. As it happens, I was there then too, briefly. How curious to think we might have met. Would we have recognised each other as La Ronde turned on the bustling night pavement of the Reeperbahn? Rainbows of neon, police in green rain slickers, furtive sailors out on the town, lustful platoons of slab-faced, pleasure-seeking German businessmen. Behind the nightclubs were several officially sanctioned streets, rookery nooks of whores' cribs. Girls in the windows. Girls on the streets. Girls practically on the rooftops and girls on the tiles. No doubt, as the old song goes on, girls with syphilis and girls with piles. At each end were brick barriers, with a narrow entry-way round which British military policemen hovered doing their best to save overheated squaddies from themselves.

Mind you, it was all less fraught in those days. The aftereffects of fifty marks' worth of speedy self-indulgence might be embarrassing to explain to the medical officer – temporarily painful, even – but at least susceptible to antibiotics. I was there for complicated reasons having to do with an elaborate and ill-conceived training exercise. The man I had come to see was anxious to be seen to be looking after me properly. Looking back, I think he was in fact professionally curious to see how I would react to odd situations. 'We'll go to see something very Kraut,' he told me in the taxi. An overheated room. A red cloth over the bedside light shaded the unambiguous stains on the frayed bedspread, battleground for so many close and brief encounters of the primary kind. Half-a-dozen men were grouped awkwardly around the bed like nervous spectators at an inquest. Two pudding-fleshed tarts – one, I swear, with braided German ringlets that she had probably first plaited when she joined the Hitler Youth – had a vigorous, if unemotional passage at arms with a perky red rubber dildo slung from the greying straps of what looked like a war-surplus truss. It was about as stimulating as watching an operation for haemorrhoids. Round one over, marked as a draw by most of the watchers, one of the girls called for a box of matches. She took three or four, moistened the non-striking ends generously between her thin lips, and stuck them like Christmas tree candles in the intimidating Brillo pad of her pubic hair. Her partner in grime switched out the light, struck a match from the box and lit the candles. As they flared perilously into life, the two girls gave us a throaty, schmaltzy chorus of 'Santa Lucia'. The matches burned down to the moistened stumps without damage or disaster. Back on with the lights. The non-combustible half of the act, dildo still harnessed and bobbing like a Japanese banker at a cocktail-party as she moved around the room, collected tributes from the audience, now each ten marks the poorer, but richer for the experience.

Round the corner we sipped reflectively on beers with a shot of raspberry juice, known even in Hamburg as a *Berliner Weisser*. 'Only the Germans can combine crudity with sentiment and charge you for it,' my host mused. We moved on. I moved on too.

Clad for illusory reasons of security in the socially far-inferior uniform of a completely different arm of the service, I paddled for a while in the kiddies' end of the intelligence swimming-pool, putting my language skills to some use initially in a nondescript building on a windswept Berlin airfield and later in a converted stable. Berlin in the late 1950s was still a battleground city, in which intelligence agents of all persuasions plotted, kidnapped, killed and conned each other with vigour, but thankfully our own work was done not, as in the novels of the time, by walking wet hostile pavements at night with your collar turned up and your eyes straining to look behind every shadow thrown by the iron bridges of the S-Bahn overhead railway. We were voyeurs, or more accurately *auditeurs*, working at a distance by the wonders of modern science, much as today the 'moan, groan, dial tone' of telephone sex chat lines substitute for the 'wham, bam, thank you, Ma'am' of the real thing. One happy, if unintended, result of it all was a lasting fascination with, and affection for, the United States. It began one rainy morning in Berlin, when, after the usual Military Police courier officer had failed to appear, I was hastily bidden to put on civilian clothes, jump, in an odd security contradiction, into an army Volkswagen with a uniformed driver, and deliver canvas pouches stuffed with secrets first to the SIS office behind the Olympia Stadium, and then to our American opposite numbers in the US sector. With the solemnity of a Masonic ritual, I was handed a large pistol in a canvas holster, which made my sports jacket bulge as though I had some curious goitre affliction of the right armpit, and a heavy brown-paper package sealed with bright red wax. Therein, I was told, lay six rounds of ammunition. If, and only if, waylaid by the Russians, I could at my discretion unseal the package, load the pistol, with trembling fingers – the Russians, no doubt, standing politely by until I was ready – and repel boarders. Heaven help me though if the package were opened in any circumstances short of dire emergency; there would be a Court of Enquiry and condign punishment. If of course I was still alive to attend.

The SIS set-up was briskly military on the outside, tweedily public school inside; you almost expected to see a couple of Labradors behind the filing cabinets. The US army Security Agency's operation was not on the face of it that secure, but clearly designed by someone with Hollywood imagination. Waved through a gate at the back of Templehof Airport by a guard interested only in the car's numberplates, we parked and I set off along what seemed a derelict façade in search of Block B. Behind the creaking door, which was standard issue for all clandestine offices, a rubble-strewn staircase led up into the darkness.

On the first landing a wire mesh gate stood open, the only evidence of a guard, his abandoned canvas chair and a comic book. I ventured further. Up one more flight, there was a light and airy landing. In the centre of a freshly painted wall was a heavy steel door, of the ponderous gravity one might expect to see guarding the treasures of deposed dictators and errant Spanish financiers in the 47th Street vaults of the Morgan Guaranty Trust Company of New York. To its left, set into the wall, was a panel of six buttons, clearly an entry code mechanism. To the right, a red Coca-Cola vending machine, of the kind I had so far only seen in films or the advertisement pages of *Life* magazine, clicked and buzzed its subliminal American Ur-melody. As I stood like Alice, wondering how I was supposed to pass through the door and gain access to the inner temple, the door opened with a slight sigh. Out stepped a bespectacled figure with hair cut *en brosse* in a style even the most ferocious British Army barbers would not have dared to emulate.

'Hi. Can I help you?' he said, without any thought that I might be representing Smersh or the *Daily Mail*. I explained my mission. 'Sure,' he waved expansively, 'just go along in. I came out to get a soda. Want one?'

My impressions then of the high-tech wizardry the Americans brought to bear on our work, compared to the Heath Robinson style of our own operations, all those whirring wall-mounted recorders, flashing lights and aerials hidden in water-tanks atop the building, were tempered only by the self-defensive conviction that while they might have the gear, they didn't seem to have the same language skills, a deficiency for which they could not be blamed, most of them having learned rudimentary Russian among the overwhelming social and climatic diversions of Monterey, California.

This first acquaintance led to secondment to another US unit in a charming South German city, which had emerged relatively unscathed from the war and was now busy prospering from the peace, blaming the unfortunate events of recent years on the evil Nazis who had destroyed the nation of Goethe and Heine, while, of course, all the solid citizens in that placid neck of the Neckar had been busily plotting against Hitler and saving Jews. The openness, the gangling good health and friendly charm of my new acquaintances were a sharp contrast to the carious furtiveness and snobbery of those with whom I lived and worked back up North.

More than that, remembering that in those far-off 1950s we are talking of times when familiarity with things American through travel and television was very limited, the richness of the home lives my contemporaries described without apparent artifice or exaggeration – two cars in every pot and a chicken in every garage, so to speak, the summers on the beach, the winters in Hobe Sound, the very variety and freshness of the food served even in mundane army messes – all seemed to me to suggest that the prevailing English attitude to Yanks was a condescending delusion born out of envy.

Sent on my way eventually by a grateful government to dead civilian streets, with a free green demob 'suit' cut a long way east of Suez, a felt hat and a pair of shoes designed for the orthopaedically challenged, I fell on reasonable times translating Russian technical and scientific journals. I was able to churn out thousands of words a day in the calm of Kensington Public Library; it was a period of considerable prosperity. There was no need to understand the underlying material – specialist dictionaries and a few back numbers of *Scientific American* usually did the trick. I tackled a wide range of subjects with ignorance and brio – Cancer Research, Chemistry, the Journal of Patents, Problems of Psychology, and even Higher Mathematics (the latter a waste of time; you were paid only for the sparse Russian text, not for the interminable equations filling most of each page). A technical editor corrected the more obvious howlers.

All of this was grist to the dynamic mill of my main customer, the bow-tied bullshit artist Robert Maxwell, then seen as a rising entrepreneurial publisher. He should have stuck to his basic business; it was, by any standards, a high-margin, cash-spinning goldmine. Hubris, a larcenous heart, the cupidity and stupidity of his bankers, and a failure to take swimming lessons, did for him in the end. As one illustration of the world's inability or unwillingness to see through the slabs of porcine flesh to the man beneath, he was allowed for years to get away with the loving burnished self-image of Bob the polyglot, chatting fluently to Eastern Bloc leaders in any one of half-a-dozen languages. Possibly his German was passable. Quite likely he imported from his native Ruthenia some familiarity with Czech and Romanian. But having once overheard him stumble ineptly through a few words of Russian, I had trouble thereafter believing any of the other aspects of the Maxwell story.

I married. We moved to the country. Buried in a nearby wood was a large Edwardian pile which housed the foreign radio monitoring station run by Reuters, the international news agency, where I applied for a job. They found I had some proficiency – hardly surprising – in listening to and reporting on Soviet radio broadcasts, and I had a great time. If one can call scoops snatching hot items from the crackly ether and banging them over the telex line before the BBC or a rival news agency had picked them up, I had a couple of nice ones. My 'snap' news of Khrushchev's decision at the nail-biting height of the Cuba missile crisis to order his ships to turn back reached John Kennedy's desk from our Hertfordshire retreat ahead even of the flash report from his National Security Agency monitors. The tranquillity of another sunny evening was broken when, buried in a stultifying Moscow radio review of the day's Soviet papers, I heard the first official confirmation that 'the English citizen Kim Philby' was alive, well and an honoured member of their Service. Philby kept the cutting of this report from *Izvestiya* for the rest of his scoundrel days.

The work attracted a somewhat eclectic group of people, mainly émigrés. A Pole who had trained for the priesthood, had studied the classics and had once scooped the world's press by picking up the result of a Papal election from a Vatican Radio news bulletin in Latin. A dour Ukrainian who swigged neat hydrochloric acid from a plain bottle on the orders of some quack doctor, to stimulate his gastric juices. A flexible former Croat emissary to the Vatican, and a kindly old gentleman in slippers who had briefly held a ministerial post in the exiled Polish Government in London. Then there was a sprightly apple-cheeked Englishman, in his sixties. He spoke Russian and Romanian. Archie Gibson had been *The Times* correspondent in Bucharest before the war.

His brother Harold, like Archie born in Moscow, had had a long career in SIS, including a spell in charge of the Intelligence Centre in Istanbul, and ending with his inexplicable suicide while Head of Station in Rome. Archie, too, was seen by informed observers as having at least a cosy relationship with his brother's organisation, and at one stage in the war seems to have been in charge of one of the super-secret communications units, known as SLUs, responsible for channelling ULTRA data from London into the hands of local commanders. His Reuters' personal file, which I happened to get hold of some years later, made this crystal clear. One of his references for the job had been the SIS veteran Colonel Monty Chidson, once Head of Station in Bucharest and later Deputy Head of Section D. The other was a Conservative MP with strong intelligence connections described as 'a friend of Reuters' Diplomatic Correspondent'. Both Gibson brothers had their entries in the Gestapo's *Wanted List, GB*.

In a lull between broadcasts one day, something was said about Hungary. I mentioned my father. Archie's leatherette typist's chair squeaked excitedly. He swung round. 'Kavan's boy – are you really? I don't believe it. I knew him very well.'

But when I started to ask about Elliott, Archie suddenly became oddly vague about where and how he had met him, other than saying their paths had often crossed in the Balkans. Did I catch a rueful echo when he remarked that my father had been 'quite a lad. Lots of girlfriends.' Time for the main evening bulletins from Moscow. The conversation petered out.

A couple of years later, after I had left Reuters and taken up usury – working for a pair of rapacious South Africans lending money at high rates of interest to small businesses teetering on the edge of insolvency – my wife and I ran into Archie in a wet suburban car park. He too had left Reuters; his file said he had taken 'temporary employment with the Foreign Office'. Indeed. Chatting before making a dawn raid on the Sainsbury's down the hill, Archie mentioned that he had heard that my father was now living back in the UK. Small world. For a short time Elliott had, I learned, rented a house only a few hundred yards from our own Edwardian home in Kew; had I passed him, unknowingly, as he clinked out of the nearby liquor store, another cheque left, more in hope than expectation, in the manager's trusting hands?

Now, Archie had heard, he was somewhere in Berkshire. A big county, Berkshire. By dint of hard work and endless cajolery with the

robotic ladies of Directory Enquiries, I eventually found an address in a
village called Chilton Foliat. How quaintly British, I remember thinking. One day in the summer of 1966, on my way back from Bristol where
I had been snatching back, a jump ahead of the rest of the creditors,
money we had lent to an over-stretched monumental mason whose cash-
flow had been depleted by the lower than expected death rate of a mild
winter, I cruised anonymously through. Not so quaint. In fact, a shabby,
single-street village. One nice house down by the river, but nothing special to be seen. A few weeks later, I was back in the neighbourhood; the
industrial finances of the Home Counties were crumbling badly.
Meanwhile, I had heard that Elliott and his second wife ran the Post
Office and General Store (nice irony that a man who had handled so
much clandestine mail for SIS should now be reduced to the mundane
real thing). But there was no sign outside the only likely premises; just
a display window, a rack of curling picture postcards, a handful of soup
tins, a few pairs of grey wool socks. It was almost as if it had been set up
as a test piece for a memory training exercise, or as a spoof re-run of
those death-dealing Bulgarian suitcases.

I knocked at the door. Elliott opened it. I felt no special emotion, just
cringing embarrassment. What in God's name was I doing? I stammered,
'Hello.' What else can one say?

'I know your face, but I can't place it, I'm afraid,' Elliott said, politely
enough.

'I'm Geoffrey.'

Elliott was the product of forty years of training, waiting for strange
knocks on the door from secret policemen, girlfriends, husbands and
bailiffs. He did not turn a hair, skip a beat, break into tears or slam the
door. Much the same man who had taken me for a walk at school. Greyer
though and lined, battered. The hair still springy, a tall lean frame,
upright, chest out, stomach in. Good military posture. The voice was
throttled back, bubbled like hookah smoke through bronchial tubes
wrecked by years of abuse. The accent undefinable. Officer overtones,
but the vowels searched for the right frequency.

'Oh! Well, you'd better come in,' laconically. I unleashed a barrage of
banalities in the 'just passing, thought I'd drop in, long time no see' vein.
I really cannot remember too much of Elliott's responses. He waved a
hand at the window, commenting that he and his wife were no longer in
business. He introduced me to a pleasant, plump woman, not much older

than I. Wet basset hounds flopped about farting. In came three round-eyed, tongue-tied children – two half-brothers and a half-sister of whose existence I had been unaware. As they, presumably, had been of mine. The whole thing was grotesque, artificial as a cheap hairpiece. Too much time had passed. I made an excuse and began to leave.

Elliott was suddenly pressing that I and my family should come down in a couple of weeks and spend a night. Spend a night, we did. The house was freezing, with a strong aroma of damp dog. There came the jingling of Bell's whisky. With the whisky, the banked fires of Elliott's mind flickered unpleasantly. There was much hostility towards my grandparents and an icy passing comment, the gist of which was that my mother had not stayed faithful to him during the war. And, offered with a straight face, the assertion that as I had seemed to do quite well in life, it showed that boys really didn't need a father around after all. We should not have gone. But having gone, with a great deal more courage and presence of mind, I should have played the White Man and objected strongly to what he said. I did not. Natural cowardice, the English desire to avoid confrontation at all costs, the weird circumstances all led me to steer the conversation gingerly away to safer ground as he slumped into incoherence.

This was a bad trip, in every sense. There are some basic rules in life. Never eat in a restaurant called Mom's. Never play cards with a man named Doc. Never sleep with a woman whose troubles are greater than yours. Never lend money to a company whose chairman has a beard, all the more if he has recently won some newspaper nomination as Young Businessman of the Year. To these add, never try to dig up a long-lost parent. In the morning, he had a hangover and was thankfully not much in evidence. We slunk away. I was ashamed and furious.

A week or so later Elliott called me. He was in financial trouble, he said ingratiatingly, and needed my help. His bank manager at the Midland, the listening bank with no hearing aid, was threatening to call in his overdraft. Someone solvent had to guarantee it. He said, unconvincingly, that I was the only person to whom he could turn. Of all the buttons that Elliott could have pressed, of all the things that he might have said and done, asking for money cut right to the bone.

Money was the worry that dogged my mother all our childhood. The alimony Elliott had been ordered to pay by the divorce court, and had never done. For him now to jump right in after one bone-grating meeting and ask for money himself tore open all the scars. I refused, as politely as I could. The pompous banker in me pontificated that before anyone could help, they would have to delve into Elliott's life and circumstances to see how a loan or guarantee could be repaid, and that I felt horribly awkward (true) about putting either of us in that situation. There would, I said, be even more difficulty when, as was inevitable, things failed to work out as promised. He hung up. He called back to try again. A little while later the bank manager himself called. He understood I could help. I said he had it wrong. That evening, a knock at the door and a brisk-looking cove with a white moustache said that, by coincidence, he lived up the road (I remember seeing him on the station platform on many commuting mornings), that he was a chum of Elliott's, and that Elliott had sent him round to ask face to face if I wouldn't change my mind. Greater love hath no man than this, that he will go round to a stranger to wheedle money for his friend. I repeated that I could not help. The anonymous friend (whom I later identified as, supposedly, another Unilever man) said that he thought I owed it to my father to do so. I shut the door. Silence. Elliott and I never met or spoke again.

In another part of my life, I met the writer and editor Auberon Waugh, whose acerbic pen belies his gentle nature and considerable kindness. I discovered, first, that he and his wife had lived for many years in the 'one nice house' that I remembered seeing in Chilton Foliat. More to the point, when I asked about my father, Waugh – himself no stranger to the difficult task of understanding a complicated parent – recollected vaguely that there had been some murky problem at the village Post Office. It might have been theft, but then again it might not.

When I heard this, I was concerned that perhaps my refusal to lend Elliott money had somehow led to whatever the problem had been. Childhood guilt is not easily erased.

Back nearly twenty-five years in the archives of the local weekly newspaper I found the story. It was actually a relatively minor affair involving only £1,200 or so, but it must have rocked the little village, in which Elliott had cut such an odd figure as a storekeeper. It was in February 1966, a year or so *before* my visit. That, then, was why the front window of the cottage bore only old traces of any attempt at shopkeeping. Why Elliott had spoken rather off-handedly about him and his wife having given up the business. Having shored themselves up for months by dipping into the till for petty cash, the inevitable day of reckoning rolled round. With the Post Office auditors due on a routine visit, and the shortfall in their books needing some convincing explanation, they went to the police with a story that, just before closing time, a burly youth had forced his way into the shop when his wife was on her own and snatched cash and stamps from behind the counter. It took a sharp-nosed Post Office investigator, helped by spiteful local tongues, only a couple of days to nail the lie. The saddest part was that only his wife was charged; she maintained stoutly that Elliott had had nothing to do with it and had known nothing about it. She had been forced by simple but harsh household financial worries, first to take the money, then to try to cover up.

That Elliott knew nothing seems to me inconceivable; it seems more likely, given his devious cast of mind, that he put her up to it. In a tearful speech at the local Assizes, she used one odd phrase, saying that she needed the cash to provide for 'my husband's three children'.

After a pompous lecture from the judge, who professed unworldly astonishment that she could have 'got through such a large sum in just five short months', probation and bankruptcy followed. At least, unlike Kati, she did not have to spend time in jail, but again Elliott's lunatic disregard for the consequences of his actions had rebounded far less on him than on someone who loved him.

Elliott had to work to live, and in any case was unlikely to be much given to introspective musings. He began commuting painfully to London. I came across traces of two jobs. Just jobs or possibly minor opportunities for him to run errands for old connections? As a tour guide and interpreter for a coach company running tourists down to Yugoslavia, I can imagine that his willingness to put up with inane questions from blue-rinsed matrons from Manchester was limited. But the opportunity to add the occasional suitcase, or even person, to the coach manifest as it chugged innocently back into Austria may have been useful to someone. Likewise a subsequent clerical job organising the loading and despatch of containers of household goods for British diplomatic and military families being posted to Eastern Europe.

It is difficult to see anything clandestine in the final occupation given on his death certificate: 'Manager of a Refrigeration Company'. But you never know!

Children's perspectives of home and family are very often much different either from those of their parents or from reality. Happy evenings at the panto, days at the zoo or on a Bermuda beach fondly recalled by parents years later may be lodged forever in the offsprings' minds as hours not just of misery but of insult and injury. Allowing for that, the flavour one gets from the offspring of Elliott's second marriage is far more bitter than sweet, once those early years in Lotusland had come to an end and it was back to England, the one journey that always ended badly.

It was not just the rented 1950s' stucco house in Kew, sooty privet instead of frangipani, the thunder of the Heathrow flightpath in place of the chatter of the tree frogs, embarrassments at the bank when so recently an expense account had splashed and flowed, the third-hand Vauxhall Viva instead of the Buick convertible, the Bendix laundromat in Sandycombe Road doing duty for a squad of domestic staff. It was, I think, the chilling realisation that this was the last lap, that the Micawber days were over. Nothing good was going to turn up now.

'What of soul was left, I wonder, when the kissing had to stop?' Not much, I think. All his life he had blamed his misfortunes on others. The Yugoslav Miljkovic for the fact that DISCLAIM had been dropped in the wrong spot on the mountains. My grandfather, who had failed to come though with the money. The 'lily-livered lot' at SIS who had manœuvred him out of happiness with Kati. My mother, whom he thought had betrayed him while he was away. His second father-in-law, who had craftily jinxed the Jamaican marriage by stipulating that his daughter would get her small and much needed allowance only if she came back every year to Jamaica without Elliott, leaving him to the rain and the bottle, and that she would inherit his estate only if she actually divorced. Even the children of his second marriage, who, he made it scornfully clear, had let him down by failing to meet his expectations, whatever they were. But eventually he ran out of excuses.

He railed at the children, derided them, pushed the boys out of school early and into the navy in some ill-considered version of the old 'make a man of you' tradition. And if they had money, and were foolish enough to let him know, it would be wheedled, bullied or, in one bitter evening, cheated out of them through a rigged card game. 'That will teach you a lesson.'

There were blimpish touches, which, had they been part of the irascible but at heart kindly persona of the Major from Fawlty Towers, might (just) have been amusing. Announcing very loudly to a crowded cinema at the high point of a John Wayne movie about the Green Berets that 'They didn't play bloody music in my war'; or switching off the TV in fury at Elton John because 'I didn't fight a bloody war for long-haired yobbos like him.' But sadly the persona was now morose, pickled in alcohol, lungs sooted, guts gnawed by guilt. In earlier times, even down on his luck, he could have seen himself as Archie the cockroach saw Mehitabel in the free-form poetry of which Elliott was once so fond:

> a cat that has seen better days . . .
> now she is thankful for
> a stray fish head from a
> garbage cart, but she is
> cheerful under it all toujours
> gai is ever her word
> toujours gai my kiddo wotto hell
> luck may change.

But now luck was never going to change. And good old Doctor Drink was increasingly a sapper of strength and a soporific, not a solution. His second wife, about in her own way to be betrayed by being led into the snare of the staged robbery, had a wild and unforgiving streak, an appetite of her own for distilled products, and a debilitating obsession about the standing she once had and to which she still aspired for herself and her children.

In a final ironic twist worthy of Jean Rhys, she divorced him a short time before his death in order to claim her father's estate, only to find that inflation, rapacity and inefficiency had reduced this to a pittance. She died only a short time ago after a long bout of cancer, a happier woman than she had been for many of the Elliott years. Sadly, I was never able to find her address and get her perspective.

Both of Elliott's sons by his second marriage eventually went into the police. One of my first leads to Elliott was the widow of his brother Basil, who also spent his working life on the force; even his other brother Leo signed up for the cape and whistle, though he only lasted a month.

What else do we have that might help us assess the man, simultaneously the hero and villain of our story? Let me try an odd one on you.

I learned many of life's lessons under the watchful, hooded eye of Sir Siegmund Warburg, a powerful cocktail of moody and mercurial genius, one day a sulky, brilliant Montagu Norman, the next a manipulative Don Alfonso, the day after a booming Dr Dulcamara, coat pockets filled with snake oil. '*Diplomate enthousiaste et encyclopédique, infatigable voyageur et bavard impénitent*', Siegmund was a considerable man, heir to three centuries of hard work, luck, culture, neurasthenia and the indefinable *Fingerspitzengefühl* for making money. And like all considerable men he had failings and fixations, mainly to do with colleagues who were temporarily in or out of favour, which made meetings of the firm's inner council at times seem unpleasantly like 'The Persecution and Assassination of Marat as Performed by the Inmates of the Asylum at Charenton under the Direction of the Marquis de Sade'.

He was uncompromising about recruitment to his firm. A century previously, Anthony Trollope, one of his favourite authors, had anticipated the flavour of the Warburg selection process in a gentle dig at a fictional Department of Weights and Measures and the way it chose its civil servants from the throng of aspirants:

> Some of course were sent away at once in ignominy, as evidently incapable. Many retired in the middle of it, with a conviction that they must seek their fortune at the Bar, or in medical pursuits, or in some other, comparatively easy way of life. Others were rejected on the fifth or sixth day as being deficient – or ignorant of the exact principles of hydraulic pressure. And even those who were retained, were retained, as it were, by an Act of Grace. [Warburg's] was and indeed is, like Heaven. No man can deserve it.

To those panning for gold today in London's financial markets, spread in a high-rise diaspora from the Isle of Dogs to Victoria Station, the tight-knit, clubby City of the 1960s and 1970s is already as much of a dusty relic of the past as the bowler hat, the ticker-tape and the Bill of Exchange. Back then, and into the 1990s, Warburg's was a successful, *arriviste* banking house with a great sense of style and purpose. Among its many strengths was Siegmund's willingness to recruit people without too much British regard to background, as long as they had enquiring minds and sharp elbows, and allow them far more headway and authority than was normal in any other merchant bank, or indeed most other businesses, while in fact keeping a very close eye indeed on their every move through insistence on a prompt written record of every phone call and meeting, and daily perusal by the firm's seniors of every scrap of incoming and outgoing mail.

I advanced with undeserved rapidity to giddy organisational heights, before succumbing to the siren call of Wall Street dollars, a move greeted by Siegmund with a histrionic display of self-pity worthy of Sir Donald Wolfit, and by some of his gerontocratic colleagues, themselves not widely known for their distaste for the good things in life, with a venom as chilling as though I had sold atomic secrets to the KGB. *'Just for an handful of silver he left us, Just for a Riband to stick on his coat . . . .'*

The cornerstone of the Warburg recruitment process was the necromantic semi-science of handwriting analysis. Some years after Siegmund's death, the sad triumph of reality over myth, and an eventually debilitating fondness for self-congratulation, brought about the bank's abrupt loss of form, and sent it scurrying, petticoat hoisted, dowry rapidly dwindling, from one cynical moustache-twirling suitor to another before swooning in well-faked orgasm into the manicured hands of the Swiss, a sad end which casts some doubt on the quality of its later leadership and thus on the efficacy of the technique. But none the less, as I had seen it produce quite reasonable results in years past, I thought I would put Elliott's script to the test based on one of his letters to Antony Terry. Not wanting to influence the outcome, I told the analyst only that the writer had been educated in England, had left school early and had become embroiled in difficult secret work.

Back came Elliott, dissected and laid out in careful, slightly European prose:

Looking at Elliott's handwriting it seems absurd to think that this exceptionally intelligent man left school so early. Endowed with a superior mind that had engineering aptitude and precision as well as a humanistic interest and finesse, he could have pursued a number of different academic or technical careers. Although the present handwriting sample (1969) shows some physical wear and tear, an erosion in resilience that could have borne down on his moods and stamina, it is still representative of the qualities he possessed.

The dominant feature is his global intelligence, that had the calibre to cross national borders. He had flexibility and social adeptness to adjust to change and new situations, but once he launched on a project was unwilling to let go (a militant attitude with potential tunnel vision). Within an overall rationally balanced personality, there was a tendency to become compulsive in his efforts for achievement.

(One is tempted to speculate whether his intellectual curiosity and early maturity put him so far ahead, that made it difficult for him to relate to his schoolmates. Did he get bored with the conventional education, fed up with narrow prejudices and views and limited opportunities?)

His own creative enterprising intellect made him too individualistic to fit the conventional mould. Influenced and shaped by the cultural climate, gifted far beyond average, ambitious, it must not have been easy for him to find the right outlet for his various talents.

His refinement, originality and some romantic, idealistic inclination must have been perceived somewhat dubiously by his own peers, unsuitable for a boyish environment, causing him to rebel and set him up for (future) misunderstandings and resentments. It could be that part of his decision to become involved in secret work was a compensation for his sensitivity, an effort to assert his virility, besides giving him the opportunity to get involved on a higher level that matched his multiple potential. One feels that he was pulled two ways, towards a softer side, as well as towards adventure.

Elliott had the deep-seated, unabating faith or belief in his destiny, a sense of purpose, similar to a vocation, combined with an enterprising active spirit that propelled him to mobilise his abilities and pursue his goals with determination, tenacity and perseverance. Disciplined when it counted, sustained by his inner strength (conviction) and resources, he was able to come through vicissitude and hardship.

While basically a sensitive and sympathetic man, he did not always show it. He was a very private person, if single minded in the pursuit of his interests, and often too self-orientated in his own endeavours to adjust to other people's wishes. He was an interesting, articulate and stimulating person to be with, but it was he who commanded the subject matter.

Intellectually an elitist, he was and felt superior, an awareness he could project at times. Rootless and restless, he superimposed his professional activities (where he felt at ease) over his emotional life (where he trod on less firm ground, having probably received some knocks early in his life) and repressed much of his feelings. He would have been too proud and unwilling to admit any inadequacy or expose his sensitivity and a (slight?) melancholic streak. As a result, some people probably perceived him as cold, distant and even cynical at times.

These contradictory undercurrents created a complex multi-layered personality, difficult to understand, often inconsistent and different in his public and private behaviour. As it often happens, a softer, refined inner core caused sharper (self-protective) reactions. His secret work taught him to keep much to himself, the secretiveness and reserve suited his disposition and must have been useful in his career.

Intellectually he always had the ability to sympathise, see the essential, combined with critical sharpness and resolve that empowered him to do superior work and assert himself with authority, and that is where his emphasis went. From this point of view, he was selfish, not having the desire or need to express and live all his feelings, which did not go beyond a certain depth. Elliott was a man who lived for work and causes and was loyal and dedicated to the ones he believed in the way he saw it fit.

The analyst is a shrewd and attractive lady. And like many of the ladies who crossed Elliott's path, she has put her finger on the weakness of the man within. Ethel, with a sister's bluntness, saw him in childhood as 'a coward'. His Budapest secretary Toni felt a basic insecurity. Rachel Ames scented something loose shifting about behind the tough exterior. Even the more visceral Margit described an empty space inside him.

His will, executed only the day before his death, left his estate to his second wife and the children. But, true to form, after outstanding bills and expenses, there was nothing left, just the ragbag of other people's memories of him and the fading files. '*Morientum desolatum, dum emisit spiritum*', taking his last ride in a big car, no matter that it was black, to the ecumenical Regulo 12 efficiency of the Reading crematorium. The swish of the curtain ended the play, leaving only a shimmer of dust drifting towards London Airport. His wife burned his effects too, except for a few things his sons manage to retrieve from the pyre.

He was what he was. He did the state some service, put his life at risk for something he believed in (whether it was himself or his country I'm not sure), and I wish I had known him better, though I have to add the uncomfortable rider that, if I had, my life would have been the worse for it.

Just to round it off, the rum business of the watch – appropriate really, given my childhood fascination with Elliott's possessions, rather than his personality. In the statement he, or more precisely SIS, gave to the *News Chronicle*, Elliott makes a special point about the AVO taking away 'my personal belongings, including my watch, tie and braces'. In the mid-1950s, my aborted rendezvous with Elliott at the disputed barricade of the Waldorf had ended in confused anti-climax, followed by the mildly exciting second-hand promise that he was about to send me a watch – 'his' watch, 'a' watch, I can't now remember – a promise that joined many others he had left scattered about the corridors of his life. I hadn't thought of it again until I began to dredge my mind for this book.

In the event, though, this turned out to be a promise on which he actually made good. When I went to see Kati, she told me with restrained sadness that she had something which belonged to me. She went to her bedroom and came back with a small, square object. A watch. Elliott's watch. A no-nonsense gold case, with English hallmarks. No strap by now, and the glass was fogged by scratches. As I peered at it, not knowing quite what to say, I couldn't make out the maker's name on the dial.

'I had to change the dial,' Kati said. 'The old one cracked. It had nice Roman numbers.' Not until later was I able to make out the name on the replacement dial. Taken from a Russian watch, it read 'Boctok', or 'East'.

According to Proust (who would not have been employed by SOE, but might have had a lot of fun in SIS's French Section), there is a Celtic legend that the souls of those we have lost are held captive in some animal or inanimate object – a cat, a tree or, indeed, a watch – and are effectively beyond our reach until the day when we happen to pass by, or obtain possession of the object which forms their prison. They start and tremble, and call out their name, and as soon as we have recognised them, the spell is broken, and they are delivered from death. In this case, the watch didn't actually work, and I didn't hear the old man call. But out here in Bermuda, in itself a micro-sized triumph of myth over reality, I'm still listening.

# Index

# THE SECRET WAR
# FOR THE FALKLANDS

## Nigel West

The Falklands War of 1982 was one of the most significant armed campaigns to be fought since the end of the Second World War. Although much is known about how the war was fought, little has been revealed about what really happened behind the scenes.

*The Secret War for the Falklands* is the hitherto undisclosed story of how the Argentines planned the invasion, and why the massive amphibious attack took the British Government by surprise. Based on previously classified documents and interviews with international intelligence personnel, Nigel West has reconstructed the astonishing events that led up to the conflict. Why was the *Sheffield* sunk? Who tapped the telephones of the Argentine mission to the UN in New York? Who were the people in the Current Intelligence Group who knew the real odds against success? And how did the SAS launch a clandestine raid, codenamed MIKADO, on an Exocet base in Tierra del Fuego?

'Exciting reading, mixing graphic description and studied investigation' Frank Cooper, *The Times*

'Extremely well written . . . a brilliantly researched and important book' Tam Dalyell, *Scotsman*

'A readable, plausible and intriguing addition to the Falklands literature' Lawrence Freedman, *Daily Telegraph*

# COUNTERFEIT SPIES

*Nigel West*

Of the many hundreds of accounts of wartime adventures by secret agents behind enemy lines, which are authentic and which are the fantasies of hoaxers? Have dozens of authors and their publishers been duped into peddling fiction dressed up as fact?

In this remarkable investigation of clandestine operations of the Second World War, Nigel West reveals a catalogue of bogus claims, doctored photographs, faked documents and manufactured archival records. The spurious tales of more than two dozen authors are placed under the expert's microscope, compared to the recently declassified files of hitherto secret organisations, and exposed as exaggeration, embellishment or outright fraud.

'Gripping stuff . . . in this book, West redresses the balance in favour of the true war heroes who died' *Sunday Times*

'Long-cherished icons of heroism shrink or completely vanish under his damning investigation. His uncomfortable conclusions make the book indispensable to lovers of the espionage genre' *Books Magazine*

'As a catalogue of Walter Mitty fantasies and publishers' credulity (or worse) *Counterfeit Spies* hits the mark' *Independent*

'Absorbing' *Scotsman*

# THE GENERAL AGAINST
## THE KREMLIN

### *Harold Elletson*

*The General Against the Kremlin* is not simply an account of the life of Alexander Lebed, the man who, in the year 2000, hopes to become the next President of Russia. Placing his story firmly in the context of the power struggles and conflicts which have riven Russia over the last forty years – many of which Lebed has experienced at first hand, even directly contributed to – Harold Elletson has written an authoritative, illuminating and thought-provoking exploration of the politics of a country which is still far from democracy.

'Impressive . . . a brave attempt at pinning down the elusive Lebed . . . he has also, in passing, written an excellent concise history of Russia's past two decades' *TLS*

'Entertaining, thought-provoking and unsettling . . . his insider knowledge and long historical perspective provide invaluable insight and a welcome, informed corrective to much press and TV coverage of the region's recent history' *Time Out*

'A sound biography . . . a solid history of contemporary Russia seen through the eyes of a man who has played a role in almost every flashpoint over the past thirty years' *The Times*

'For authors, as for generals who aspire to political power, a sense of timing is important. This book is well timed. If, by the end of it, the reader is still in some doubt as to where Lebed might lead Russia, the fault lies with the man himself, not the author' *Daily Telegraph*

# FALSE FLAG

## *Zeev Avni*

A 'false flag' is the most complex and dangerous of intelligence operations: the recruitment of an agent who believes he is working for an entirely different country.

Zeev Avni's speciality in Mossad was to cultivate former Nazis employed as military advisers to rebuild Egypt's army. None would have willingly co-operated with him if they had suspected for one moment that he was a professional Israeli intelligence officer. And nor would Mossad have promoted him if it had been realised that their star performer in Brussels and Belgrade was a long-term mole, dedicated to penetrating right to the heart of the agency.

For the first time, Avni tells the story Mossad would prefer you to forget: his adventures as a GRU agent in Switzerland; the ease with which he was accepted by Mossad; the harrowing circumstances of his imprisonment and his eventual rejection of Marxism. Avni's unique story of commitment, duplicity and betrayal is the only documented case of Mossad's penetration by the Soviets, and will be regarded as a classic by espionage aficionados.

**Other bestselling Warner titles available by mail:**

- [ ] The Secret War for the Falklands     Nigel West     £7.99
- [ ] Counterfeit Spies     Nigel West     £7.99
- [ ] The General Against the Kremlin     Harold Elletson     £7.99
- [ ] False Flag     Zeev Avni     £7.99

**WARNER BOOKS**

**WARNER BOOKS**
**Cash Sales Department, P.O. Box 11, Falmouth, Cornwall, TR10 9EN**
**Tel: +44 (0) 1326 372400, Fax: +44 (0) 1326 374888**
**Email: books@barni.avel.co.uk**

**POST AND PACKING:**
Payments can be made as follows: cheque, postal order (payable to Warner Books) or by credit cards. Do not send cash or currency.

| | |
|---|---|
| All U.K. Orders | **FREE OF CHARGE** |
| E.E.C. & Overseas | 25% of order value |

Name (Block letters) . . . . . . . . . . . . . . . . . . . . . . . . . . . . . . . . . . . . . . . . . . .

Address . . . . . . . . . . . . . . . . . . . . . . . . . . . . . . . . . . . . . . . . . . . . . . . . . . . . . . .

. . . . . . . . . . . . . . . . . . . . . . . . . . . . . . . . . . . . . . . . . . . . . . . . . . . . . . . . . . . . . .

Post/zip code: . . . . . . . . . . . . . . . . . . . . . . . . . . . . . . . . . . . . . . . . . . . . . . . . . .

- [ ] Please keep me in touch with future Warner publications
- [ ] I enclose my remittance £
- [ ] I wish to pay by Visa/Access/Mastercard/Eurocard

Card Expiry Date